GLOSSARY

Scottish a... ...Terms

Members of the LexisNexis Group worldwide

United Kingdom	LexisNexis UK, a Division of Reed Elsevier (UK) Ltd, 4 Hill Street, EDINBURGH EH2 3JZ and Halsbury House, 35 Chancery Lane, LONDON WC2A 1EL
Argentina	LexisNexis Argentina, BUENOS AIRES
Australia	LexisNexis Butterworths, CHATSWOOD, New South Wales
Austria	LexisNexis Verlag ARD Orac GmbH & Co KG, VIENNA
Canada	LexisNexis Butterworths, MARKHAM, Ontario
Chile	LexisNexis Chile Ltda, SANTIAGO DE CHILE
Czech Republic	Nakladatelství Orac sro, PRAGUE
France	Editions du Juris-Classeur SA, PARIS
Germany	LexisNexis Deutschland GmbH, FRANKFURT, MUNSTER
Hong Kong	LexisNexis Butterworths, HONG KONG
Hungary	HVG-Orac, BUDAPEST
India	LexisNexis Butterworths, NEW DELHI
Ireland	LexisNexis, DUBLIN
Italy	Giuffrè Editore, MILAN
Malaysia	Malayan Law Journal Sdn Bhd, KUALA LUMPUR
New Zealand	LexisNexis Butterworths, WELLINGTON
Poland	Wydawnictwo Prawnicze LexisNexis, WARSAW
Singapore	LexisNexis Butterworths, SINGAPORE
South Africa	LexisNexis Butterworths, DURBAN
Switzerland	Stämpfli Verlag AG, BERNE
USA	LexisNexis, DAYTON, Ohio

The Law Society of Scotland
26 Drumsheugh Gardens, Edinburgh EH3 7YR

© The Law Society of Scotland 2003

A CIP Catalogue record for this book is available from the British Library.

First edition published 1988
Reprinted 1992, 1996, 1998, 2000

ISBN 0 406 94947 6
Typeset by Phoenix Photosetting, Chatham, Kent
Printed by Thomson Litho Ltd, East Kilbride, Scotland

Visit LexisNexis UK at www.lexisnexis.co.uk

GLOSSARY

Scottish and European Union Legal Terms and Latin Phrases

The Law Society of Scotland

LexisNexis™ UK

Scottish and European Union Legal Terms and Latin Phrases

Second edition

Compiled and edited by

SCOTT STYLES MA LLB DIP LP
Senior Lecturer in Law,
University of Aberdeen

NIALL R WHITTY MA LLB FRSE
General Editor, *The Laws of Scotland,*
Stair Memorial Encyclopaedia;
Visiting Professor, The Law School,
University of Edinburgh

European Union and European Community Terms updated by

R C LANE MA PHD
Senior Lecturer in the School of Law
University of Edinburgh

This edition of the Glossary is based on the First Edition of the Glossary compiled by

ANN D SMITH BA PHD
Formerly Lecturer in Criminology
University of Edinburgh

HAMISH MCN HENDERSON MA LLB
Advocate in Aberdeen
University Fellow and Formerly
Senior Lecturer in Scots Law,
University of Edinburgh

The late JOHN S BOYLE BL

And including a part on European Community Law compiled by

K P E LASOK MA LLM PHD
of the Middle Temple, Barrister

D A O EDWARD CMG QC
Judge of the European Court of Justice
Honorary Professor of the
University of Edinburgh
(Salvesen Professor of
European Institutions 1985–89)

R C LANE MA PHD
Lecturer in the Europa Institute
University of Edinburgh

INTRODUCTION

The over-all object of this second edition of the Glossary remains the same as in the first edition published in 1988 namely to give a succinct explanation of words and phrases used by Scots lawyers the meanings of which might not be immediately apparent. This edition also retains many of the characteristics of the first edition.

It continues to include for example a large number of words and phrases which are no longer in common use. Their inclusion is necessary because they will be found in old (but still relevant) books, reports and statutes. Sometimes a principle which is valid and applicable in modern law may be illustrated or formulated in old cases and texts using old terminology which requires to be explained if the principle itself or its application is to be understood.

As in the first edition, a large number of Latin words and phrases have been included, reflecting the fundamental importance of Roman law and the European *jus commune* as a source of Scots law. Indeed it has proved necessary to add some Latin phrases not included in the first edition. This is partly because advances in Scottish legal scholarship since 1988, for example in the conceptualisation and structure of property law as exemplified in volume 18 of the *Stair Memorial Encyclopaedia,* and in aspects of the law of obligations, such as unjustified enrichment and *negotiorum gestio*, have highlighted their importance. Partly also it is the result of the renewal of links with European legal culture. The title to the first edition referred to Latin Maxims but in fact covered Latin phrases and names as well. The change in the title to this edition reflects this fact and not a change in content.

The changes in legal language since 1988 have been significant. New categories with their own terminology have arisen (eg legislative devolution to Scotland; statutory rights of access to land and community rights to buy) or increased in importance (eg discrimination; judicial review). Other categories have been transposed to Scots law from international conventions (eg human rights) or European Union law (eg competition). Some statutory changes to existing categories have introduced important new terminology for example in the context of legal capacity of minors; child law; requirements of writing; adults with incapacity; and (with effect from 28 November 2004) real burdens on land. Recent legislation has abolished feudal tenure (with effect from that date), tutory and poindings, thereby making many legal concepts obsolete. New terms are also found in new rules of court.

The first edition of the Glossary sought to exclude statutory definitions so far as practicable but, in view of the conceptual and terminological implications of the statutory changes just mentioned, too rigid an adherence to that approach would have greatly diminished the utility of this edition. Reference to statutory definitions however remains relatively sparing lest they overload the text.

The coverage of the proper names of legal, legislative or official bodies or offices has been considerably expanded, and now includes some acronyms which are so much a feature of modern legal and business life. A few concepts which are not strictly legal but are specially relevant to the practice of law have been included.

In the first edition, Part I covered Scottish legal terms and Latin phrases while Part II contained terms used in European Community law. This edition is unitary combining European Union law and European Community law terms (each of which is marked with an **E**) together with Scottish legal terms and Latin phrases in one list.

The editors wish to thank Professor K G C Reid for assistance with definitions relating to land tenure and title conditions.

SCOTTISH AND EUROPEAN UNION LEGAL TERMS, AND LATIN PHRASES

a

a coelo usque ad centrum — from the sky to the centre of the earth. This description of the scope of ownership of land was formerly generally accepted but has now been qualified by planning and other legislation.

a fortiori — by a stronger argument: a phrase used to emphasise the strength of an argument by contrasting it with an earlier weaker proposition founded on the same or similar reasoning.

a mensa et thoro — from bed and board; judicial separation of husband and wife.

a morte testatoris — from the death of the testator: a phrase distinguishing bequests which vest upon a testator's death from those where vesting is postponed to a later date.

a non domino — from one who is not the owner: used to describe a title given by one who does not pretend to be the owner, as when land is sold by a lawful occupier when all trace of the identity of the true owner has been lost. The purchaser's defective title is cured by prescription.

a posteriori — viewed from after; reasoning from effect to cause.

a priori — viewed from before; reasoning from cause to effect.

a vinculo matrimonii — from the bond of marriage; divorce, permitting remarriage.

ab initio — from the beginning. Thus a bigamous marriage is said to be void *ab initio*.

ab intestato — from a person dying intestate; description of property acquired according to the rules of intestate succession.

abandonment —
(1) in civil procedure, the process by which a party to a court action formally withdraws from it, subject to such conditions as to **expenses** (qv) or otherwise as the court may impose. An **appeal** (qv) may be abandoned;
(2) in insurance law the giving up by the insured of the proprietary rights in insured property to the insurer in consideration for payment of a **constructive total loss** (qv) or an **actual total loss** (qv);
(3) in property law, abandoned property is property which has once been owned but the ownership of which has been given up by its owner.

abatement —
(1) in general, a reduction or decrease in the amount, degree, intensity or worth;
(2) termination of a legal nuisance;
(3) abatement of legacies: where a testator's estate is insufficient to satisfy all his bequests in full, they are reduced in an order fixed by law.

abbreviate — an abstract of a writ and warrant recorded in an official register in bankruptcy proceedings to give public notice thereof.

abdicate — (of a monarch) to renounce the crown.

abduction — the taking away of a person, especially a child from the parent with whom the child resides without the parent's consent.

abet — to help or encourage.

ABI — Association of British Insurers.

abortion — termination of a pregnancy and destruction of the foetus.

abrogate — to abolish, especially a rule of the common law. Compare **repeal** and **revoke**.

abscond — to depart secretly; to flee the jurisdiction of a court.

absolute discharge — an order which may be made by a court instead of imposing a sentence when the court has found a person guilty of a crime or offence but considers that any punishment would be inappropriate. An offender cannot receive an absolute discharge if the penalty is fixed by statute. A court of summary jurisdiction may make the order without the offender being convicted, but may also order an absolute discharge after conviction. When an offender is tried and convicted on indictment, the conviction is always recorded.

absolute disposition — the conveyance of property unqualified by any reservation in favour of the disponer or of a third party. At one time securities over heritable property could be created by *ex facie* absolute disposition qualified by a back-bond but these were made ineffectual by the Conveyancing and Feudal Reform (Scotland) Act 1970, s 9(3).

absolute exclusivity — the quality of an agreement (such as a licence or assignation of an industrial, commercial or intellectual property right) by which one party agrees:
(1) to supply goods for resale in a particular geographical area to the other party and to no other person;
(2) not to compete with the other party in that area; and
(3) to prevent other persons from competing with the other party. Cf **open exclusivity**.

absolute insolvency — the state of a debtor whose liabilities are greater than his assets as distinct from the less serious state of inability to pay debts as they fall due, that is, practical insolvency or **apparent insolvency** (qv).

absolute warrandice. *See* **warrandice**.

absolvitor — (noun) a final decree in a civil case giving judgment in favour of and exonerating the defender so that the pursuer is precluded from raising a new action on the same grounds (*see res judicata*). The verbs are to absolve or to **assoilzie** (qv).

abstract — a summary of a document.

abstract system of transfer — in property law, a system whereby the validity of the act of transfer or conveyance is determined independently of (that is, in abstraction from) the underlying contract or promise to transfer. A reduction of the underlying contract or promise does not by itself reduce the conveyance. Contrast **causal system of transfer** (qv). Scots law has an abstract system in heritable property but the true position in moveable property is debated.

abuse of a dominant position — prohibited conduct in competition law whereby an **undertaking** (qv) with overwhelming **market power** (qv) engages in practices which take unfair advantage of that power to the detriment of competition and/or the consumer.

abuse of legal process — the delict of causing harm to a person by using legal process against him with malice and want of probable cause. The legal process may be criminal proceedings or diligence. It is not a delict to raise an unfounded civil action and there is some doubt whether the existence of malice and want of probable cause would make the action delictual.

abuse of rights — the exercise, or purported exercise, of a right maliciously and with the predominant motive of harming another without benefit to oneself. A delict of wider scope in some civil law systems. Scots law recognises one form of the doctrine in neighbourhood relations namely *aemulatio vicini* (qv) but has not, or not yet, developed a general doctrine of abuse of rights.

accelerated procedure — the hearing of a reference for a **preliminary ruling** (qv) by the European Court of Justice by special, speedy procedure where the circumstances require a judgment as a matter of exceptional urgency. **[E]**

acceleration decision — a decision speeding up the establishment of the **customs union** (qv) of the European Community. **[E]**

acceptance — expression, by words or conduct, by the recipient of an offer of unqualified assent to the terms of the offer with the effect that a contract is concluded. As a general rule silence or inactivity on the part of the offeree does not in itself amount to acceptance.

acceptilatio or **acceptilation** — the discharge of an obligation by complete or partial remission of performance.

acceptor — the party which is primarily liable for the payment of a **bill of exchange** (qv). An acceptor is the drawee of a bill who has made written acceptance of that liability upon the face of the bill.

access —
(1) in property law, a means of reaching property which may involve crossing another's property for example to reach landlocked property. A right of access may be created as a **servitude** (qv) either expressly or by implication from a conveyance;
(2) at one time in family law denoted the rights conferred by a court on the parent or other relative of a child under sixteen who is not given the right of custody. *See* now **contact order**.

access rights — statutory rights, which were conferred on everyone by the Land Reform (Scotland) Act 2003, Part I, to be on land or to cross land for purposes defined in the Act such as recreation or educational activity.

accession or *accessio*—
(1) the natural or **industrial** (qv) accretion of additional objects to existing property (eg by reproduction or building);
(2) an arrangement set out in a deed approved by the creditors of an insolvent person as an alternative to sequestration.
(3) the admission to the European Union of a state other than a **founding member** (qv). *See also* **Treaty of Accession, Act of Accession** and **accession criteria**. **[E]**

accession countries — also candidate countries; **applicant countries** (qv) which have signed a **Treaty of Accession** (qv) with, but have not yet joined, the European Union. In 2003 there are ten accession countries from central, eastern and southern Europe, expected to accede in 2004. **[E]**

accession criteria — also 'Copenhagen criteria'; criteria by which fitness for accession to the European Union is to be judged; from a 1993 resolution of the European Council in Copenhagen. **[E]**

accessorium principale sequitur — the accessory follows the principal thing to which it is attached. Thus the owner of land owns buildings attached to it and its fruits, and the owner of cattle has a right to their offspring.

accessory — a person who aids or advises the perpetrator of a crime. Cf **art and part**.

accessory action — an action intended to achieve some further procedural objective. Such an action involves eg **proving the tenor** (qv) so as to base a claim for a later action.

accessory obligation — an obligation imposed to increase the effectiveness of an earlier obligation, eg caution.

accidentalia — accidents: incidental, as contrasted with essential, parts of a contract.

accommodation bill — a bill of exchange to which a party has put his name (whether as drawer, acceptor or indorser) gratuitously in order to accommodate another party who wishes to raise money on the bill.

account of charge and discharge — a form of account of transactions of property committed to the care of trustees, executors, factors etc or their agents. The account is generally drawn up annually and deals with credits, debits and capital in hand.

Accountant in Bankruptcy — the Accountant of Court in his capacity as the officer supervising the administration of sequestration (bankruptcy) and personal insolvency.

Accountant of Court — the officer of the Court of Session who supervises the conduct of judicial factors; holds *ex officio* certain statutory offices such as **Accountant in Bankruptcy** (qv) and **Public Guardian** (qv); and performs other statutory functions.

accretion —
(1) the passing of the share of a deceased joint legatee to the other joint legatee or legatees;
(2) in the case of a conveyance of title to heritable property, the perfection of a formerly imperfect title of the granter may cause validation of the grantee's title by accretion;
(3) *alluvio* (qv).

accumulation of income — investing the income of a trust fund for the benefit of beneficiaries at some time in the future. There are statutory restrictions on accumulation: Trusts (Scotland) Act 1961, s 5; Law Reform (Miscellaneous Provisions) (Scotland) Act 1966, s 6.

accusatorial —
   (1) a system of criminal procedure found in Common Law and mixed legal systems in which the responsibility if any of the accused is determined by the process of prosecution and defence according to the strict rules of evidence before a judge acting impartially;
   (2) in civil proceedings a system of procedure in which the determination of the rights of parties is governed by a system of adversary pleading and of fact-finding and truth-telling according to the strict rules of evidence, also before an impartial judge.

accused — a person charged with committing a crime or offence, more properly referred to in Scots law as the **panel** (qv); 'defendant' is an English legal term of art.

ACP countries — African, Caribbean and Pacific countries which are parties to the **Cotonou Agreement** (qv). **[E]**

acquiescence — a **personal bar** (qv) which arises through failure by a person whose rights have been infringed to object within the time allowed, proof of knowledge of the acts done being essential to infer consent.

acquis communautaire — lit. Community assets or patrimony; the term used to describe at a point in time the state of the development of the law which embodies the principles and objectives, essential rights, obligations and remedies of Community law. Maintaining and building upon the *acquis communautaire* is a fundamental objective of the European Union. **Accession countries** (qv) are required to accept and adapt to the *acquis* at the time of accession. **[E]**

acquisita et acquirenda — things acquired and to be acquired, relevant in the execution of diligence and the law of bankruptcy.

acquit — to find the accused in a criminal trial not guilty or not proven.

act. *See* **Act of Parliament**

act adversely affecting an official or servant — an act adopted by or on behalf of a **Community institution** (qv) or other body which affects (not necessarily 'adversely') the legal position of a Community official or other servant employed by that institution or body. The official or servant may seise the European Court of Justice of a dispute against his employer only where the dispute concerns such an act. **[E]**

act and warrant — in sequestration, a judicial order confirming the appointment of a permanent trustee in terms of the Bankruptcy Act 1985.

Act of Accession — an instrument ancillary to a **Treaty of Accession** (qv) setting out the detailed conditions upon which a state other than a founding member is admitted to the European Union. **[E]**

Act of God. *See* **damnum fatale**.

Act of Parliament — primary legislation; a law passed by the Houses of Common and Lords of the United Kingdom Parliament and enacted with assent by the sovereign (until then it is a Bill); also referred to as legislation, or as a statute.

Act of the Scottish Parliament — primary legislation; a law passed by the Scottish Parliament and enacted with assent by the sovereign (until then it is a Bill).

acte clair — a principle deriving from the separation of powers resulting from the French revolution whereby a legislative measure the meaning of which is so clear that it can give rise to no reasonable doubt need not be, and cannot be, subjected to interpretative challenge in a court. **[E]**

actings — conduct or acts.

actio injuriarum — a Roman action for penal damages to vindicate offensive behaviour. In Scots law the phrase has been correctly applied to an action for **affront** (qv) and more recently but incorrectly, though with judicial recognition, to an action for *solatium* for the death of a relative, now replaced by a **loss of society award** (qv).

actio de effusis vel dejectis — in Roman law, action classified as a **quasi-delict** (qv); anyone from whose dwelling something was thrown or poured out on the street was strictly liable to a person injured thereby. After initial hesitation it seems generally accepted that this doctrine is not part of Scots law.

actio de in rem verso — in Roman law where a slave or son-in-power acquired from another party money, property or the product of services which were not due to him and applied them for the benefit (*in rem versum*) of his master or *paterfamilias*, the other party could raise an *actio de in rem verso* against the master or *paterfamilias* to recover his loss up to the value of the enrichment of the master or *paterfamilias*. Justinian extended this to cover a principal's obligation to redress his enrichment arising from the acts of a person not in power, thereby laying the basis for claims in the European *jus commune* (qv) for redress of indirect enrichment and for aspects of the Scots obligation to redress unjustified enrichment.

actio de positis vel suspensis — in Roman law, action classified as a **quasi-delict** (qv); where a thing which had been placed on or suspended from a building fell down and injured a person, the owner of the building was strictly liable to that person. After initial hesitation it seems generally accepted that this doctrine is not part of Scots law.

actio mandati — in Roman law an action by the mandator against the mandatory for the proper execution of the mandate in terms of the contract and for the restoration or delivery of things received for the purpose of the mandate by the mandatory from the mandator or from a third party including the surrender of secret profits. A main foundation of the Scots law of **mandate** (qv).

actio negotiorum gestorum contraria and *directa* — in Roman law when a legal relationship of *negotiorum gestio* was created by a person (*gestor*) managing the affairs of another (called the *dominus negotii*) in accordance with certain rules, then reciprocal rights and duties were created. These were enforceable by reciprocal actions, called the *actio negotiorum gestorum directa* brought by the *dominus negotii* against the *gestor*, and the *actio negotiorum gestorum contraria* brought by the *gestor* against the *dominus*. These actions form the basis of the remedies in the Scots law of *negotiorum gestio* (qv).

actio Pauliana — in Roman law an action for restitutionary remedies giving protection to the creditors of an insolvent against transactions by a debtor to the detriment of his creditors. One of the historical roots of the Scots law on the reduction of unfair preferences by a bankrupt in fraud of his creditors and equivalent laws in civilian European systems.

actio popularis — in Roman law a person could bring a penal *actio popularis* to restrain and punish socially reprehensible forms of conduct such as violation of sepulchres. In Scots law there is no *actio popularis* of that type. On the other hand, a person who is within the class of persons entitled to enjoy a public right (such as a public right of passage) has a title and interest to enforce it by an action and such an action is sometimes called an *actio popularis*.

actio quanti minoris — an action in Roman law whereby the purchaser of goods could retain them and seek from the seller the difference between their actual value and the value they should have had under the contract. The action was not in general recognised by the common law of Scotland but was effectively introduced into Scots law by ss 15B and 53A of the Sale of Goods Act 1979 and s 1 of the Contract (Scotland) Act 1997.

actio spolii — a possessory action in romano-canonical procedure from which is derived the Scottish action and doctrine of **spuilzie** (qv).

action — civil (but not criminal) proceedings to obtain from the court some civil remedy of advantage to the pursuer.

action of annulment — proceedings raised before the European Court of Justice or the Court of First Instance in order to obtain the **annulment** (qv) of a measure adopted by a Community institution. **[E]**

actor debet sequi forum rei — a pursuer must follow the court of the defender. Thus jurisdiction is normally determined by the residence of the defender.

Acts of Adjournal — type of delegated legislation made by the High Court of Justiciary regulating procedure there and in inferior criminal courts, published as **statutory instruments** (qv).

Acts of Sederunt — type of delegated legislation made by the Court of Session regulating procedure in the Court of Session, the sheriff court (in civil matters) and administrative tribunals, published as **statutory instruments** (qv).

actual total loss — in insurance law occurs when the insured property is completely destroyed; or the assured is irretrievably deprived of the insured property; or the insured property changes in character so that it is no longer the thing that was insured (eg wood becomes ashes); or when a ship is posted 'missing' at **Lloyd's** (qv).

actus non facit reum, nisi mens sit rea — an act does not infer criminality unless the actor had criminal intent or criminal negligence. The maxim is usually now simply expressed in references to *mens rea* (qv).

actus reus — the physical act or conduct prohibited in a crime or offence.

ad civilem effectum — as to the civil effect, contrasted with effect in criminal law. An activity may have separate civil and criminal effects.

ad factum praestandum — for the performance of an act. In modern practice a decree or an obligation *ad factum praestandum* requires the performance or fulfilment of some physical rather than pecuniary obligation. A decree *ad factum praestandum* is an order to do something, and as such is the opposite of an **interdict** (qv) which is a court order not to do something.

ad fundandam jurisdictionem — for the purposes of founding jurisdiction.

ad hunc effectum — literally 'to this effect' but used to mean 'with limited effect'. In a ranking of creditors, where an ordinary creditor had registered an **inhibition** (qv) and then obtained a decree of reduction of a conveyance by the debtor of his heritable property violating the inhibition, the decree does not annul the conveyance for all purposes so as to benefit the general body of creditors but only *ad hunc effectum* (with limited effect) to give the inhibiting creditor a preference in the ranking under the special rules for ranking inhibitions.

ad interim — in the meantime.

ad litem — as regards the action. Thus a curator *ad litem* is a curator appointed for the purposes of a specific action to look after the interests of a party under legal disability.

ad longum — at length, used of documents or statements in contrast to a precis or summary.

ad medium filum — to the middle line, normally used of the rights of proprietors of opposite banks of a river.

ad omissa vel male appretiata — as regards things omitted or undervalued, in the context of a confirmation and inventory submitted by executors.

ad valorem — according to value; proportionally, as of stamp duties.

ad vindictam publicam — for the maintenance and defence of the public interest: the particular concern of the Lord Advocate and procurators fiscal as public prosecutors.

ad vitam aut culpam — for life or until fault is established; formerly included in the terms of appointment to certain public offices such as judges and professors of law; now mostly superseded by specific contracts or by statutory retirement ages.

ademptione — by ademption. Specific legacies are revoked by ademption when the thing bequeathed has ceased to exist or has been disposed of by the testator before the time of death.

adhere —
(1) by a court, to confirm the judgment given by a lower court;
(2) by a husband or wife, to cohabit at bed and board (the action to secure adherence was abolished in 1984).

adhesion contract — a contract where the bargaining power of the parties is so unequal that the terms are offered on a 'take it or leave it' basis, with no opportunity to negotiate by the weaker party.

adjudication —
(1) (generally) judicial determination;
(2) the means by which the Court of Session vests a title to land in a claimant entitled thereto or attaches the heritable property of a debtor in security or in satisfaction of a debt. *See also* **foreclosure; attachment;**
(3) a decision on stamp duties made by the Commissionersof the Inland Revenue.

adjust — to alter written pleadings in a civil action before the court closes the **record** (qv).

adjustment roll. *See* **rolls**.

adminicle — an item of helpful evidence.

administration order — an order made under a procedure introduced by Part II of the Insolvency Act 1986 (ss 8–27) which is designed to secure the rehabilitation of an ailing company or the better realisation of its assets than would follow upon a formal winding up of the company.

administrator — a person appointed by the court to manage the affairs of a company under an **administration order** (qv).

administrator at (*or* in) law — a title of a parent as the tutor of a pupil child or the curator of a minor child. Tutory and curatory are now replaced in respect of persons under sixteen by guardianship: see the Age of Legal Capacity (Scotland) Act 1991, s 5.

admiralty — the maritime law jurisdiction of the Court of Session and sheriff court, derived from the former Courts of Admiralty.

admissible evidence — testimony given to a court or tribunal which conforms with the law of evidence in respect of competency and relevance.

admissibility — competence; the quality of a cause of action, claim or pleading which entitles it to be heard on its merits by a given court. For example, a case may be dismissed as inadmissable by the Court of First Instance for want of sufficient standing of the person raising the action or because it is time-barred. **[E]**

admonition — a form of disposal by a court, in criminal cases, after an offender has been found guilty, where the court considers that a censure or warning would be a more appropriate means of dealing with the accused than the imposition of a greater punishment.

adopted as holograph — a phrase written by the subscriber to a deed immediately above his signature which implies his acceptance of the deed as though it were handwritten by him throughout. Witnesses to his signature are then unnecessary. Abolished in respect of documents executed on or after 1 August 1995: see the Requirements of Writing (Scotland) Act 1995, ss 1, 11(3).

adoption —
(1) the acceptance as valid of a document which would otherwise be defective on grounds of informality. *See also* **adopted as holograph**.
(2) the vesting of parental rights and duties in an individual when those of the natural parents are extinguished.
(3) the making by a Community institution of a measure having legal effect. **[E]**

ADR — alternative dispute resolution; informal methods of resolving disputes without resort to litigation including **arbitration** (qv), and conciliation or **mediation** (qv).

adults with incapacity — person aged 16 or over who lacks the capacity to take some or all decisions for themselves, because of mental disorder or inability to communicate.

advance fixing — the fixing, before a transaction is entered into, of the amount of levy to be charged or refund to be allowed on the import or export of certain **agricultural products** (qv) under the **common agricultural policy** (qv). **[E]**

adversary procedure. *See* **accusatorial**.

advise — to give judgment after having taken time for consideration. *See also* *avizandum*.

advocate —
(1) A person who has been admitted to the Faculty of Advocates and is thereby a member of the Scottish Bar (*English law*: barrister); a lawyer who specialises in court pleadings and writing opinions. Until 1992 advocates had a monopoly right of audience in the Court of Session and High Court of Justiciary, but this was abolished by the Law Reform (Miscellaneous Provisions) (Scotland) Act 1990. Successful advocates usually become **Queen's Counsel** (qv) after about 15 years in practice. The term 'advocate' is never used in court where the correct term is '**counsel**' (qv);
(2) a solicitor who is a member of the Society of Advocates in Aberdeen;
(3) to submit the judgment of an inferior court for review. In modern practice this procedure is rare and is restricted to criminal jurisdiction by means of a bill of **advocation** (qv).

Advocate Depute (plural advocates depute) — an advocate appointed by the Lord Advocate to act as Crown counsel and to assist or represent him in the prosecution of crime in the High Court of Justiciary. The most senior advocate depute is known as the Home Depute.

Advocate-General — a judicial officer of the European Court of Justice, of whom there are (in 2003) eight. To each case before the Court is assigned an Advocate-General, who attends the hearing and delivers in open court an impartial reasoned opinion discussing the issues of fact and law raised and recommending to the Court a solution to them. **[E]**

Advocate General for Scotland — the Scottish law officer of the British government, responsible for giving the government legal advice on non-devolved matters, the post was created by the Scotland Act 1998.

advocates' clerk — administrative support officer for a particular group of advocates with the task of liasing with instructing solicitors, distributing work and negotiating fees etc. *See also* **stable**.

advocation — an old form of appeal to a superior court. It now survives only in criminal procedure where it is occasionally used by the Crown to bring irregularities in an inferior court before the High Court of Justiciary. It proceeds upon a writ known as a **bill** (qv).

aedificatum solo, solo cedit — what is built upon the ground accrues to it.

aemulatio vicini — the purpose of annoying or injuring a neighbour, a motive which may render unlawful an otherwise lawful act.

affidavit — a written statement of fact made on oath and signed before a **notary public** (qv). Previously rarely used in Scotland but now in general use in undefended actions for divorce and certain other actions.

affiliation *or* **filiation** — an action raised to determine the paternity of a child, usually an illegitimate child.

affinity — the relationship arising between the husband and the blood-relations of the wife and between the wife and the blood-relations of the husband.

affirm — to declare solemnly as a witness the truth of one's evidence when one objects to taking an oath. In practice the form of words is 'I solemnly, sincerely and truly declare and affirm that I will tell the truth, the whole truth and nothing but the truth'.

affirmative —

(1) in the law of property a real burden is affirmative if it imposes an obligation to do something including an obligation to defray or contribute towards some cost. Contrast **negative burden**. See Title Conditions (Scotland) Act 2003, s 2(1)(a), (2)(a);

(2) in the law of negligence, an affirmative duty of action is a duty of care whose implementation involves positive conduct on the part of the person bound.

affirmative resolution — a method of imposing a measure of parliamentary control on **subordinate legislation** (qv) under which a **statutory instrument** (qv) is required to be laid before Parliament and approved (1) in the case of control by the United Kingdom Parliament, by a resolution of either House of Parliament or in some cases of the House of Commons or (2) in the case of control by the Scottish Parliament, by a resolution of the Parliament. Contrast **negative resolution**.

affreightment — a contract for the carriage of goods in a ship, either under a **bill of lading** (qv) or a **charterparty** (qv).

affront — insulting or threatening words or conduct.

aforementioned — mentioned already; slightly old fashioned word, much used by drafters of contracts.

age of legal capacity — as a general rule (subject to some exceptions) persons of 16 or over have legal capacity to enter into any transaction and persons under that age lack that capacity: Age of Legal Capacity (Scotland) Act 1991.

agency — a contract under which one person, an agent, is given authority by another person, called a principal, to represent the principal and to enter into contracts with third parties binding the principal as well as the third parties. Unlike the contract of mandate, agency is not gratuitous.

agent —

(1) a person authorised expressly, or by implication, to act or make legally binding agreements on behalf of another, known as the principal. *See also* **law agent**; **principal**.

(2) the representative of a member state or **Community institution** (qv) in proceedings before the European Court of Justice and the Court of First Instance. **[E]**

agent disburser — a solicitor who has advanced or incurred the costs of an action and who may be entitled to seek in his own name a decree for the expenses awarded to his client.

aggravation — a circumstance in a criminal case which adds to the seriousness of the case, eg the existence of a previous conviction, or the circumstances or purpose of an assault.

agreement — in competition law, a stated 'concurrence of wills' or common scheme (which may fall short of a contract generally recognised) between or amongst **undertakings** (qv) by which they align, or limit, their individual commercial conduct in the market.

aggregated discount — a discount granted to a buyer which is calculated by reference to the total volume sold to all buyers during a specified period, and not to the amount sold to the buyer in question during that period. **[E]**

aggregation and apportionment — a system used in the European Community social security regulations of adding up the contributions made and qualifying periods completed in different member states for the purpose of acquiring and retaining the right to a benefit or determining its amount (aggregation) and then dividing the responsibility for paying the benefit between or among the member states concerned (apportionment). **[E]**

agnate — a person related to another on the father's side, as distinct from a cognate, who is related on the mother's side.

agricultural holding — a tenancy of a farm or agricultural land. *See also* **croft**, **small tenancy**, **small landholding**.

agricultural product — a product subject to the **common agricultural policy** (qv) of the European Community, defined by art 32(1) of the EC Treaty as a product of the soil, stock farming or fisheries, or a product of first stage processing directly related to a product of the soil, stock farming or fisheries. **[E]**

aid —

(1) assistance;

(2) assistance whether pecuniary or in some other form, under European Community law. *See also* **state aid**. **[E]**

alias — an assumed or alternative name, usually assumed for criminal purposes.

alibi — elsewhere: a defence to a criminal charge that the accused was not at the *locus* of the crime but at some other specified place.

alien — any person who is not a British citizen.

alienation — the transfer of property from one party to another.

aliment — provision for maintenance for the support of a spouse or child. Formerly the law recognised a mutual obligation of support between ancestors and dependants. See now the Family Law (Scotland) Act 1985, ss 1–7.

alimentary — (as a description of a fund) not available to meet the claims of creditors, eg alimentary liferent. Formerly common in antenuptial contracts of marriage where property was provided by the wife; since 1984 the privilege may extend only to funds provided by third persons.

aliud est celare, aliud tacere — it is one thing to conceal, another to remain silent: Cicero, *De Officiis*. Thus a seller in some situations may remain silent, but must not conceal defects.

aliunde — otherwise, or from some other source or direction. Eg certain contractual obligations may be proved only by writ or oath when more than the relevant statutory period had elapsed after it fell due; before then it could be proved *aliunde* in any lawful manner.

allenarly (adv) — only; solely; exclusively. Usually applied in cases of liferent to emphasise the restriction of an interest, preventing its being construed as a fee.

allodial (adj) — applied to absolute land tenure (eg church property, property acquired by compulsory purchase and property in udal tenure) in contradistinction to feudal property held of a feudal superior. On the abolition of the feudal system of land tenure on 28 November 2004 (*see* **feu**; **feudal tenure**), an estate of *dominium utile* (ie the estate of the feuar or vassal) will cease to exist as a feudal estate but shall forthwith become the ownership of the land: Abolition of Feudal Tenure etc (Scotland) Act 2000, s 2.

allotment —
(1) a plot of land let by a local authority for cultivation;
(2) the allocation of shares in a company.

alluvio — alluvion, the gradual accretion of new land by the deposit of sand and earth through the action of the sea or river to the benefit of the owner of land to which it becomes attached.

ALT — Association of Law Teachers.

alternative dispute resolution. *See* **ADR**

alterum non laedere — to harm no one: a basic legal principle or duty.

altius non tollendi — of not raising higher, a **servitude** (qv) preventing an owner of ground from erecting buildings beyond a certain height.

alveus — the bed of a river, stream or loch.

amand — a financial penalty: an obsolete term traditionally applied to the payment of an award of expenses as a condition precedent to further procedure or proceedings.

amend — to alter the written pleadings in an action, by leave of the court, after the record is closed, or to alter the instance, crave or conclusions at any time. Cf **adjust**.

amerce — to assess a financial penalty: an obsolescent term now usually found only in proceedings for contempt of court.

amicus curiae — a friend of the court; one who argues at the request or with the leave of the court for an unrepresented party or in the public interest.

AMS — Additional Member System – one of the two methods of voting for electing members of the **Scottish Parliament** (qv)

Amsterdam Treaty. *See* **Treaty of Amsterdam. [E]**

ancillary real burden — a **real burden** (qv) is ancillary if it consists of a right to enter or otherwise make use of property, or makes provision for management or administration, but only for a purpose ancillary to those of an **affirmative** (qv) real burden or a **negative** (qv) **real burden** (qv).

anent — concerning.

animo et facto — by act and intention: factors determining the acquisition of a domicile of choice or the possession of some thing, in contrast with its custody.

animus donandi — the intention of giving as a gift, rarely presumed by the law except as between husband and wife.

animus injuriandi — the intention of harming or insulting.

animus negotia aliena gerendi — the intention to manage another's affairs; one of the requirements of *negotiorum gestio.*

animus possidendi — for some purposes acquisition of possession requires both *animus* (mind) and *corpus* (body).

animus remanendi — the intention of remaining; where domicile is in issue, used to indicate the intention of creating a permanent residence.

animus revertendi — the intention of returning, as of domesticated animals, pigeons in a dovecot etc, of whom ownership is not lost by their merely temporary absence because they are presumed to intend to return to their accustomed habitations.

annual rent — interest on money. To evade pre-Reformation prohibitions on lending at interest lenders contracted to receive a yearly rent from land, thus 'annual rent' became synonymous with 'interest'.

annuity — a right to a yearly payment of money.

annulment — reduction; a judicial declaration that a measure (eg of a Community institution) otherwise having legal effect is void and thereby depriving it of legal effect. **[E]**

answer — a written pleading given to a court in replication to the written claim of a pursuer.

ante — before.

ante litem motam — before an action is raised.

ante omnia — before everything; before anything else.

anticipatory breach of contract — an indication given by one contracting party to the other contracting party that he will breach the contract in the future sometimes called a repudiation of the contract. Such an indication or repudiation does not by itself terminate the contract but it does entitle the injured contracting party to rescind the contract and claim damages.

anti-dumping — measures under European Community, or other, law against the **dumping** (qv) of goods. **[E]**

anti-dumping duty — a charge imposed under European Community law upon the importation of dumped goods. **[E]**

apocha trium annorum — receipt for three years: a presumption arising from the discharge or formal receipt of three consecutive periodical (though not necessarily annual) payments that all similar prior payments have been made.

apparent heir — prior to 1964, the person to whom succession to heritable property had actually opened by the death of the ancestor, but who had not yet completed title. Cf **heir-apparent**.

apparent insolvency — the circumstances, replacing the concept of notour bankruptcy, which must be established under the Bankruptcy (Scotland) Act 1985 (see s 7) as a prerequisite to the initiation of sequestration proceedings by creditors.

appeal — an action raised by the losing party in a case which takes the case to a higher court in the hope of having the existing decision reversed.

appeal court. *See* **appellate court.**

appearance — a step taken or notice given by the defender in a civil action indicating that he proposes to defend the action.

appellant — a person appealing to a higher court from the decision of a lower court (eg in a criminal case from the sheriff court or district court to the High Court of Justiciary, or in a civil case from the Court of Session to the House of Lords).

appellate court — a court which reviews the decisions of courts of **first instance** (qv) at the request of a party. In Scotland these include the **Sheriff Principal** (qv), the **Inner House** (qv) and the **House of Lords** (qv) (and in devolution cases the **Privy Council** (qv)).

applicant countries — states which have applied to join the European Union; in 2003 there were 14 applicant countries. *See* **accession countries. [E]**

appointment. *See* **power of appointment.**

apportion — to divide property or rights into appropriate shares as between those entitled, eg as between **liferenter** (qv) and **fiar** (qv).

appraiser — in diligence, the person entrusted with the valuation of goods.

apprehend — to arrest.

approbate and reprobate — to take advantage of one part of a deed and reject the rest. This is forbidden by law. A deed must be accepted or rejected as a whole.

approximation of laws. *See* **harmonisation of laws. [E]**

APR — Annual Percentage Rate, the percentage rate which a loan will cost each year, including all charges.

APS — Acts of the Parliaments of Scotland, the statutes enacted by the Pre-1707 Scottish Parliament.

apud acta — among the acts, referring to orders judicially pronounced in open court in the presence of the parties and which must be obeyed without further notice.

aquaeductus — the rural servitude of aqueduct conferring on the owner of the dominant tenement the right to convey water through the servient tenement by pipes or canals.

aquaehaustus — a rural servitude conferring on the owner of the dominant tenement the right to water cattle on the servient tenement.

arbiter — a person appointed to adjudicate outside the courts in a dispute. On a question of fact, his decision is final; on a question of law, unless otherwise agreed, he may (on the application of either party) and must (if the Court of Session so directs) state a case for the court's opinion on the question of law.

arbitrage — financial term for finding the difference in prices between two financial instruments and exploiting the difference for profit eg by the simultaneous purchase and sale on different markets, of the same or equivalent financial instruments to profit from price or currency differentials.

arbitration — the settlement of a dispute between parties by the decision of experts of their choice rather than by the courts. Arbitration is usually made under laws and procedures agreed upon in advance.

area of freedom, security and justice — a goal of the European Union, to be 'established progressively' by means of the adoption of rules on the **free movement of persons** (qv) with 'flanking' measures on border controls, asylum, immigration and police, judicial and administrative co-operation amongst competent national authorities. **[E]**

arles — a small sum of money or small part of a commodity given as an earnest (arrhae) or token of the completion of a bargain.

arms —
(1) weapons;
(2) heraldic emblems or armorial bearings unique to, and belonging to, a person, *see* **coat of arms**.

arrest —
(1) to apprehend or detain a person in execution of a warrant for arrest or in virtue of powers of arrest such as are vested in a police constable or other officer of the law in virtue of citizens' powers of arrest;
(2) to lay an **arrestment** (qv).

arrestee — a person subject to an arrestment in whose hands the arrestment is laid and who owes the arrested debt or has possession or detention of the **arrested** (qv)property.

arrestment — in the law of **diligence** (qv) the attachment of the property of a debtor or **defender** (qv) which is in the hands of a third party to obtain security against the debtor for payment of the debt or to found jurisdiction against a defender. In the case of an admiralty arrestment of a ship, the ship may be and usually is in the possession of the debtor. *See* **furthcoming**.

arrestment in execution - arrestment used to enforce (execute) a court decree, or an order by a tribunal for payment, or an extract registered document of debt. *See* **summary diligence**.

arrestment on the dependence — an **arrestment** (qv) is on the dependence when it is in force, while a court action is proceeding, for the purpose of securing the amount claimed in the action.

arrestment to found jurisdiction — an arrestment used for the purpose of bringing a foreigner within the jurisdiction of the Scottish courts.

arrhae — earnest: *see* **arles**.

art and part — in the capacity of accessory or accomplice in relation to a criminal act.

Article 6 letter — a response from the European Commission to a **complaint** (qv) alleging anticompetitive conduct by which the Commission adopts and justifies a decision not to pursue the matter. **[E]**

articles — clauses, paragraphs or sections of a legal document.

articles of association — management regulations of a registered company.

articles of roup — conditions of the contract prescribed for a public auction, especially of land.

artificial person — a person (other than a natural person) to which juristic identity is given by law.

ARTL — Automated Registration of Title to Land; a project which aims eventually to bring about paper-free registration of title to rights in land in Scotland.

as accords — agreeable or conformable to law.

ascendant — kin to a deceased person from a previous generation, eg parent or great-uncle.

ascription — the application of payments to particular debts.

ASP — act of the **Scottish Parliament** (qv) made from 1999 onwards.

assault — an attack upon the person of another which is both a crime and a civil delict.

Assembly — original, now obsolete, name for the **European Parliament** (qv). **[E]**

assent — term applied in Community law where a measure may be adopted by the Community institutions only with the positive endorsement ('assent') of the European Parliament. **[E]**

assessor —
 (1) a person with specialised knowledge relevant to the subject matter of an action who assists a judge;
 (2) in local government, a person who assesses the annual value of property for rating purposes;
 (3) a representative on a council or board appointed by another council or person.

assignation —
 (1) act of transferring rights in incorporeal moveable property from one party to another;
 (2) the document transferring such rights.

assignatus utitur jure auctoris — an assignee exercises the right of his cedent, and no more.

assize —
 (1) the sittings of a court;
 (2) a jury.

associate — in the law of bankruptcy and insolvency, a person within certain categories of relationship with another person: see the Bankruptcy (Scotland) Act 1985, s 74, and the Insolvency Act 1986, s 435.

association — a degree of integration with the European Community which falls short of **accession** (qv). Association applies in different ways to non-European countries and territories of several member states and to third countries or international organisations. **[E]**

association agreement — an agreement concluded under article 310 of the EC Treaty between the European Community and a third country, a union of third countries or an international organisation, which establishes an association involving reciprocal rights and obligations, common action and special procedures. **[E]**

assoilzie (pronounced 'a-soil(y)i') — to absolve; to decide finally a civil action in favour of the defender. The judgment is termed 'absolvitor'; the cognate verb (transitive) is 'assoilzie'. In a criminal case when the panel is acquitted, he is 'assoilzied *simpliciter*'.

assumption — adoption of eg an additional trustee or a partner; assumption of risk. *See* **volenti non fit inuria**.

assurance policy — a policy of insurance on a person's life in which in return for premiums the insurance company undertakes to pay the assured person an indemnity if dies or suffers harm.

assythment — an obsolete claim for compensation for injury to feelings formerly made by relatives of a person killed by the defender's criminal act. It was abolished by the Damages (Scotland) Act 1976, s 8.

asylum — the claiming of residence in one country in order to avoid persecution in another.

at arm's length — where two parties are independent of each other they are said to be at arm's length.

at will — as of a contract (eg partnership or tenancy) terminable by either party on reasonable notice, as contrasted with terminable on the expiry of a fixed term.

ATM — automated telling machine; ie a cash dispenser.

attachment —
 (1) a form of diligence by which corporeal moveables owned by a debtor may be seized and sold by an officer of **court** (qv) on the instructions of a creditor holding a warrant for attachment. Attachment was introduced by the Debt Arrangement and

Attachment (Scotland) Act 2002 to replace the diligence of poinding and warrant sale which was abolished;

(2) a generic term for the effect of an inchoate diligence in imposing a nexus on property.

attempt — an attempt to commit a crime is itself a crime under the Criminal Justice (Scotland) Act 1975.

attestation — the authentication of a deed or other instrument by the signatures and designations of witnesses before whom the granter signed or to whom he acknowledged his signature.

attorney — a person acting under the authority of a power of attorney.

attour — besides; as well as; over and above.

auctor in rem suam — one who acts in his own interest. A trustee, agent, *negotiorum gestor* or other fiduciary may not so act.

audi alteram partem — hear the other side: the rule of natural justice that no decision should be reached by a court or tribunal until all parties have been given an opportunity to be heard.

Audit Scotland — agency which audits funds spent by the **Scottish Executive** (qv) and or public sector bodies in Scotland.

auditor — a person appointed to check and verify the accounts of companies, partnerships, trusts, public and local authorities and other organisations.

Auditor General for Scotland — officer appointed by the **sovereign** (qv) on the **Scottish Parliament's** (qv) nomination, who acts independently of the Parliament and the Executive to exercise statutory functions of financial control, accounting and audit.

Auditor of Court — the court officer or other person responsible for the examination and **taxation** (qv) of accounts in the Court of Session or a sheriff court.

augmentation — an increase in the payment of periodic sums, eg rent or stipend.

authentication — features establishing the validity of a deed, eg the signatures of witnesses.

author — a person from whom title is derived.

authorised lay representative — a person other than a lawyer who represents a party to a court action.

authority — a judicial decision, authoritative textbook or statute justifying a proposition or statement of law.

automatism — where, through illness or other grounds, an individual acts without being conscious of his acts and therefore is not legally responsible for his actions.

autonomous duty — a customs tariff of the European Community fixed other than pursuant to an agreement with a third country or an international organisation. **[E]**

AVCs — Additional Voluntary Contributions, method of enhancing an occupational pension scheme by making extra payments.

aver — to make an **averment** (qv).

average. *See* **general average**.

average rate — the level of **turnover equalisation taxes** (qv) under European Community law calculated at a single rate deemed to correspond to the aggregate tax burden borne by domestic products where it is difficult to calculate the precise level of compensation required in the case of imports. **[E]**

averment — a statement of fact made (usually in written pleadings) which the party making it asserts that he can prove in court.

avizandum — to be looked into or considered: the taking of time for consideration before a judgment is given.

avoid — to reduce or set aside a contract.

avulsio **or avulsion** — the violent severance of land by the action of a river, eg by flood or where the river changes its course, having no effect on rights of property.

award — the decision of a tribunal or arbiter; more rarely, the ruling of a court.

b

back; back up —
(1) to indorse details (eg name and type of deed) on the back of a folded document;
(2) to indorse a warrant so as to permit its execution outwith the original jurisdiction.

back bond; back letter — an agreement in the form of a letter, qualifying the provisions of another document that is unqualified, eg a standard security, and formerly an *ex facie* absolute disposition (which is obsolescent since 1970).

backdate —
(1) to make a court order have effect retrospectively as for example by awarding aliment for a past period;
(2) to put an earlier date on a cheque or invoice.

backhand rent — rent agreed to be paid in arrear, ie after the period of the lease to which it relates, as distinct from **forehand rent** (qv).

bail — security for the release of a person charged with a crime or an offence on conditions designed to ensure that he appears before the court: see the Bail (Scotland) Act 1980.

bailie —
(1) prior to the reorganisation of local government in 1975, a magistrate in a Scottish burgh;
(2) formerly the representative of the superior who appeared on the ground to grant infeftment in feudal conveyances;
(3) formerly an officer of a barony or regality;
(4) there is still a Bailie of the Abbey of Holyrood, the precinct of the royal palace.

bairns' part — the part of the moveable estate of a deceased person to which his issue, natural or adopted, have a legal right. *See* **legitim**.

balance of probabilities — the normal standard of proof of facts in civil proceedings is proof on balance of probabilities as compared with the standard in criminal proceedings namely proof beyond reasonable doubt.

balance sheet — a statement presenting a true and fair view of the financial position, assets and liabilities of a business at a specific point of time such as the end of a financial year or other accounting period.

bank — an institution which accepts money and collects **cheques** (qv) for customers; honours cheques or orders drawn on bankers by customers; and keeps running accounts for customers in which debits and credits are entered.

banknote — printed paper money.

bankruptcy. *See* **sequestration; apparent insolvency**.

Bar —
(1) the members of the Faculty of Advocates in Scotland;
(2) solicitors practising in a local court, eg members of the Glasgow Bar Association.

bar of trial. *See* **plea in bar of trial**.

bareboat charter — type of maritime contract which is effectively a 'lease on a boat' where the charterer takes over all responsibility for the vessel for the duration of charter; also known as a demise charter.

baron —
(1) in Scotland the holder of a **barony** (qv);
(2) in the **peerage** (qv) other than the Scots peerage the lowest rank of peer.

barony — a direct grant by the Crown of an estate in land *in liberam baroniam* (that is 'in free barony') often referred to as a feudal barony to distinguish it from a **peerage** (qv). Few practical benefits remain, and the privileges in the form of civil and criminal jurisdiction are obsolete and will be abolished when the Abolition of Feudal Tenure etc. (Scotland) Act 2000 comes into force. Barony titles may be sold for significant sums and for this reason the dignity of baron is to be retained by the 2000 Act as a form of incorporeal heritable property.

barony court — an inferior court under the hereditary jurisdiction of a baron, whose jurisdiction is obsolete and which will be abolished on 28 November 2004 when the relevant provisions of the Abolition of Feudal Tenure etc. (Scotland) Act 2000 come into force.

barter — a contract of exchange (in Roman law *permutatio*) under which the ownership of one moveable thing is exchanged for the ownership of another moveable thing, neither thing being money. Cf **excambion** (qv) of land.

base holding — a holding, under the feudal system of land tenure, from a person who does not hold directly from the Crown but whose holding has been subfeued from an original superior holder.

basic price — the price used to determine the level of market prices at which **agricultural products** (qv) covered by certain common organisations of the market within the **common agricultural policy** (qv) may be sold into **intervention** (qv). **[E]**

battle of the forms — dispute as to which one of two or more differing standard form contracts governs a particular contract.

before answer — before deciding the main question raised in civil proceedings. The relevancy of a proof offered for example may be questionable, and the court may pronounce an **interlocutor** (qv) allowing a proof 'before answer' to the question of relevancy.

behoof — advantage; benefit.

bench — (colloquial) the judiciary; derived from the raised bench upon which judges sit in court.

benefice — the living or provision for a minister of a parish.

beneficiary — a person who benefits or will benefit from the terms of a deed such as a will or a trust instrument.

beneficium — a right, privilege or benefit.

beneficium cedendarum actionum — the benefit of cession (assignation) of actions:
(1) in Roman law the right of a cautioner, who has paid the debt for the principal debtor, to compel the creditor to asign to the cautioner his right of action to enable the cautioner to exercise a right of relief against the principal debtor;
(2) in Scots law a cautioner, co-cautioner and co-obligant have a right of relief against respectively the principal debtor, other co-cautioners and other co-obligants, without the need for an assignation from the creditor.

beneficium competentiae — the right of a bankrupt to retain from his estate sufficient funds for his own maintenance; and the similar right of a person who is liable to aliment dependants.

beneficium discussionis. See beneficium ordinis.

beneficium divisionis — benefit of division; the right of a cautioner that all co-cautioners should share the obligation *pro rata*.

beneficium ordinis — benefit of discussion, the right of a debtor to insist that the creditor proceed first against the principal debtor (amended by the Mercantile Law Amendment (Scotland) Act 1856).

benefited property. See **real burden.**

Berne Convention — Convention for the Protection of Literary and Artistic Works, signed at Berne, Switzerland in 1886; the leading international copyright treaty.

beyond reasonable doubt — the standard of proof in criminal proceedings. See **balance of probabilities**.

bid rigging — collusion amongst **undertakings** (qv) to agree a response to a tender; prohibited by competition law and, if dishonest, may constitute a **cartel offence** (qv).

bill —
(1) a form of procedure now used only in certain proceedings in the Court of Session or the High Court of Justiciary;
(2) a document asserting an obligation for the payment of money on a debt;
(3) provisions presented to a parliament for the purpose of being passed into law as a

statute (qv), whereafter it is known as an act.

Bill Chamber — a former department of the Court of Session, with responsibility among other things for proceedings begun by bill, abolished in 1933 and replaced by the Petition Department.

bill of exchange — a three-party instrument written, dated, and signed containing an unconditional order by a drawer that directs a drawee to pay a definite sum of money to a payee on demand or at a specified future date.

bill of lading — a document by which goods are loaded and unloaded by ship (the term 'lading' is a corruption of 'loading'); the instrument is issued by a warehouseman or carrier to a shipper and serves as a receipt for goods shipped, as evidence of the contract of carriage, and as a document of title for the goods.

billet — an order requiring the occupier of premises to provide accommodation for members of HM forces or their vehicles.

black clause — a clause in an agreement which causes the agreement to infringe the competition rules or fall outside the scope of a **block exemption** (qv).

black letter law — (in informal legal usage)
(1) legal doctrine; the formal law set out in books of the law;
(2) the antithesis of the law in action and of law reform;
(3) the study of law as practised by lawyers and applied in the courts – sometimes called lawyer's law – as distinct from the social, economic and political aspects of law.

black list — terms set out in a **block exemption** (qv) which, if breached, cause an agreement to fall outwith the application of the block exemption.

blackmail — the extortion of money by the use of illegal force or threats. Originally it was an annual extortion paid to armed bands for 'protection'.

blanch. *See* **blench**.

blank bond — a bond, long since invalidated by statute, containing a blank in place of the creditor's name, and which accordingly circulated as a bearer bond.

blench *or* **blanch** — a feudal holding where the feuduty takes only a nominal form, eg one penny Scots, if asked only. *See* **feu**; **feudal tenure**.

block exemption — in competition law, **exemption** (qv) from a prohibition for certain defined categories of agreements or restrictive practices. The exemption then applies automatically to every agreement falling within the defined category and conditions without the need for **notification** (qv) and individual exemption; the benefit of exemption may be withdrawn in a particular case where appropriate by a competent administrative authority.

blood relationship — the relationship between two people who have either one common parent (relationship of the half blood) or two common parents (relationship of the whole blood), as distinguished from relationship by marriage, where no parent is shared. Compare **affinity**.

blood test —
(1) a test on a sample of blood to determine whether the alcohol level exceeds the limit prescribed under road traffic legislation;
(2) a test on a sample of blood to determine whether paternity can be excluded.

boilerplate clause — colloquial term for standard clauses in commercial agreements, eg clauses governing jurisdiction, indemnity, arbitration etc.

boll — a measure of grain or pulse. 16 bolls amount to a chalder.

bona fide(s) — in good faith, acting honestly, even if negligently or mistakenly, or even foolishly, but not fraudulently or deceptively or without inquiry where reasonable suspicion is raised.

bona fides non patitur ut bis idem exigatur — good faith does not allow the same debt to be exacted twice.

bona fide perceptio et consumptio — gathering and consumption of crops in good faith by persons having an apparently good but in fact defective title.

bona vacantia — property of persons dying without successors, and other ownerless property, which falls to the Crown and is administered by the Crown Agent who has taken over the functions of the Queen's and Lord Treasurer's Remembrancer.

bond —
(1) a written obligation to pay money or to do or refrain from doing an act.
(2) in the stock market, a bond usually refers to a document evidencing a debt, and bearing a stated rate or stated rates of interest, or stating a formula for determining that rate, and maturing on a fixed date. Government Bonds are instruments of this sort issued by government as a means of raising finance from the markets;
(3) until replaced by the standard security in 1970, the bond and disposition in security was the normal form of securing a debt with heritable property.

bond of corroboration — in conveyancing, an additional obligation granted by the debtor in a bond by which he corroborates the original obligation.

booking — a form of land tenure in the Burgh of Paisley under which rights were secured by registration in the Register of Booking, and now secured by registration in the Land Register of Scotland.

Books of Adjournal — the records of the High Court of Justiciary.

Books of Council and Session —
(1) the Registers of Deeds and Probative Writs, kept by the Keeper of the Registers of Scotland, in which a wide variety of deeds may be registered;
(2) the Register of Judgments kept by the Keeper of the Registers of Scotland in compliance with the Civil Jurisdiction and Judgments Act 1982 in order to register certificates of foreign judgments passed in the

Books of Sederunt — records kept by the Court of Session in which Acts of Sederunt require to be inserted.

border tax adjustment — an adjustment under European Community law of the tax burden on imported goods comprising (1) remission of the tax imposed in the country of exportation, and (2) the imposition of a **compensatory tax** (qv) in the country of importation, in order to make the tax borne by the import equal to that borne by the same product when produced and consumed in the country of importation. **[E]**

border warrant — an obsolete form of warrant for the arrest of the effects and person of someone in England for debts owed in Scotland.

bounding charter; bounding title — a deed which defines the land comprised in it by reference to its boundaries, thus preventing any increase in land held by possession for the prescriptive period. Reference may be to walls, roads, the land of another person, or by measurement or a plan.

bowing — a form of agricultural contract whereby one party lets his herd to the other (the bower) for the bower to graze it on the former's land, while the bower retains the profits from eg dairy produce.

box — to lodge papers required in proceedings in the Court of Session for the clerk to place in the box for the appropriate judge or court officer (obsolete).

bracket tariff — a tariff under European Community law which, instead of prescribing a fixed amount for each item, sets upper and lower limits within which the amount applicable to each item is to be fixed by the competent authority. **[E]**

breach — the breaking, infringement or violation of a law, legal right, contract, unilateral promise other obligation, arrestment or other **diligence** (qv) or duty, by either act or omission.

breach of arrestment — the wrongful paying away by an arrestee of funds or property arrested in his hands to the common debtor or another party in breach of the prohibition in the arrestment.

breach of confidence — a civil wrong (whether a breach of a contract to maintain confidentiality or a delict) consisting of the disclosure of information to a third party which the wrongdoer has an obligation owed to the confider to keep confidential.

breach of contract — the failure by a party to a contract to implement any of its terms which are binding on him. If the breach is proved the injured party may claim damages, refuse to perform his obligations, rescind the contract or seek specific implement as appropriate in the circumstances.

breach of interdict — non-compliance with the terms of an interdict is punishable by the court pronouncing the interdict as a contempt of court, on a petition and complaint by the injured party with the concurrence of the public prosecutor (Lord Advocate in the Court of Session; procurator fiscal in the sheriff court).

breach of the peace — a common law offence of causing a public disturbance, such as fighting, shouting or swearing in a public place, or conduct causing or likely to cause annoyance, disturbance or disruption of the peace of the neighbourhood.

breach of trust — an act or default of a trustee consisting of embezzlement or failure to account for secret profits or intromissions, or an irregularity or error of judgment imposing on the trustee a personal liability to make good to the trust estate the loss he has caused and to account for profits.

breath test — a preliminary test to obtain from a person's breath an indication whether the proportion of alcohol in his blood is likely to exceed the limit prescribed by road traffic legislation.

brevi manu — summarily; action taken to correct a wrong without seeking a remedy through the courts.

brevitatis causa — for the sake of brevity: a phrase frequently found in written pleadings to explain the incorporation by reference of the terms of some other document.

brieve —
(1) a document once founding almost all civil actions in Scotland, but now in practice obsolete;
(2) a warrant issued from Chancery to a judge, ordering an inquest by jury into certain specified matters.

brocard — a legal maxim derived from Roman law or ancient custom and accounted part of the common law.

Brussels — colloquial term for the European Union derived from the fact that the **Commission of the European Communities** (qv) and the **Council of the European Union** (qv) have their official seats there. **[E]**

Brussels Convention 1968 — The Convention on Jurisdiction and the Enforcement of Judgments in Civil and Commercial Matters, adopted at Brussels on 27 September 1968 and in force as of 1 February 1973 which provides uniform rules on jurisdiction and the recognition and enforcement of judgments for all member states of the European Community; now largely replaced by the **Brussels Regulation** (qv). **[E]**

Brussels Regulation — Council Regulation No 44/2001 of 22 December 2000 on jurisdiction and the recognition and enforcement of judgments in civil and commercial matters. It came into force on 1 March 2002, replacing the **Brussels Convention** (qv) except for matters between Denmark and any other contracting party to the Convention. **[E]**

building contract — not a term of art; a contract for the construction of a building. *See* **construction contract**. Standard form building contracts are issued by the Joint Contracts Tribunal (JCT) and by the Scottish Building Contract Committee which issues the Scottish Building Contract.

building society — a society established under the Building Societies Acts whose principal object is to raise funds from its members and to make secured loans to them to assist them to purchase dwelling houses.

building warrant — a warrant granted under the Building (Scotland) Acts by a buildings authority authorising the construction or alteration of a building or other structure.

bulk goods — a mass of goods of the same kind contained in a defined space or area which are interchangeable with any other goods in the bulk of the same number or quantity. In a sale of unascertained goods forming part of an identified bulk, special statutory rules provide for the buyer becoming owner in common of a share in the bulk.

bumping — the displacement of an employee by another who, because of reorganisation, is moved from one department to another.

burden — a limitation, restriction or incumbrance on the use, enjoyment, ownership etc of property. Burdens may be real or impose mere personal obligations. *See* **real burden**.

burden of proof. *See* **onus of proof.**

burdened property. *See* **real burden.**

burgage — an obsolete type of feudal tenure whereby property in royal burghs was held from the Crown.

burgh — a town brought into being or incorporated by royal charter or by or in accordance with statute. Since local government reorganisation in 1975 burghs no longer have any political or legal functions, having been absorbed by the new forms of local authority. District courts have replaced the former burgh courts.

byelaw — a form of **subordinate legislation** (qv) made eg by a local authority under power delegated by Parliament, and usually confirmed by some higher authority eg the Secretary of State.

C

cabinet —
   (1) a committee of senior government ministers, in the United Kingdom government, headed by the Prime Minister which determines government policy and is governed by the doctrine of **collective responsibility** (qv). *See also* **Scottish Cabinet**.
   (2) the private office and supporting staff of a **European Commissioner** (qv), or judge of the **European Court of Justice** (qv) or the **Court of First Instance** (qv) personally appointed by the commissioner or judge; in this usage generally pronounced the French way (cabinay).**[E]**

caduciary — subject to lapse or escheat.

CAJR — the **Chancery and Judicial Registers** (qv).

call — a demand for payment made by a company or its liquidators to those shareholders whose shares are not fully paid up.

calling — the publication of a summons in the Court of Session by posting, in a list on the walls of the court and in the printed rolls of court, the names of the parties and of the pursuer's legal representative. The time for 'entering appearance' is determined by reference to the date of calling.

calling date — the day on which a **summary cause** (qv) summons in the sheriff court is first called before the sheriff clerk. The date is stated in the summons. Cf **return day**.

calling list. *See* **roll**.

camera — the chambers of a judge. Proceedings conducted there are heard *in camera*, ie in private.

candidate countries. *See* **accession countries**. **[E]**

Candlemas — a quarter day in Scotland (28 February: Term and Quarter Days (Scotland) Act 1990, s 1).

Canon law — law made by the church, especially the Roman Catholic Church, historically much Scots **consistorial** (qv) law derived from the pre-Reformation canon law; derived from the Greek word *kanon,* a rule or practical direction.

CAP. *See* **common agricultural policy**. **[E]**

capacity. *See* **legal capacity**.

capax — capable. Cf *incapax*.

capax doli — capable of or of an age to commit a crime.

caption — formerly a warrant for arrest in a civil process. As a 'process caption' it competently survives as a summary warrant to apprehend a solicitor to compel him to return to court a civil process which he has borrowed. As other normally effective remedies are available, it must be regarded now as a last resort!

carriage — the act or activity of carrying goods or passengers by air, or by land (eg road or rail) or by sea.

carrier — a person who holds himself out to the public as willing to carry goods or passengers for hire under a contract of carriage.

cartel — two or more competing **undertakings** (qv) which enter into **agreements** (qv) or practices for the purpose of diminishing competition in a particular product or service market to their mutual advantage; generally prohibited in competition law.

cartel offence — the **offence** (qv) of engaging dishonestly in certain types of cartel practices: Enterprise Act 2002, s 183.

case —
  (1) an action or proceeding before a court;
  (2) the written report of such proceedings;
  (3) the arguments of a party in court proceedings.

case law — judicial decisions as a source of law. *See also* **common law** and **precedents**.

cash credit — a contract of loan under which the borrower may withdraw sums required up to a prescribed limit, and repay the sums periodically, paying interest only on the amount actually borrowed.

Cassis de Dijon **rule**. *See* **rule of reason**. **[E]**

casual homicide — accidental killing where there is no fault on the part of the person causing the death.

casualty — a payment formerly due to a feudal superior or landlord on the occurrence of uncertain events. These payments are no longer exigible in respect of feus and are disallowed in respect of leases entered into after 1 September 1974.

casus amissionis — the occasion of circumstances of the loss, which must be shown when proving the tenor of a lost document.

casus improvisus — a case not provided for or not foreseen, frequently considered in the construction of rules, contracts and statutes.

casus incogitatus — unforeseen case.

casus omissus — a case omitted, where a situation has not been provided for within the existing law, especially in a statute.

catholic creditor — a creditor whose debt is secured over several subjects or the whole property of the debtor. He is bound to claim his debt according to equitable rules so as not to injure unnecessarily the claims of secondary creditors whose securities are postponed to his rights. Cf **secondary creditor**.

causa causans — the immediate cause; the effective or proximate cause of the harm occasioned where a duty has been breached.

causa cognita — a case known, heard and ready for judgment.

causa proxima, et non remota, spectatur — the near, and not the remote, cause is regarded. Eg a claimed loss must be a direct and not a remote consequence of a delict.

causa sine qua non — in the law of obligations, the cause but for which the harm would not have resulted. This is not necessarily the immediate cause.

causal system of transfer — in property law, a system whereby the validity of the act of transfer or conveyance depends on the validity of the underlying contract or promise to transfer. In such a system there must be a *justa causa traditionis,* that is to say, a valid legal ground (such as a contract or promise) underlying the transfer of ownership. A reduction of the underlying contract or promise will, by necessary implication, have the effect of reducing the conveyance. Contrast **abstract system of transfer**.

cause — an action or proceeding in a civil court.

cause of action — factual grounds of action which if proved or admitted will entitle the pursuer to the remedy which he concludes for or craves. The *facta probanda* (facts requiring to be proved).

caution (pronounced 'kay-shun') —
  (1) in civil matters, security by which one party guarantees the payment of anothers debt or the due performance of another's obligation or of some other legal act such as the administration of a trust estate;
  (2) in criminal practice, security for future good behaviour or as a condition of bail.

cautionary obligation — an obligation by way of **caution** (qv).

cautioner — person who is bound by a **cautionary obligation** (qv).

caveat — a formal notice to a court given by a party to proceedings to secure that no step affecting him will be taken in his absence or unless intimation is first given to him.

caveat emptor — let the buyer beware: a rule, basically of English law, much eroded by exceptions, both statutory and at common law.

CCP — **common commercial policy** (qv). **[E]**

CCT — **Common Customs Tariff**. (qv). **[E]**

CELEX — *Communitatis Europae Lex,* the official on-line database of **European Union** (qv) law, covering primary and secondary legislation including draft proposals published in the **Official Journal** (qv), **European Parliament** (qv) and **ECOSOC** (qv) and **Committee of the Regions** (qv) opinions and case law from the **European Court of Justice** (qv) and the **Court of First Instance** (qv). **[E]**

CEN — *Comité européen de normalisation* (European Committee for Standardisation) European bodies responsible for promoting greater uniformity in product regulations. **[E]**

censure — a motion put before the **European Parliament** (qv) which, if successfully carried, requires the European Commission to resign *en bloc.* **[E]**

certificate —
  (1) a document authorised by some person authenticaticating or authorising some mater within his authority;
  (2) in e-commerce a secure document containing information about the issuer (the certification authority), the certificate's owners, a public key, the period for which the certificate is valid, and the host to whom the certificate was issued. The token is designed in such a way that none of its details can be changed without invalidating the digital signature.

certification — an assurance to a party to proceedings of the implied or specified consequences of his failure to obey the will of the writ or court order. Where the order invites appearance in court, the consequences of failure are usually that the case will proceed in that party's absence or, occasionally, a warrant for his arrest.

certification authority — in e commerce the third party organisation which approves and provides the **public key infrastructure** (qv) technology necessary for the provision of secure e commerce by providing **public keys** (qv) and **private keys** (qv).

certiorate — to notify a fact formally.

certum est quod certum reddi potest — that is certain which can be made certain, such as a price, which may be established by reference to an authorised list or by measurement.

cess — an obsolete form of land tax.

cessante ratione legis cessat ipsa lex — when the reason for a law ceases, the law itself ceases to operate.

cessio bonorum — an obsolete action in which an insolvent debtor brought his creditors into court to surrender his assets to them in order to avoid imprisonment for debt.

ceteris paribus — other things being equal.

CFI — **Court of First Instance** (qv) of the **European Communities** (qv). **[E]**

CFP — common fisheries policy. **[E]**

CFSP — **common foreign and security policy** (qv). **[E]**

CGT — capital gains tax.

chamber —
  (1) The division in which the European Court of Justice and the Court of First Instance sits when not in plenary session (qv); **[E]**
  (2) a division of the ECtHR consisting of seven judges;
  (3) the hall where a parliament meets.

chambers — term given by lawyers to their office. A hearing by a judge other than in open court is said to be 'in chambers.' A lawyer who works only from his office, and who does no court work, is said to have a 'chambers practice'.

chancellor — an obsolete term for the foreman of a jury. *See also* Lord Chancellor.

chancery — the sheriff of chancery has jurisdiction in questions relating to the service of heirs in successions opening before 10 September 1964

Chancery and Judicial Registers — collective name for those registers administered by the **Registers of Scotland** (qv) other than those pertaining to land, eg the Register of Inhibitions and Adjudications, the Register of Deeds and Probative Writs in the Books of Council and Session, and the Register of Judgments in the Books of Council and Session.

Chancery Office — an office derived from that of the Lord Chancellor of Scotland, an appointment in abeyance since 1730. Certain Crown writs and commissions are issued from the Chancery Office by the Director of Chancery.

CHAPS — Clearing House Automated Payment System.

Chapter I prohibition, the — the prohibition of restrictive agreements and practices: from the Competition Act 1998.

Chapter II prohibition, the — the prohibition of **abuse of a dominant position** (qv): from the Competition Act 1998.

charge —
  (1) an order to obey a decree of court, including a written command served on a debtor to pay, on pain of **diligence** (qv);
  (2) a security over the property of a company;
  (3) a formal accusation of crime;
  (4) the direction given by a judge to a jury;
  (5) English legal term for a security, a usage now found in Scots law in the **floating charge** (qv).

charge having equivalent effect to a customs duty — any pecuniary charge, however small, whatever its designation and mode of application, which is unilaterally imposed on goods imported into a member state of the European Community from another by reason of the fact that the goods cross a frontier. **[E]**

charter —
  (1) a deed comprising a grant of land by a feudal superior;
  (2) a royal grant of incorporation, with powers and privileges, to a public institution.

Charter of Fundamental Rights — a codification of rights deriving mainly from the **European Convention on Human Rights** (qv), the **European Social Charter** (qv) and general principles of **Community law** (qv) 'solemnly proclaimed' by the member states of the European Union at Nice in 2000. It is intended to regulate the conduct of the Community institutions and of the member states when acting within the sphere of Community law. But it is afforded no binding force. The Charter is written into the draft **Constitution of the European Union** (qv), and the Union is to be bound to 'recognise' it. **[E]**

charterer — party which has hired a ship under a **charterparty** (qv) from its owner.

charterparty — a contract whereby a ship or part of a ship is hired for a fixed period or a specified voyage. *See also* **bareboat charterparty**, **time charter** and **voyage charterparty**.

charters by progress — charters of confirmation or resignation formerly used to renew a right to land already held. They were so designated to distinguish them from the original **charter** (qv) creating the right.

chartulary — a mediaeval register containing copies of the owner's charters and other deeds.

cheque — a bill of exchange drawn on a banker payable on demand.

child assessment order — a sheriff court order, on the application of a local authority, for an assessment of the state of a child's health or development. See the Children (Scotland) Act 1995, s 55.

child protection order — a sheriff court order made under the Children (Scotland) Act 1995 where there are reasonable grounds to believe that a child is or will be so treated or neglected as to suffer significant harm. The order may authorise the removal of the child by the applicant to a place of safety and other measures for the emergency protection of the child.

child-stealing. *See plagium.*

Child Support Agency — government agency responsible for the assessment, review, collection and enforcement of child maintenance under the Child Support Act 1991 and amending legislation notably the Child Support, Pensions and Social Security Act 2000.

child support maintenance — the amount which a nonresident parent must pay as a contribution for the upkeep of his or her child to a parent with care or a person in whose favour a **residence order** (qv) is made.

children's hearing — a hearing by three members of the children's panel for a local authority area set up under the Children (Scotland) Act 1995 (formerly the Social Work (Scotland) Act 1968) to deal with children who may be in need of compulsory measures of supervision including measures taken for the protection, guidance, treatment or control of the child.

chirographum apud debitorem repertum presumitur solutum — a bond or other document of debt, found in the possession of the debtor who granted it, is presumed to have been discharged.

cif — carriage, insurance, freight; type of maritime contract where the seller has to arrange for the carriage and insurance of the goods.

circuit court — a court held by the judges of the High Court of Justiciary when sitting on circuit out of Edinburgh.

circumstantial evidence — indirect evidence of a fact when the fact cannot be established by direct evidence.

circumvention *or* **facility and circumvention** — conduct to persuade a weak minded or facile person to act against his interest. Any contract thus entered into would be thereby rendered voidable.

CISG — Convention on Contracts for the International Sale of Goods, a 1980 **UN** (qv) convention, more generally known as the Vienna Convention. The Convention is a model draft code which aims to harmonise the sale betwen different countries. It may be adopted in whole or part by a state; and it may also be invoked by agreement of the parties as a basis of terms in international contracts.

citation —
(1) the procedure whereby a defender is called to court to answer an action or a witness to give evidence;
(2) a reference in legal debate, argument or judgment to a supporting authority.
(3) the exact reference to the year, volume and series within which a case is cited eg 2001 SLT 123.

cite — to effect or make a **citation** (qv).

citizen — a person who is a full legal member of a state.

citizenship of the European Union — a status created by the **Treaty on European Union** (qv) in 1993 (and made part of the EC Treaty), adhering to anyone who is a citizen of a member state of the European Union as defined by its nationality laws. **[E]**

civil law —
(1) all law (whether public or private) which is not **criminal law** (qv);
(2) 'private law' concerned with the rights. and duties of persons in their private capacity and with settling disputes between them, as opposed to **public law** (qv);
(3) Roman law or legal systems (such as German law or French law) based on Roman law;
(4) law other than military law.

civilian — *noun* a person learned in Roman law.

civil possession — **possession** (qv) of an object by a person through another's **detention** (qv) of the object for that person. Cf **natural possession** (qv).

claim —
(1) a demand for what is due whether a payment of money, delivery or conveyance of property or performance of an obligation;
(2) an assertion of a right to property;
(3) a right to begin an action in court. *See also* **claim form, small claim**.

claim form — in English law since April 1999 the document by which a **claim** (qv) is made in the civil courts previously known as a summons. It is a formal written statement setting out details of the claimant, the defendant and the remedy sought. The particulars of claim may be included in the claim form or served separately.

Claim of Right —
(1) the declaration of the pre-**Union** (qv) Scotland's constitutional rights and liberties

following the Glorious Revolution of 1688–89 (akin to the English Parliament's Bill of Rights);

(2) the declaration issued by the **Scottish Constitutional Convention** (qv) in 1989 in favour of a Scottish assembly based on popular sovereignty which constituted a significant political step towards **devolution** (qv).

claimant — (1) (colloquial) a person who claims; (2) in English law since April 1999 a person who makes a claim in the civil courts, a new English legal term of art replacing plaintiff, equivalent to **pursuer** (qv) in Scots law.

clare constat — it clearly appears: a precept (later a writ) granted by a superior in favour of the heir of a deceased vassal declaring that from the documents produced it clearly appears that the grantee is the heir. It was rendered unnecessary by the Succession (Scotland) Act 1964.

clause —

(1) a provision in a deed or instrument;

(2) a provision in a parliamentary Bill equivalent to a section in an Act of Parliament.

Clerk of Justiciary — an official who provides procedural and administrative support to the High Court of Justiciary.

Clerk of the Parliament — The head official and chief executive of the Scottish Parliament administration.

click-wrap agreements — web jargon for acceptance of terms which take effect once the 'I Agree' button on the screen is clicked.

close season — a statutory period during which specified fish, animals or birds may not be taken or killed.

closed record — a document comprising the final written pleadings of the parties to a civil action. The court has 'closed' the record of the pleadings and leave is required for later amendments.

closer cooperation. *See* **enhanced cooperation. [E]**

club — an association of people bound together by agreement for a particular purpose. Their rights and responsibilities are usually set forth in a constitution with rules. Where the assets and property of the club belong to the members, it is a members' club. Where they belong to an individual to whom the members pay a subscription, it is a proprietary club.

coat of arms — a symbol or icon designed to represent a particular family name and its members. In Scotland coats of arms may only be granted by the **Lord Lyon** (qv), so called because such heraldic symbols were originally worn as coat by medieval knights. A coat of arms belongs to only one party at a time and is a form of heritable incorporeal property.

code —

(1) a piece of legislation which consolidates and collates all the law on a particular subject. In most European states much of the law will be found in the national code(s);

(2) a non-legally binding set of practices agreed by significant actors within a particular area of activity eg the Banking Code, Insurance code. Such codes may be considered as soft law.

Codex or **Code** — part of the *Corpus Juris* (qv) of the Roman Emperor Justinian promulgated in the year 534 AD and containing an edited collection of Imperial enactments going back to the reign of the Emperor Hadrian (117–138 AD).

co-decision procedure — a legislative procedure introduced by the Treaty on European Union in 1993, set out now in article 251 of the EC Treaty, which requires close collaboration between the European Parliament and the Council for the adoption of European Community legislation; a measure adopted by the co-decision procedure is, uniquely, an act 'of the European Parliament and the Council'. **[E]**

codicil — an addition to or alteration or revocation of a previous testamentary writing. The codicil is then construed with previous testamentary writings as a single document.

codifying Act — an Act which consolidates and collates all law from statutory and other sources on a particular subject into one piece of legislation. It is not to be confused with a **consolidation Act** (qv).

cognate — a person related to another on the mother's side, as distinct from an agnate, who is related on the father's side.

cognition — an obsolete legal process by which a person could be found insane by a jury and a curator appointed.

cognitionis causa tantum — have the amount of the debt ascertained; an action of declarator raised by the creditor of a deceased debtor for the purpose of constituting his debt.

cohesion — the European Community policy of removing economic and social imbalances within the Community, given the varying standards of living and that is one of the main reasons for providing regional aid. **[E]**

collateral — a relative descended from the same ancestor but not in a direct line, eg a cousin.

collateral security — an additional security reinforcing the primary security for the performance of an obligation.

collatio inter haeredes — a bringing together among heirs. In the common law of succession, an heir-at-law who wished to participate in the legitum fund required to collate or bring in the heritable property to which he was heir as part of the fund. The principle was rendered obsolete by the Succession (Scotland) Act 1964.

collatio inter liberos — a bringing together among children. In the law of succession it still applies to the succession to the legitim fund of children of the deceased. Any advances made to a child by the deceased ancestor during his or her lifetime must be taken into account in calculating and distributing the legitim fund.

collective dominant position — also joint dominant position; a term of competition law which describes an oligopolistic (or oligopsonistic) market in which a **dominant position** (qv) is shared by a small number of **undertakings** (qv), but no one undertaking is itself dominant, and those undertakings are linked in such a way that they adopt the same conduct in the market.

collective responsibility — a cardinal principle of cabinet government: that all ministers are jointly responsible for any decisions taken by the government.

College of Justice — the Court of Session, established in 1532, comprising the Senators of the College of Justice (who are the judges of the Court of Session, addressed officially as Lords of Council and Session), advocates, Writers to the Signet, clerks of Session, keepers of the rolls and macers. The Law Society of Scotland and its members are not, as such, members of the College of Justice.

combined nomenclature — a list of goods used to meet the requirements of the **common customs tariff** (qv) and the external trade statistics of the European Community. **[E]**

comfort letter —
   (1) a letter from one party to another giving assurance on some matter which may or may not include a legally enforceable obligation;
   (2) a letter from an official of the European Commission responding to a **notification** (qv) seeking **exemption** (qv) or **negative clearance** (qv) for a possible infringement of the competition rules stating that the Commission intends to close the file and not proceed to a formal decision. **[E]**

Comhairle Eilean Siar — (Gaelic) the Western Isles Council.

comitology — a term for the administrative procedures, using various types of committees (hence, 'comitology'), deployed by the European Commission when adopting measures by authority delegated to it by the Council. **[E]**

commercial action — action in the Court of Session under special rules to allow the case to be heard more quickly and flexibly than under ordinary action procedure.

commissary — originally an ecclesiastical judge with jurisdiction in matters of personal status, eg legitimacy, marriage and succession. The Reformation did not abolish the functions of the Courts of the Officials in dioceses, but in 1563 a new Commissary Court was established in Edinburgh and each diocese. Until the 19th century the commissaries virtually monopolised jurisdiction in matters of status and succession. However, in 1832 the inferior commissaries were merged in the sheriff court, though they were not abolished until 1876, and the expression 'commissary' survives in the description or executing matters as 'commissary business'. Today commissary business consists largely of matters to do with executries.

commission —

(1) the authorisation by the court granted in the course of an action to a qualified person to take evidence from a witness who cannot attend court or, with diligence, to recover documents;

(2) common abbreviation for the **Commission of the European Communities** (qv).

Commission for Racial Equality — a publicly funded, non-governmental body set up under the Race Relations Act 1976 to combat racial discrimination and promote racial equality.

Commission of the European Communities — commonly called the European Commission; an institution, one of the five created by the EC Treaty, comprising (in 2003) 20 members nominated by the member states and approved by the European Parliament for a five year term. Commissioners act in the interests of the Community as a whole and take an oath of independence to that effect. The Commission enjoys a monopoly in the initiation of virtually all EC legislation and significant legislative powers in its own right delegated to it by the Council. It also 'safeguards the Treaty' by monitoring member state compliance with Community law, and has authority to raise an action before the **European Court of Justice** (qv) to enforce compliance. It has its seat in Brussels. **[E]**

Commissioner for Local Administration in Scotland — the local government ombudsman. On a complaint by a member of the public who may have suffered an injustice through maladministration, the commissioner has power to investigate the acts and actions of certain authorities and may make recommendations and state his conclusions to the appropriate authorities or government departments. See the Local Government (Scotland) Act 1975, s 23.

Commissioner of Teinds — a judge of the Court of Session appointed to sit in the Court of Teinds, which is in effect a function of the Court of Session. Since the business of the Court of Teinds is now almost entirely formal and unopposed, usually a Lord Ordinary sits as a Lord Commissioner of Teinds, with the Teind Clerk, and deals with its ministerial and judicial functions. *See* **teind**.

commissioners in a sequestration — up to five persons who may be appointed by creditors from their own number or their mandatories following a sequestration under the Bankruptcy (Scotland) Act 1985 to supervise the permanent trustee in bankruptcy.

committal — the ordering of a person charged under a petition of the procurator fiscal to be detained in custody pending further inquiry or, when 'fully committed', until liberated in due course of law.

Committee of the Regions — an advisory body established by the EC Treaty (as amended in 1993 by the Treaty on European Union), comprising representatives of local and regional authorities; must be consulted by the Community institutions prior to the adoption of EC legislation in certain fields. **[E]**

commixtion — (Latin *commixtio*) the mixing of solid (as contrasted with liquid) moveables belonging to different owners, thus affecting their property rights. The consequences vary depending upon whether the mixture is or is not capable of subsequent separation or has been made as a result of consent, accident or fault.

commodatum — the gratuitous loan of an article which the borrower must return in the same form and state as when borrowed.

common agent — a solicitor employed to conduct a cause in which several parties have a common interest, eg ranking and sale or multiplepoinding.

common agricultural policy (CAP) — the agricultural policy of the **European Community** (qv). Its objectives are set out in article 33 of the EC Treaty (qv) and include an increase in productivity, technical progress, rational development of production, a fair standard of living for producers, market stability, assured availability of supplies and reasonable prices. CAP expenditure accounts for some 45 per cent of the Community budget. **[E]**

common calamity — a fatal event in which two or more persons die with no indication of which predeceased. If they were husband and wife, neither is presumed to have survived the other; otherwise, generally the older is presumed to have predeceased the younger. See the Succession (Scotland) Act 1964, s 31.

common commercial policy — the policy of the European Community with regard to trade between the European Community and third countries; – embraces application of the **common customs tariff** (qv), import and export policies, protective measures, association agreements of various types with third countries and Community policy within the World Trade Organisation. **[E]**

common customs tariff (CCT) — the uniform tariff of customs duties applied by the member states of the European Community to all goods imported from third countries. **[E]**

common debtor — where the effects of a debtor have been arrested and several creditors claim a share of them, the debtor, as being debtor to all, is designated as the common debtor in related proceedings.

common good — property of a local authority derived otherwise than from rates or central government grants. Former royal burghs received grants of land, taxes, tolls etc from the Crown to sustain the dignity of the burgh.

common interest — an interest less than a right of property which justifies the party exercising it in having some control in the use of the property; eg in the case of a mutual wall between two houses, a party with common interest may resist any injurious alteration.

common foreign and security policy (CFSP) — provision for the gradual approximation of the foreign policies of the member states of the **European Union** (qv), providing now for the eventual framing of a common defence policy; governed by Title V of the **Treaty on European Union** (qv). **[E]**

common law —
(1) law which does not stem from a statute but is laid down in judicial decisions. Influences on the Scots common law include authoritative writings (*see* Institutional Writers), and Roman, canon and feudal law and custom.
(2) the Law of England, so called because it was common to the entire country, and to those systems derived from English Law, eg US, Canada, Australia etc.

common market —
(1) the form of integration between states involving the fusion of national domestic markets into one market having the characteristic of a domestic market and covering all factors of production, including goods, persons, services and capital;
(2) an old fashioned term loosely used as a synonym for the European Community or its territorial area. **[E]**

common organisation of the markets — an interventionist legal regime adopted within the **common agricultural policy** (qv) regulating the market of a particular **agricultural product** (qv) or group of products (eg cereals, oils and fats, bananas) and applied uniformly throughout the European Community. **[E]**

common policies. *See* **Community policies**. **[E]**

common position —
(1) in EC law, an agreed position adopted by the Council early in the legislative process which serves as a basis for negotiation with the European Parliament under both the **cooperation procedure** (qv) and the **co-decision procedure** (qv); **[E]**
(2) under the Treaty on European Union, a measure adopted by the Council either (a) within the framework of **common foreign and security policy** (qv), defining the approach of the Union to a particular matter of a geographic or thematic nature, or (b) within the framework of **police and judicial co-operation in criminal matters** (qv), defining the approach of the Union to a certain matter. **[E]**

common property — property, either immoveable or moveable, belonging to two or more owners *pro indiviso*, ie in an undivided manner with no separation of shares. Each co-owner may sell his undivided share. In matters of administration, except in the case of necessary operations, the wishes of an owner objecting to a course of action prevail. However, any owner may compel division of the property. *See also* ***pro indiviso***.

common seal — the **seal** (qv) of a corporation or limited company.

common strategy — a device adopted by the **European Council** (qv) within the framework of **common foreign and security policy** (qv) which sets out the objectives, duration and means to be provided by the European Union and the member states in areas in which there is common interest. **[E]**

common transport policy — European Community policy, implemented piecemeal, to establish common rules applicable to international transport to or from the territory of the member states or passing across the territory of one or more of them; applies now to rail, road and inland waterways, maritime transport, cabotage and some aspects of commercial air transport. **[E]**

commonty — a right neither of common property nor of common interest but of joint perpetual use of land by adjoining commoners eg for pasturing. The Division of Commonties Act 1695 (c 38) provides for division, and commonty is now virtually obsolete.

communings — negotiations which do or may result in a contract, usually called 'prior communings'.

communitisation — jargon for the transfer of a matter within the European Union constitutional framework from the intergovernmental method (second and third pillars) to the Community method (first pillar). *See also* **European Union**. **[E]**

Community — informal shorthand for either the **European Community** (qv) or the two European Communities (so including the **European Atomic Energy Community** (qv)); to be distinguished from the **European Union** (qv). **[E]**

community burden — a **real burden** (qv) which regulates a group or 'community' of properties which is mutually enforceable among the owners of those properties: Title Conditions (Scotland) Act 2003, s 25(1). Each property in the community is thus both a **burdened property** (qv) and a **benefited property** (qv), and enforcement is reciprocal. Compare **neighbour burden**.

community charge — a *per capita* charge imposed by a local authority on persons resident in its area for the purpose of providing funds to enable the authority to discharge its statutory functions so far as the cost thereof is not otherwise met or provided for. From 1 April 1989 to 31 March 1993 community charges were payable in Scotland.

community council — an elected body established by a scheme made by a local authority to ascertain, co-ordinate and express the views of the community which it represents and to take such action in the interests of the community as appears to it to be expedient and practicable.

Community courts. *See* **Community judicature** (qv). **[E]**

Community institution — a body set up under, and described as such in, the **founding treaties** (qv) for the purpose of carrying out the tasks of the **European Community** (qv) and of the **European Union** (qv). There are five institutions properly so-called: the (European) Parliament (previously, 'the Assembly'), the Council (of the European Union), the Commission, the Court of Justice and the Court of Auditors. **[E]**

Community judicature — also 'Community courts'; shorthand for the two courts established by the EC Treaty, the **European Court of Justice** (qv) and the **Court of First Instance** (qv) taken together. **[E]**

Community language — a language recognised by the Community institutions as an 'official' or 'working' language; in 2003 there were 11 Community languages (plus a partial status for Irish, which is recognised as a language of the Court of Justice); following anticipated enlargement in 2004 there will be a further nine Community languages. **[E]**

Community law — the law laid down in and derived from the treaties establishing the European Communities. **[E]**

Community policies — Part Three of the EC Treaty, comprising now 159 articles and setting out the great bulk of the substantive law of the European Community. **[E]**

community right to buy — a right of members of a community to buy land, introduced by the Land Reform (Scotland) Act 2003, Part 2.

community service order — an order of a criminal court under the Criminal Procedure (Scotland) Act 1995, requiring an offender to do useful work within the community instead of being fined or imprisoned.

Community Trade Mark — a trade mark granted by the European Community, uniform and valid throughout the territory of the Community; governed by Council Regulation No 40/94 of 20 December 1993 on the Community Trade Mark. **[E]**

Community transit — the regime governing the movement of goods through the European Community or a part of it. **[E]**

commute — to change into another form, eg when feudal casualties were converted into increased annual feuduty, or cancelled by a lump sum payment.

company — a business organisation registered, ie 'incorporated' under the Companies Act 1985 or its predecessors.

compear — to appear as a party in court, in person or by counsel or agent.

compensatio injuriarum — compensation of wrongs; an obsolete plea, formerly found in actions of defamation, to set off claims for mutual injuries against each other.

compensation — the extinction of mutual similar claims by setting one off against the other. There must be *concursus debiti et crediti* (qv).

compensation order — an order for the payment of compensation to an injured party by a person convicted of an offence which has caused injury, loss or damage. See the Criminal Procedure (Scotland) Act 1995, ss 249–253.

compensating products — products produced by certain processes under the **inward or outward processing** (qv) arrangements of the European Community. **[E]**

compensatory justification — a contribution by the beneficiary of a **state aid** (qv) to the achievement of the objectives of the European Community which is over and above the effects of the normal play of market forces and which may justify the European Commission in exercising its discretion to allow the implementation of a proposed aid scheme. **[E]**

compensatory tax — a tax imposed on imports in order to make the final tax burden on the goods the same as that imposed on domestic products. **[E]**

competence — the authority of a court to entertain a particular type of case or form of procedure.

competency — the admissibility of evidence or of a particular witness are matters of competency.

competent and omitted — describes a preliminary plea against an argument which could have been but was not advanced in an earlier litigation.

competition —
(1) commercial rivalry between or amongst **undertakings** (qv);
(2) the system used (the *concours*) to recruit officials to the **Community institutions** (qv). **[E]**

competition law — the body of rules used to ensure fair commercial competition; includes such matters as **restrictive agreements** (qv) and practices, monopolies and mergers and takeovers. There is an established body of competition law within the **European Community** (qv), now imported *mutatis mutandis* into United Kingdom law by the Competition Act 1998. **[E]**

competition policy — the course of action adopted by the European Community or by appropriate national authorities (in the United Kingdom, the Office of Fair Trading) in order to maintain a desired level of rivalry between commercial **undertakings** (qv).

competition rules. *See* **competition law**.

complaint —
(1) a document instituting summary criminal proceedings in a sheriff or district court, setting out the offence charged;
(2) in **competition law** (qv), objection lodged by an **undertaking** (qv) with the European Commission alleging unlawful anticompetitive conduct on the part of a competitor, and inviting the Commission to intervene. **[E]**

composition — an arrangement between a debtor and his creditors whereby the debtor's debts are discharged in exchange for agreed partial payment. Composition may take the form of an extra-judicial contract or, after sequestration, proceed under the Bankruptcy (Scotland) Act 1985, Sch 4.

compulsory expenditure — those parts of the budget of the European Community disbursed by legal obligation to do so, and not at the discretion of the **Community institutions** (qv); the bulk of compulsory expenditure is in support of the **common agricultural policy** (qv). **[E]**

compulsory measures of supervision — such measures of supervising a child as may be imposed on the child by a **children's hearing** (qv) under the Children (Scotland) Act 1995 (formerly called compulsory measures of care).

concentration — the merger of two or more **undertakings** (qv); the takeover by one undertaking of another; the acquisition by one undertaking of effective control of another. **[E]**

concerted practice — a form of co-ordination between competing **undertakings** (qv) which, without having reached the stage at which an **agreement** (qv) properly so-called has been reached, knowingly substitutes practical co-operation between them for the risks of competition.

conciliation committee — a committee comprising representatives in equal numbers of the Council and the European Parliament, convened when the Community institutions are acting under the **co-decision procedure** (qv) and fail initially to reach agreement, for the purpose of agreeing a joint text which, if adopted, is then subject to the approval of both institutions in order to become law. **[E]**

conclude — to claim a remedy in a summons in civil procedure in the Court of Session. *See* **conclusion**.

conclusion — the statement in a summons in civil proceedings in the Court of Session of the precise remedy claimed. *See also* **crave**.

concourse — the concurrence of the public prosecutor in a private prosecution.

concursus debiti et crediti — concourse or concurrence of debt and credit: a prerequisite of a plea of compensation, which can be founded only where each party is debtor and creditor, each in his own right, at the same time. *See* **compensation**.

condescendence — statement(s) of fact by the pursuer in civil pleadings.

condictio — (plural *condictiones*) in Roman law a form of personal action to enforce performance of a personal obligation, contrasted with *vindicatio* (qv), a real action. In Scots law a *condictio* is no longer regarded (as in Roman law) as a form of action or remedy but rather as an element in the grounds of an action for redress of unjustified enrichment. Proof of facts amounting to a *condictio* provides a good legal reason for reversing a defender's enrichment at the pursuer's expense by showing that the enrichment is unjustified in law.

condictio causa data causa non secuta — claim under the principles of unjustified enrichment to recover money paid or property transferred or performance rendered for a lawful future purpose which failed.

condictio indebiti — claim under the principles of unjustified enrichment for recovery of money paid or property transferred or for value of services performed without legal ground when not due in circumstances where the claimant made the payment or transfer or performance erroneously believing it to be due by the claimant to the recipient.

condictio ob turpem vel iniustam causam — claim under the principles of unjustified enrichment for recovery of money paid or property transferred or value of services performed for an immoral or illegal purpose. The plea of immoral or illegal purpose is sometimes seen only as a defence to an action and not as a distinct ground of action.

condictio sine causa — claim under the principles of unjustified enrichment for recovery of money paid or property transferred or value of services performed without legal ground otherwise than through an error of the claimant as to the claimant's obligation to make that performance. Sometimes called a *condictio sine causa (specialis)* to differentiate it from a *condictio sine causa (generalis)* which is a generic name for all the *condictiones*.

conditio si institutus sine liberis decesserit — the condition if the beneficiary dies childless: an implied condition in a will that where a bequest is made to a group of the testator's family, and a named beneficiary in that group dies before the testator, the issue of that beneficiary takes the beneficiary's share in preference to other legatees and heirs.

conditio si testator sine liberis decesserit — the condition if the testator dies childless: a rebuttable presumption applicable where a parent who makes a will without provision for a child then has a child and dies without altering it. The law may presume that the will has been revoked because the deceased testator would have wished to make provision for the child.

condition — a clause in a contract or disposition qualifying an obligation therein contained. Conditions may be suspensive or precedent, indicating postponement of the obligation until the condition is fulfilled, or resolutive, indicating that the obligation ceases upon fulfilment of the condition.

conditions of employment — the rules governing the employment by a European Community institution of persons other than officials. **[E]**

confer — compare (abbreviated 'cf').

configurations — a term describing the various compositions (for example: general affairs and external relations; economic and financial affairs) in which the **Council of the European Union** (qv) meets; formerly 'formations'. **[E]**

confirmation — power judicially conferred on the executor of a deceased person's estate to administer the estate. By confirmation an executor gains title to the property and assets of the deceased and to ingather and distribute the estate.

confiscation — the proceeds of certain criminal offences may be confiscated by order of the court under the Proceeds of Crime (Scotland) Act 1995. Contrast **forfeiture** (which relates to the means of committing crime).

conflict of laws — rules determining issues of jurisdiction and applicable law in disputes which have involve more than one legal system.

conform (adj) — in conformity. A 'decree conform' is a judgment by one court giving effect to the judgment of another, eg so as to enable diligence to be done.

confusio —
(1) the commingling of liquids: *see* **commixtion**;
(2) a form of accession by which an obligation may be extinguished, eg where a debtor acquires the rights of his creditor, or where the proprietor of a servient tenement becomes proprietor of the dominant tenement.

conjoin — to join two causes into one. The court has a discretion to conjoin causes which are related to the same subject matter, raise the same question or are otherwise so connected that it is expedient that they be tried together and disposed of in the same manner. On conjunction the two causes become one.

conjoined arrestment order — an order by way of diligence against the earnings of a debtor in the hands of his employer to enforce the payment of two or more debts owed to different creditors against the same earnings.

conjunct — rights taken by two or more persons jointly. Thus a grant to two unrelated persons 'in conjunct fee and liferent and their heirs' makes them equal fiars during the joint lives, the survivor taking the liferent of the whole, and on his death the fee divides equally between the heirs of both.

conjunct and several obligation — an obligation (also called a 'joint and several obligation') in which each obligant is individually bound, irrespective of the duties of co-obligants, to render complete performance if called upon to do so.

conjunct or confident persons — persons closely related by blood or affinity or being in a situation of 'intimate and confidential intercourse'. Alienations to conjunct or confident persons without due cause by a person verging on insolvency were to be annulled under the Bankruptcy Act 1621. The Bankruptcy (Scotland) Act 1985 repeals the earlier statute and now uses the term associate (s 74).

conjunct probation or proof — the process of disproving by evidence an opponent's averments while also proving one's own averments.

conjunctural policy — the policy of the European Community intended to rectify cyclical problems or short-term trends in the economy. **[E]**

conjunction. *See* **conjoin**.

consanguinean — describes relations descended from the same father, but not from the same mother, eg half sisters. Cf **uterine**.

consanguinity — relationship of persons descended from the same ancestor.

conscious parallelism — co-ordinated behaviour between **undertakings** (qv) which arises in the apparent absence of any direct or indirect contact between them; constituent element of a **concerted practice** (qv).

consensus in idem — consent as to the same essentials; agreement as to those matters in a contract which are essential to make the contract binding. There is no consent if eg one party consents to hire and the other consents to sale.

consequential loss — a financial loss occurring as the result of some other loss, also known as an indirect loss. (eg if a shop is destroyed by fire then the loss of the building, stock etc is the direct loss and the loss of trading profit is the consequential loss).

conservation burden — a **personal real burden** (qv) held either by a conservation body or Scottish Ministers and which preserves the built or natural environment for the benefit of the public: see the Title Conditions (Scotland) Act 2003, s 38(1).

consideration — in the context of a contract, some right, interest, profit or benefit accruing to one party or some forbearance, detriment, loss or responsibility given, suffered or undertaken by the other; consideration is essential to the valid formation of a contract under English law but not to one made under Scots law.

consignation — the deposit with the clerk of court or a third party, under the authority of the court, of money or a moveable in dispute.

consistorial action — proceedings derived from the jurisdiction formerly exercised by the Commissary Courts in matters of marital status. It included actions of divorce, of separation, of declarator of marriage, of legitimacy, of freedom and putting to silence, of adherence and of aliment between husband and wife. For certain purposes it remains an important term of art. The sheriff court has had concurrent jurisdiction with the Court of Session in actions of separation since 1907 and in divorce since 1984.

consolidation — the bringing together in the same person of the two estates in land of superiority (*dominium directum*) and of vassalage (*dominium utile*) which have hitherto been separately vested in that person. *See* **feu**; **feudal tenure**.

consolidation Act — an Act which incorporates in one Act and supersedes some or all of the provisions of a number of earlier Acts relating to the same subject matter.

constituency — electoral boundaries, defined by population and rural or urban location, which return an MP or **MSP** (qv).

constitute — to establish (usually through a judgment) the fact that a debt exists. This may be necessary after the debtor or original creditor has died.

constitution — a document which sets out basic principles and laws of a nation. These principles and laws determine the powers and duties of a government and guarantee certain rights to the people under it. The United Kingdom has no written constitution.

Constitution of the European Union — a draft treaty concluded in Spring 2003 and proposing the fusion of all basic EC and EU documents into a 'constitution' of the European Union; it will be considered at the 2004 **intergovernmental conference** (qv). **[E]**

constitutional — in accordance with the relevant **constitution** (qv).

constitutional convention — an *ad hoc* convention called for by the **European Council** (qv) at Laeken in 2001, convened in 2002 and consisting of 105 members drawn from existing member states and **accession countries** (qv) under the chairmanship of M. Valéry Giscard d'Estaing, it reported in Spring 2003 proposing the draft **Constitution of the European Union** (qv). **[E]**

constitutum possessorium — a transfer of possession in which the transferor retains actual physical control of the thing. By a declaration or agreement with the transferee, the transferor changes his legal **possession** (qv) (holding for himself) into **detention** (qv) (holding for the transferee).

construction contract — a synonym of **building contract** (qv) and defined for some purposes by the Housing Grants, Construction and Regeneration Act 1996, s 104, as an agreement for any of the following, (a) the carrying out of construction operations by a person; (b) arranging for the carrying out of construction operations by others, whether under sub-contract or otherwise; (c) providing for his own labour, or the labour of others, for the carrying out of construction operations.

constructive — having legal effect, even though the thing described may not exist as a fact, eg constructive knowledge or constructive total loss.

consuetudo pro lege servatur — custom is observed as law. All Scots law, except legislation, is ultimately customary or common law.

consultation —
(1) a power of the judges of a Division of the Inner House of the Court of Session, in cases of importance or difficulty or where the judges are equally divided, to state questions of law for the opinion of the other judges of the court;
(2) a meeting between counsel and solicitor, with or without the client, to discuss a case.

consultation procedure — a legislative procedure set out in the EC Treaty whereby the Council is required to consult the European Parliament prior to the adoption of legislation; it is not bound by Parliament's position but only by the obligation of consultation. **[E]**

consumer — private individual who buys property (usually goods) and services for use or consumption otherwise than in the course of business. Consumers are protected by several enactments which define 'consumer' differently for different purposes. Cognate concepts like consumer-credit agreement, consumer-credit business, consumer-credit register, consumer-hire agreement and consumer-hire business are all defined by the Consumer Credit Act 1974.

consumer credit — lending and other transactions with a **consumer** (qv) are regulated under the Consumer Credit Act 1974 which establishes a system of licensing and control of providers of credit and regulates the supply of goods to consumers on hire or **hire purchase** (qv).

contact order — in family law means a court order regulating the arrangements for maintaining personal relations and direct contact between a child under sixteen and a person with whom the child is not living. See the Children (Scotland) Act 1995, s 11(2)(d).

contemporanea expositio — contemporaneous construction: a rule that the meaning or construction of old Acts of Parliament, deeds and contracts which they had or were given at the time they were made should, in case of doubt, prevail.

contempt of court — insulting, disorderly or disobedient behaviour towards a court, or acts calculated to obstruct the course of justice or flouting the court's authority. Courts have summary power to punish for contempt, subject to a right of appeal.

continental shelf — that part of the sea-bed and subsoil of the submarine areas that extend beyond the territorial sea a coastal State by the natural prolongation of its land territory to the outer edge of the continental margin, or to a distance of 200 nautical miles.

contingency — a situation which warrants a court remitting an action *ob contingentiam* to another court dealing with another action. It arises eg where in the two actions the same parties are in dispute about the same matter, or where the second action arises directly out of the first, or where, though the parties are different, the subject matter is the same and the decision in one will decide the matter as regards the whole world. On remission the actions remain distinct, but one may be sisted to await the result of the other. Cf **conjoin**.

contingent debt — one which depends on the occurrence of an uncertain future event, which may not happen. Contrast **future debt** (qv).

continue — to defer or adjourn proceedings to a later date.

continuing attorney — a person appointed to manage affairs under a continuing power of attorney.

continuing power of attorney — a **power of attorney** (qv) which relates to the granter's property or financial affairs and which continues to have effect after the granter has become incapable.

contra — against, to the contrary.

contra bonos mores — against decent moral standards. Thus contracts or obligations for an immoral consideration are unenforceable.

contra proferentem — against the person putting it forward. Thus an ambiguous term in a contract may be construed against the person who inserted it.

contract — a legally binding voluntary agreement.

contributory negligence — some careless or blameworthy act or omission by the pursuer which contributed, with the defender's fault or negligence, to the pursuer's loss or injury. Since 1945 the court may reduce an award of damages in proportion to the pursuer's share of responsibility for what happened.

contumacy — stubborn or wilful refusal to obey a court order, whence contumacious.

convenor — traditional Scots term for the person who chairs a meeting, especially common usage in local government, and has the advantage of being a gender neutral expression.

convention —
(1) an agreement, especially an international treaty;
(2) shorthand for the European Convention of Human Rights (usually with a capital letter);
(3) a custom or practice;
(4) a meeting or gathering of states or individuals;
(5) under the Treaty on European Union, an agreement amongst the member states within the framework of **police and judicial cooperation in criminal matters** (qv) which is 'established' by the Council and is then subject to adoption procedures in each of the member states. **[E]**

Convention rights — rights under the **European Convention of Human Rights** (qv).

conventional duties — customs duties fixed in accordance with an agreement concluded between the **European Community** (qv) and a third country or international organisation. **[E]**

conventional obligation — an obligation arising from an agreement or contract, as distinct from one created by the general law, as in the case of delict or unjust enrichment.

convergence criteria — also 'Maastricht Criteria' the five criteria a member state of the European Community must meet prior to admission to the final stage of **economic and monetary union** (qv). **[E]**

conveyancing — the transfer of property rights, especially those over land and buildings.

convicium — a delict involving the communication of true or false material designed to hold a person up to hatred, ridicule or contempt.

cooling off period — a specified period of time, allowed in certain circumstances, during which a person who has entered into a contract (for example, an insurance policy or a personal loan) may cancel it without incurring any penalty.

cooperation agreement —
(1) an agreement between the European Community and one or more third countries to cooperate in some particular field of activity;
(2) an agreement between two or more **undertakings** (qv) by which the parties agree to work together in some aspect of their business. **[E]**

cooperation procedure — a legislative procedure introduced by the Single European Act in 1987, set out now in article 252 of the EC Treaty, which requires the cooperation of the European Parliament and the Council in the adoption of European Community legislation. Since the **Treaty of Amsterdam** (qv) the cooperation procedure has been largely replaced by the **co-decision procedure** (qv). **[E]**

co-ordination of laws. *See* **harmonisation of laws**. **[E]**

copyright — an incorporeal property right in (a) original literary, dramatic, musical or artistic works; (b) sound recordings, films and broadcasts and (c) the typographical arrangements of published texts.

COPFS — **Crown Office** (qv)/**Procurator Fiscal Service** (qv).

COREPER — committee comprising the permanent representatives (ambassadors) of the member states of the European Community or their deputies, responsible for preparing the work of the **Council of the European Union** (qv) and carrying out the tasks assigned to it by the Council; from *COmité des REprésentants PERmanents.* **[E]**

corporate veil — a metaphor used to express the principle that the shareholders in limited company are not liable for the debts of the company beyond the extent of the price they have paid for their shares: the existence of the corporation veils the shareholders from the eyes of the company's creditors. Where this principle is breached this is said to be 'piercing or lifting of the corporate veil'.

corporeal moveables — physical objects which are capable of being moved, as distinct from heritable property.

corpus — body.

corpus delicti — the substance or body of facts constituting a crime or offence charged.

Corpus Juris — the **European Union** (qv) project for harmonising criminal procedures. **[E]**.

Corpus Juris Civilis — Collective term for the great compilation and synthesis of classical Roman Law made at the command of the Emperor Justinian I (reigned 527-562). The *Corpus Juris Civilis* comprises four works: the **Institutes** (qv), the **Digest** (qv), the **Codex** or **Code** (qv), and the **Novels** (qv). The *Corpus Juris Civilis* is both a monument to the law of ancient Rome, as an attempt to systematize 1,000 years of classical Roman law, and the foundation stone of all western legal systems, and was especially influential in Continental Europe.

corroboration — evidence which confirms other evidence of fact. Corroboration was normally required for 'full proof' in Scots law but is no longer essential in civil proceedings: see the Civil Evidence (Scotland) Act 1988, s 1. Subject to certain exceptions, a crucial or primary fact cannot be proved by the testimony of one witness alone. There had to be either the direct testimony of two witnesses or two or more evidential facts each spoken to by one or more witnesses from which a crucial fact could be inferred. Documentary or real evidence may provide corroboration.

Cotonou Agreement — a 'partnership' agreement signed in 2000 in Cotonou (Benin) between the European Community and its member states on the one hand and 77 developing countries (the **ACP countries** (qv)) on the other governing trade, commercial and other relationships between the two groups. Replacing the **Lomé Agreements** (qv), the Cotonou Agreement is to cover a 20 year period, subject to revision every five years. **[E]**

council —
(1) an assembly or decision making body;
(2) a local authority in Scotland, since 1996 all councils have been unitary, and there are 32 in total;
(3) the **Council of the European Union** (qv). **[E]**

Council of Europe — organisation comprising (in 2003) 45 European states with the aim of promoting democracy and protecting human rights. It is a separate institution from the European Union and should not be confused with it, but the 15 member states and all the candidate countries for the EU are members. The Council of Europe is based in Strasbourg and was established in 1949 as a forum for discussion between European states. The Council makes recommendations but does not have any legislative power. The European Convention on Human Rights was made under the auspices of the Council and the European Court of Human Rights is an institution of the Council.

Council of the European Union — an institution, one of the five, created by the EC Treaty, called therein simply 'the Council', frequently referred to as the Council of Ministers, but restyled (by itself) the Council of the European Union in 1993. It is the European Community's principal decision and law making institution, and enjoys significant powers under the Treaty on European Union, insofar as that Treaty allows, to conduct Union activities. The Council consists of the ministers of the fifteen member states responsible for the matters falling within the **configuration** (qv) on the agenda. Although the Council consists of various different configurations, often meeting simultaneously, it is nonetheless a single institution. It is assisted by **COREPER** (qv), by a

General Secretariat, and by working parties of national government officials. It should not be confused with the **European Council** (qv) or with the **Council of Europe** (qv). **[E]**

Council of Ministers. *See* **Council of the European Union**. **[E]**

counsel — an advocate; a member of the Faculty of Advocates; in court the term counsel is always used when referring to an advocate.

count, reckoning and payment — an action to require the defender to render an account of his dealings or intromissions with property which does not belong to him but which has been entrusted to him, and to pay to the person entitled any balance which may be found to be due on the account.

counter action — an action raised by the defender to another action in order to clarify his position. The defender is not bound to await the pleasure of the pursuer as to the prosecution of the first action; hence his right to raise a counter action, although there must be a slight difference between the issues or a plea of *lis alibi pendens* will be sustained. *See also*, in the context of divorce, **cross action**.

counterclaim — a claim by a defender which may competently be made and dealt with in the principal action even though it could have formed the basis of independent proceedings initiated by the defender.

countervailing duty *or* **countervailing measure** — a charge or duty, usually imposed on imports, which compensates for an advantage enjoyed by the goods in question in their country of origin, such as a government subsidy granted by the exporting state, national marketing rules which favour their competitive position or fiscal measures. Cf **compensatory tax**. **[E]**

county — ancient geographical areas of Scotland, abolished as local government divisions in 1973 but retained for the purposes of postal addresses and the registration of land.

court —

    (1) the institution of state which decides on disputed cases brought before it, consisting of a judge or judges and, where appropriate a **jury** (qv);

    (2) the building where justice is administered;

    (3) the official retinue of the **sovereign** (qv).

Court of Auditors — an institution, one of the five, created by the EC Treaty, entrusted with auditing the accounts of the European Communityand the European Union; composed of fifteen members appointed for six years by unanimous decision of the Council after consulting the European Parliament. It audits Community and Union revenue and expenditure to make sure it is lawful and proper and ensures that financial management is sound. Despite the name the institution has no judicial powers; if irregularities are uncovered, appropriate steps may be taken only by other Community institutions. **[E]**

Court of Criminal Appeal — a court, of which three **Lords Commissioners of Justiciary** (qv) form a quorum, constituted to hear appeals against conviction and sentence by persons convicted on **indictment** (qv). No further appeal is competent. *See also* **High Court of Justiciary**.

Court of Exchequer — a court created after the Union of 1707 to determine revenue matters. It was merged with the Court of Session in 1856, although revenue matters are still heard as Exchequer causes.

Court of First Instance — the Court of First Instance of the European Communities; created in 1989, originally 'attached' to the European Court of Justice by a council decision, since the Treaty of Nice enjoying autonomous personality under the EC Treaty. It now enjoys first instance jurisdiction in a large number of matters falling within the jurisdiction of the **Community judicature** (qv). The **Constitution of the European Union** (qv) proposes that it be restyled the 'High Court'. **[E]**

Court of Justice of the European Communities. *See* **European Court of Justice** (qv). **[E]**

Court of Session — the supreme civil court in Scotland, which sits only in Edinburgh, established in 1532 and whose existence is protected by article 19 of the **Treaty of Union** (qv). The judges of the court's **Outer House** (qv), sitting alone, determine cases at first instance. The two **Divisions** (qv) of the **Inner House** (qv) have primarily an appellate jurisdiction. In certain conditions the decisions of the Inner House are appealable to the House of Lords.

court of summary jurisdiction — a court where criminal cases are dealt with by a judge sitting alone without a jury. The district court has summary jurisdiction only, but the sheriff court exercises both summary and solemn jurisdiction.

Court of Teinds. *See* **Commissioner of Teinds.**

Court of the Official — Pre-Reformation church court which dealt with issues of canon law, replaced after 1560 by the Commissary Court.

courtesy — the liferent in the heritage of a deceased wife, conferred on a widower (obsolete since 1964).

court-martial — a court appointed to hear charges of breach of service discipline by members of HM forces or civilian employees of the forces. The court usually comprises a number of officers advised by a **judge advocate** (qv).

Courts Group — the office of the **Scottish Executive Justice Department** (qv) responsible for the judiciary.

Courts-Martial Appeal Court — a United Kingdom court constituted to hear appeals against conviction by court-martial.

cover — in insurance terms to describe either the monetary value insured (eg £1,000) or the peril insured (e.g. theft, fire, death).

cover note — a temporary certificate confirming that an insurance policy is in force, often obtained over the phone; commonly used in motor insurance for taxation/registration purposes and in some other contexts such as life assurance to confirm that cover is effective on a temporary basis while further information is being gathered.

CPAC — Children's Panel Advisory Committee.

CPAG — Children's Panel Advisory Group.

CPCG — Children's Panel Chairmen's Group.

crave —
(1) the statement in an initial writ in a sheriff court action of the precise remedy sought, cf **conclusion**;
(2) to ask a court for something.

CRE. *See* **Commission for Racial Equality.**

credit — the provision of goods or money in advance of repayment, generally done in return for a commission in the from of interest on the sum lent..

creditor — a person to whom a debtor is obliged. In Scots law the term is not restricted to monetary obligations. A secured creditor is one to whom the debtor has granted security for the sum due. Some creditors may have preferential claims.

crime. *See* **offence.**

crimen falsi — the crime of falsehood: any crime known to the law consisting in falsehood, eg forgery, perjury and fraud.

criminal —
(1) contrary to the criminal law;
(2) a person who breaks the criminal law.

Criminal Injuries Compensation Authority — government agency which administers the **criminal injuries compensation scheme** (qv).

criminal injuries compensation scheme — government scheme which provided financial compensation out of state funds to the victims of violent crime.

criminal law — conduct prohibited by the state on pain of the imposition of penalties which may include imprisonment or some other penalty.

critical illness policy — type of insurance policy which provides a lump sum payment to the insured should he or she be diagnosed as having one of a number of specified illnesses, conditions or diseases.

croft — an agricultural holding situated in one of the **crofting counties** (qv). Such holdings have been regulated exclusively by statute. A crofter who has not purchased the land which forms his croft does not own the croft land or croft house but is a tenant of both and has security of tenure as tenant.

crofting counties — the area to which the statutes relating to crofting apply, comprising the seven former counties of Argyll, Caithness, Inverness, Orkney, Ross and Cromarty, Sutherland and Shetland.

cross action — an action for divorce raised by a party to a marriage who is being sued by the other for divorce.

cross-examination — the examination of a witness by the other party or parties after examination-in-chief. Leading questions are allowed in cross-examination, but not in examination-in-chief. The questions must be relevant to the issues in dispute, but considerable latitude is allowed.

Crown —

(1) ceremonial headgear worn by a monarch which has become a symbol of the monarchy, and in the United Kingdom the state;

(2) in criminal proceedings the state prosecution service headed by the **Lord Advocate** (qv) and composed of the **procurators fiscal** (qv) and the **Crown Office** (qv);

(3) Her Majesty's government, analogous to the term 'the state', 'the people' or 'the Commonwealth' in other jurisdictions. Probably the concept of 'the Crown' has discouraged constitutional analysis of the concept of 'the state' within the United Kingdom.

Crown Agent — the most senior official on the staff of the **Crown Office** (qv). The Crown Agent, whose primary concern is with the criminal process, also acts as the government solicitor if the Crown Office or Lord Advocate's Department become involved in a civil action.

Crown Court — senior English criminal court, consisting of a judge and a jury of 12, which deals which the more serious offences such as rape and murder.

Crown Office — a department under the Lord Advocate responsible for the public prosecution of crime within Scotland. Crown counsel in the High Court of Justiciary are assisted by Crown Office officials, who also administer the procurator fiscal service. Some functions of the Queen's and Lord Treasurer's Remembrancer have been transferred to the Crown Office.

CSA. *See* **Child Support Agency**.

CTP. *See* **common transport policy**. **[E]**

cujus est solum, ejus est usque ad coelum — whoever owns the land owns everything above it, eg buildings and fruits.

culpa — fault. Derived from the *Lex Aquilia* of Roman law as developed by the civilians, in its broadest sense *culpa* implies fault generally, whether intentional or negligent. In modern practice *culpa* in the narrower sense of negligence is more familiar, ie a breach of a legal duty to take reasonable care in the particular circumstances, but the comprehensive concept of *culpa* distinguishes Scots delict from English tort.

culpa lata dolo aequiparatur — gross negligence is treated as fraud, ie as if it were intentional.

culpable homicide — comprises all aspects of homicide which are neither casual nor justifiable, on the one hand, nor murderous on the other. Death which results from assault or negligent criminal acts are prosecuted as culpable homicide. The crime also includes cases where there has been no intent to kill but there are circumstances of diminished responsibility or provocation. (in English law manslaughter)

cum decimis inclusis — including teinds. If land is feued *cum decimis inclusis*, the titular (ie the person entitled to teinds) cannot claim payment.

cum nota — with a mark; describes evidence admitted with some reservation, eg the evidence of an accomplice.

cumulative multi-stage turnover tax — a sales tax imposed at each transaction from production to consumption without deduction of the tax imposed at earlier taxable events. **[E]**

cumulative obligations and remedies — where a party has a right of action to enforce two or more different obligations owed to him by another party and arising from the same set of facts (eg an obligation in contract and in delict), the obligations are normally treated as being alternative and not cumulative and accordingly the first party generally is not entitled to enforce both obligations but must (and may) choose between them. On the other hand, as a general rule the remedies enforcing an obligation are cumulative (eg a party's claim for damages does not normally exclude a claim for specific implement) unless they are incompatible (eg reduction of a contract is incompatible with specific implement of it).

curator. *See* **curatory**.

curator ad litem — a curator appointed by the court to act for a person under disability (eg by reason of youth or mental disorder) whose interests have to be safeguarded in legal proceedings.

curator bonis — a curator appointed to act generally for a person incapable through illness or absence of administering his own affairs.

curatory — the office of an administrator who acts for or consents to the legal actings of an *incapax* (ie a person legally incapable of acting on his own account). Thus a curator supplements the capacity of minors by consenting to their acts.

Curia —
(1) Latin for court;
(2) the civil service and government of the Roman Catholic Church, based in the Vatican, Rome.

CURIA — internet portal of the European Court of Justice, available at: http://curia.eu.int/en/index.htm.

current maintenance arrestment — a form of diligence against the earnings of a debtor in the hands of his employer to enforce the payment of current maintenance.

current payment — a transfer of foreign exchange which constitutes the consideration passing within the context of an underlying transaction. Cf **free movement of capital. [E]**

custom —
(1) judicial custom or *usus fori*, the method by which the judges developed the common law through judicial decisions;
(2) a generally accepted unwritten rule which, if embodied in the common law by reason of its acceptance by the community, need not be proved; such a rule, not recognised by the law, but which may, if reasonable, be binding on the parties to a contract if they or their community or trade accept it, although it must be proved by evidence.

Customs & Excise — the Government department responsible for collecting customs duties, VAT and other taxes, and also responsible for preventing illegal imports of drugs, alcohol and tobacco smuggling.

customs duty — a pecuniary charge imposed on goods by reason of the fact that they are listed in a customs tariff and cross a frontier. **[E]**

customs territory — a territory subject to a single customs regime. **[E]**

customs union — a single customs territory defined by a common customs or common external tariff formed by merging the customs territories of several states. **[E]**

CVA — company voluntary arrangement.

cyber-crime — crime committed via the medium of computers or the internet.

cy-près scheme — a 'so-near' scheme approved by the Court of Session, in the exercise of its *nobile officium*, under which, where literal effect cannot be given to the intention of the donor or testator under a charitable gift or bequest, or where it would be unreasonable or in excess of what the law permits to do so, or where the circumstances have changed, the court allows the funds to be applied as nearly as possible or practicable to the apparent intended purpose.

d

damages — a sum of money claimed as compensation for loss, injury or damage resulting from an act or omission of the defender which is in breach of a duty owed, either as a result of voluntary obligation or by force of law. The amount of damages awarded is intended to put the person entitled thereto as nearly as may be in the same position as he was before the harm ocurred.

damnum — loss or damage, injury or harm.

damnum absque (or sine) injuria — loss or damage suffered, but not as the result of a legal wrong, and therefore not reparable.

damnum fatale — loss caused by an unusual accident, such as exceptional storm or other natural calamity which could not reasonably have been foreseen, and consequently the resulting loss could not have been prevented. It is sometimes called an Act of God (its equivalent in English law).

damnum injuria datum — loss caused by a legal wrong or fault: the basis of liability in delict. If there is no legal wrong (eg if there is statutory authority for the act causing the loss) there may be no liability.

data — information recorded in a form in which it can be processed by equipment operating automatically in response to instructions given for that purpose: see the Data Protection Act 1984, s 1(2).

data user — the person holding **data** (qv) who must register under the Data Protection Act 1984.

de die in diem — from day to day; daily.

de facto — in fact; existing as an objective fact, albeit not necessarily based on any rule of law. Thus the *de facto* situation is the actual or factual situation. Cf *de jure*.

de fideli administratione officii — of the faithful administration of the office: the oath taken by a person appointed to perform some public office or duty, undertaking to carry it out faithfully.

de futuro — in the future.

de jure — as a matter of law or in point of law; rightful, by right. Cf *de facto*.

de lege ferenda — concerning what the law ought to be.

de lege lata — concerning what the law is.

de liquido in liquidum — of a liquid claim against a liquid claim; compensation or set-off.

de minimis non curat lex — the law does not concern itself with trifles. Thus the courts will not provide an equitable remedy for a trivial complaint. The maxim is not usually found in criminal procedure.

de minimis non curat praetor — the judge does not concern himself with trifles. A less familiar but more strictly accurate version of *de minimis non curat lex* (qv).

de momento in momentum — from moment to moment. Thus prescription runs *de momento in momentum*, ie to the very last minute.

de novo — anew, afresh; starting again from the beginning.

de plano — immediately; summarily, without further formality.

de presenti — now, at the present time.

de recenti — recent. Thus a *de recenti* statement made by a victim soon after the alleged commission of eg a sexual offence may reinforce the victim's evidence by enhancing its credibility, but does not provide corroboration. Possession *de recenti* of stolen goods may create the presumption that the possessor is the thief.

dead's part — that part of the moveable estate of a deceased person which, after the legal rights of any surviving spouse, children or their issue have been deducted, the deceased may dispose of by will in any way he wishes.

deadfreight — the sum of damages payable by the charterer to the shipowner or intermediate charterer where the charterer loads less cargo than promised in the **charter-party** (qv).

Dean of Faculty — the elected leader of the **Faculty of Advocates** (qv), or of a local Faculty or society of solicitors.

Dean of Guild — formerly the head of the Guild, Brethren or Merchant Company in certain burghs, with jurisdiction in mercantile and maritime causes, and latterly elected by a town council to preside over a **Dean of Guild Court** (qv).

Dean of Guild Court — a court constituted, until the reorganisation of local government in 1975, by the Dean of Guild, sitting alone or with others, with jurisdiction in respect of the construction of buildings throughout certain burghs. From 1959, in other burghs and in the landward area of counties, this jurisdiction was exercised by a buildings authority consisting of not less than three councillors.

debitum fundi or *debitum reale* — a real debt, lien or obligation over land which attaches to the land itself.

debitum in presenti solvendum in futuro — a debt now due but not payable until a future date, eg a legacy payable out of an estate on the expiry of a liferent.

debitum reale. See debitum fundi.

debt — money legally owed.

debt adjusting — third party negotiating or brokering terms for settlement of a debt or debts.

debt collecting — third party taking steps to recover debts.

decern — to give a final and extractable decree or judgment. Actual use of this formal expression is no longer necessary to warrant the issue of extract.

decimae — tenth parts or teinds. *See also* **cum decimis inclusis**.

decision —
(1) the final result of a case brought before a **court** (qv) for consideration, especially, but not only, a written judicial opinion giving reasons;
(2) a lawmaking measure, normally of an administrative character, adopted by a **Community institution** (qv); it is binding in its entirety, but only upon those to whom it is addressed; **[E]**
(3) under the **Treaty on European Union** (qv), an act adopted by the **Council of the European Union** (qv) within the sphere of **police and judicial cooperation in criminal matters** (qv) for any purpose other than approximation of national laws. **[E]**

declaration — a formal statement before a sheriff made by an accused person at or after his first appearance in court.

Declaration of Arbroath — a letter, made in 1320, from the earls and barons of Scotland to the Pope, stressing Scotland's independence from England, and asking him to recognize Scotland's independence and acknowledge Robert the Bruce as the country's lawful king.

declaration of incompatibility — a declaration that can be made by a **higher court** (qv) that a provision of primary legislation (or inevitably incompatible subordinate legislation) is incompatible with a **Convention right** (qv). A declaration of incompatibility does not affect the validity and continuing operation or enforcement of the legislation but it does trigger a power to make a remedial order to amend the incompatible legislation.

declarator — a declaration by the court of a person's rights, made in an action for declarator. The declarator does not itself actually enforce the rights. There has to be a practical rather than a theoretical purpose to the action.

declaratory power — power of the High Court of Justiciary of the Court of Session to declare a new law.

declinature — the rule that a judge must decline to hear a cause in which he has an interest, whether because of relationship to the parties (Declinature Act 1681) or because of pecuniary interest. The rule extends to the refusal of other appointments, eg as trustee.

decree (the first syllable is stressed) — the final order of a court or arbiter in civil proceedings. A decree may for example modify rights (eg divorce) or declare rights (qv **declarator**), or order the defender to pay, perform or abstain from performing some act (qv **petitory**), or may exonerate him if the pursuer has failed to establish his claim. *See also* **extract decree.**

decree arbitral — the final judgment of an arbiter.

decree condemnator — technically correct term (now little used) for a decree in favour of the pursuer; cf decree **absolvitor**.

decree conform — a decree authorising the enforcement of an order or decree of some other court or body.

decree dative — a judgment appointing a person to be an executor.

decryption — the process of making a secure, encrypted file readable as plain text.

deed — a formal document, executed and authenticated in accordance with prescribed formalities and incorporating the terms of an agreement, contract or obligation.

deed of arrangement — a contract between competing claimants, such as creditors or beneficiaries, in which the distribution of property is agreed.

deeming — a legal fiction often adopted in legislation whereby a thing or situation is stated to be as stated, whether or not this corresponds to fact or reality. Thus something can be deemed to be something else.

defamation — a delict involving the making of a statement or the communication of an idea concerning another which harms his or her character, honour and reputation and is made maliciously to the person's loss, injury or damage.

default — to fail to comply with a legal duty, eg to pay a sum of money owing on the due date.

defences — a statement lodged by the defender in a civil action, setting out in numbered paragraphs the facts and legal propositions constituting his answers to the pursuer's claim.

defender — the party against whom a civil action has been raised.

defer sentence — to adjourn a criminal case after a person has been convicted or found to have committed an offence for his good behaviour or to enable inquiries to be made to help the court to determine sentence or final disposal.

deflection of trade — deviation of trade from its normal course. **[E]**

deforcement — the crime of resisting or obstructing officers of the law who are enforcing a decree or judicial warrant.

del credere — describes an agreement with an agent whereby, for additional remuneration, the agent guarantees to his principal the performance by a third person of a contract into which the principal has entered.

delectus personae — the choice of a specific person because of personal considerations. A person so chosen may not delegate or assign any duty imposed on him.

delegated legislation. *See* **subordinate legislation**.

delegation —

(1) the substitution, with the creditor's consent, of a new debtor for the old, thus extinguishing the liability of the old debtor;

(2) generally one party authorising another to act for agreed purposes.

delegatus non potest delegare — a representative cannot devolve the powers entrusted to him by another.

deliberation room — the room in which the judges of the **European Court of Justice** (qv) meet in private to discuss and vote upon cases before the court. **[E]**

delict —a civil wrong created by the deliberate or negligent breach of a legal duty, from which a liability to compensate consequential loss and injury may arise. Delictual liability is involuntary in that it is obediential or imposed by law, and as such may be contrasted with voluntary obligations, viz those created by contract or unilateral promise.

delictual — adjectival form of **delict** (qv).

deliverance — an interlocutor or court order commonly used in sequestration proceedings.

delivery —

(1) in moveables: the transfer of possession of a corporeal moveable from one person to another;

(2) in heritable (immoveable) property: the delivery of a disposition or other deed followed by registration of a right in the appropriate register, which functions as the legally significant equivalent of physical delivery;

(3) in assignation of debts and similar incorporeal moveables: delivery of an assignation and intimation thereof to the debtor.

demise charter. *See* **bareboat charter.**

demit — to leave or resign office.

demonstrative legacy — legacy payable out of a specific fund; classified as a **specific legacy** (qv) and not a **general legacy** (qv).

demonstrative plan — a plan of property referred to in a disposition is demonstrative if in the event of an inconsistency between the plan and the verbal description of the property in the disposition, the verbal description is deemed to be correct. The opposite of 'demonstrative' is '**taxative**' (qv).

demurrage — an agreed amount payable to the shipowner by the charterer, In a voyage charterparty, for any delay in loading or unloading the vessel beyond the agreed **laytime** (qv), for which the owner is not responsible; is a type of **liquidated damages** (qv).

denuding — the divesting by a trustee of the trust estate on his demitting office.

deponent — a witness who makes a **deposition** (qv).

deportation order — an order requiring an alien to leave the United Kingdom and prohibiting his re-entry.

deposit; deposition —
(1) strictly, a gratuitous contract under which corporeal moveable property is entrusted by the depositor to the depository for safe custody, the contract being for the sole benefit of the depositor (the term is now extended to include custody for reward);
(2) a sum deposited as a pledge;
(3) the initial payment under a hire purchase agreement;
(4) a payment made to the credit of a bank account.

deposition — a statement made by a witness (a deponent) on oath and recorded in writing.

Deputy First Minister — the second most senior member of the **Scottish Executive** (qv), if the government is a coalition the post is likely to be held the leader of the minority partner in the coalition.

Deputy Presiding Officers (DPO) — the two deputies of the Scottish Parliament's (qv) **Presiding Officer** (qv), who can fulfill his duties in his absence.

dereliction — definitive abandonment of property.

derivative acquisition of property — refers to the transmission of a right in a thing from a prior owner to the acquirer usually as a result of a conveyance, assignation, or other voluntary transfer but could be by involuntary conveyance (such as adjudication in implement or compulsory purchase). Derivative acquisition is so called because the title of the acquirer derives from the title of the transferor which is transmitted to the acquirer. By contrast in the other mode namely original acquisition of **property** (qv) the acquirer's title does not derive from the title of a previous owner (if any).

derivative action —
(1) in English law, an action (whose existence derives from the rules of procedure) brought by the holder of shares in a company to enforce rights of the company which the company itself does not wish to enforce by court action;
(2) in Scots law, there is strictly no shareholder's derivative action, but a shareholder has a right (broadly comparable but derived from substantive law not rules of procedure) to raise an action in certain circumstances to protect a company's interests and to seek a remedy on its behalf.

derogation —
(1) generally, to take away from or to evade; an exception to a rule;
(2) more especially, an exemption of a state, sometimes temporarily, from the provisions of an international treaty or a provision of the EC Treaty or of Community legislation. **[E]**

desert the diet — to abandon a criminal charge, either *simpliciter* (irrevocably) or *pro loco et tempore* (for this place and time). In the latter case a new charge may be brought.

design — to set out a person's **designation** (qv).

designation — a person's style, title, name, description, address, marital status etc.

destination — a direction, usually in a deposition or will, prescribing the order of succession to moveable and heritable property.

destination over — a clause providing that if a designated beneficiary fails to take a gift, it is to pass to another.

destination principle — a system under which goods are taxed in the country of consumption instead of in the country of production. The country of consumption imposes the same tax burdens on both domestic and imported products, but imposes no tax on domestic goods intended for export. **[E]**

detention —
(1) in criminal law a punishment whereby young persons under the age of twenty-one are kept or detained in custody for a fixed period of time;
(2) in property law, exclusive physical control of an object; an important element in the legal concept of **possession** (qv).

development value burden — a **feudal real burden** (qv) which reserves development value to the feudal superior and the imposition of which caused a significant reduction in the consideration for the feu: Abolition of Feudal Tenure (Scotland) Act 2000, s 33(1).

devolution — the transfer of legislative power from the United Kingdom parliament to parliaments or assemblies representing Scotland, Wales and Northern Ireland. Scottish devolution was finally achieved by means of the Scotland Act 1998.

devolution case — a case where the disputed issue is over the functions and/or legal competences of the devolved legislative and executive authorities in Scotland, Wales and Northern Ireland; the final court of appeal in such matters is the **Judicial Committee of the Privy Council** (qv).

devolved power — legislative authority within the competence of the **Scottish Parliament**. (qv)

devil — an aspirant for admission to the **Faculty of Advocates** (qv) who trains as an assistant to an established advocate, who is known as his or her 'devil master'.

deviling — the period of training undergone by an aspirant for admission to the **Faculty of Advocates** (qv); this period lasts approximately 9 months and is unpaid.

DG. *See* **directorates-general**. **[E]**

dictum — a statement made by a judge in the course of a judgment.

dies cedit — *dies cedit* imports that an obligation has come into existence but is not yet prestable, and *dies venit* imports that the time for its enforcement has arrived.

dies dominicus non est juridicus — Sunday is not a 'lawful' day, in the sense that it is not a day recognised as appropriate for most judicial or legal proceedings.

dies incertus pro conditione habetur — an uncertain day is treated as a condition. Thus a promise of payment on the occasion of one's marriage is a conditional obligation which comes into effect only on the marriage.

dies interpellat pro homine — the day interrupts the man: the arrival of the stipulated day of performance of an obligation is enough, and no further action by the creditor is required. Failure to perform will attract the appropriate penalties, eg interest on any sum due.

dies non — a day (eg a Sunday or public holiday) when judicial proceedings are not conducted.

dies venit. *See* **dies cedit**.

diet — a date fixed by a court for the hearing of a case.

Digest, the — the most important part of the *Corpus Juris Civilis* (qv) consisting of the collection of extracts of the 39 leading Roman jurists; commissioned by the Emperor Justinian I, completed in 533 AD and the foundation of western law.

digest — a compilation of summaries of decided cases.

digital certificate — a public key that has been digitally signed by a third party (eg a financial institution) to identify the user of the public key. Digital certificates are used for encrypting information exchanged in online transactions.

digital receipt infrastructure (DRI) — method allowing web users to prove that electronic transactions and events actually took place, by providing a 'digital trail', a sort of online equivalent of a paper trail.

digital signature — an electronic signature encrypted digitally for security. An electronic signature is generated from an encrypted digest of the text (*see* public key) that is sent with the text message. The recipient decrypts the signature and retrieves the digest from the received text using a **private key** (qv). If the digests match, the message is authenticated and proved to be from the sender. Legally binding like a traditional signature under the Electronic Communications Act 2000 and must be backed by a digital certificate, issued by a **certification authority** (qv). *See also* **digital certificate**.

dilatory defence — a defence in civil proceedings that does not go to the merits of the case and is designed to delay it.

diligence —
(1) the methods of enforcing unpaid debts and other obligations either on the **dependence** (qv) or in execution of decrees of the Scottish courts or their equivalents (eg decrees of foreign courts or awards of statutory tribunals): enforcement of judgments;
(2) in litigation, the process of enforcing the recovery of evidence from an opponent or third person.

diligence on the dependence — diligence over assets of the defender executed while an action is continuing in order to secure implementation of the decree in the action which automatically converts diligence on the dependence into diligence in execution of the decree.

diminished responsibility — a state of mental instability or weakness, falling short of insanity, which, if established, may justify reducing the quality of the crime of murder to culpable homicide or otherwise mitigate the guilt of the accused.

direct action — contentious legal proceedings which commence and terminate in the European Court of Justice or in the Court of First Instance. **[E]**

direct applicability — that quality of a provision of European Community law which causes it to become law in each member state without the necessity of incorporation in or transformation into national law. **[E]**

direct concern — describing a quality of a measure adopted by a Community institution which bears directly upon the legal rights or obligations of a person without any discretionary intervening or intermediate act; a natural or juristic person (other than the addressee) must show direct concern in order competently to raise an action of **annulment** (qv) against the measure. **[E]**

direct effect — that quality of a provision of European Community law which causes it to confer upon individuals rights which national courts must protect. 'Vertical direct effect' is sometimes used to describe cases where the right conveyed by the provision lies against a member state or a public authority generally, and 'horizontal direct effect' is sometimes used to describe cases where the right lies against another natural or juristic person. **[E]**

direct racial discrimination — the treatment, on racial grounds, of one individual less favourably than another in similar circumstances, examples include discrimination in filling jobs, racist abuse and harassment.

directive — a legislative measure adopted by a **Community institution** (qv) which is addressed to the member states and is binding upon them as to a result to be achieved, but leaves to the appropriate national authorities the choice of the form and methods to be used to achieve that result. A directive must be incorporated into national legislation by all addressee member states within a time limit set by the directive; but even where no incorporation occurs, a directive may of itself create vertical (but not horizontal) directly effective rights; *see* **direct effect**. **[E]**

director —
(1) a person elected by the shareholders to manage the affairs of a registered company;
(2) a senior manager in an organisation, eg a local authority.

Directorates-General — the administrative departments into which the services (or civil service) of the European Commission are divided. The DGs and their staff are located mainly in Brussels, but some are based in Luxembourg. **[E]**

disability — a disabled person is 'anyone with a physical or mental impairment, which has a substantial and long-term adverse effect upon their ability to carry out normal day-to-day activities' DDA 1995.

Disability Rights Commission — government agency established to promote civil rights for disabled people and combat discrimination against them.

discharge —
(1) the formal release of a debtor from an obligation, sometimes without full payment or performance;
(2) the release of a bankrupt from the disabilities of sequestration;
(3) a receipt;
(4) the implementation of an obligation;
(5) part of an account of **charge and discharge** (qv);
(6) in environmental law, to allow effluent to enter a river.

discretionary power — power granted to a person or body to act according to his or its own judgment.

discuss — to use diligence against the principal debtor before using it against a cautioner. *See also beneficium ordinis.*

disgorge — to surrender or to give up (as distinct from to restore or to give back) money or property; the duty of a trustee or other fiduciary to give up unauthorised gains acquired by virtue of his fiduciary position; a synonym for payment of '**restitutionary damages**' (qv). *See also auctor in rem suam,* **damages, fiduciary, restitution**

dismissal — a decree bringing to an end proceedings in a civil action which does not have the effect of excluding a new action: that is to say, it does not constitute *res judicata* (qv).

dispone — to convey land. Formerly the use of the word in a deed was indispensible for the validity of a disposition of land.

disposition — a formal deed transferring heritable or moveable property.

dispositive clause — the clause in a disposition by which the property is transferred.

dissent — to disagree with the majority opinion. Thus a dissenting judgment disagrees with the opinions of the majority of the bench.

dissolution — the termination of parliament made by Royal Proclamation which ends that parliament, and calls a new General Election; made either at the request of the Prime Minister or when five years has expired since the previous General Election.

distortion — the act of changing to an unnatural form, or the condition of being so changed. Thus distortion of competition under European or United Kingdom competition law is an unnatural change in the desired level of commercial rivalry.

district — a sub-division of a **region** (qv) for local government purposes prior to local government reorganisation in 1996. The local authority was the district council.

district court — a court established in each area of a local authority by the District Courts (Scotland) Act 1975 with a jurisdiction, concerned with less serious criminal offences, exercised by **justices of the peace** (qv) (who need not be legally qualified) or legally-qualified stipendiary magistrates. On the introduction of district courts the former justice of the peace courts, quarter sessions, burgh courts and the Court of the Bailie of the River and Firth of Clyde were abolished.

dividend — the percentage of a company's after-tax profits paid to shareholders.

Division —
(1) a component of the **Inner House** (qv) of the **Court of Session** (qv). The First Division is composed of four judges, presided over by the Lord President and the Second Division is composed of four judges, presided over by the Lord Justice-Clerk; but in practice Division normally sits with only three judges on the bench. There is occasionally an Extra Division.
(2) a vote in the Houses of Commons or Lords;
(3) **scission** — the operation by which the business of one legal person is transferred to more than one legal person. **[E]**

division — an action by a *pro indiviso* proprietor for the division of property held in common with other proprietors.

divorce — judicial dissolution of marriage. *See* **irretrievable breakdown**.

divot. *See* **feal and divot**.

dock — an enclosure in a courtroom where the accused person sits during a criminal trial.

docket *or* **docquet** —
(1) an authenticating indorsement on a deed or other document;
(2) in obsolete conveyancing practice, a holograph attestation appended to a notarial instrument.

document of debt — a document constituting evidence of a legal transaction or itself creating indebtedness, eg a bill of exchange.

document of title — a document which provides evidence of a legal entitlement to property.

dole. *See **malus animus**.*

doli incapax — incapable of crime, eg on grounds of age or insanity.

dolus — fraud; 'every trick, falsehood or device employed for the purpose of circumventing, cheating or deceiving another' (Dig 4, 3, 1, 2).

domicile — the place where a person is considered by law to have his permanent home.

dominant position — a term of competition law which describes an **undertaking** (qv) or group of undertakings which enjoys such market power as to be effectively immune from competitive forces. In European and United Kingdom competition law a dominant position is not of itself prohibited, it is abuse of that privileged position which is prohibited.

dominant tenement — land the ownership of which includes a servitude over adjoining land, called the 'servient tenement'.

dominium directum — the residual but radical rights in land enjoyed by the feudal superior who has granted the effective ownership (the *dominium utile*) to a vassal. For the abolition of the *dominium directum, see* **allodial**; **feu**; **feudal tenure**.

dominium utile — the effective right of ownership of land enjoyed by a vassal, generally regarded as full ownership subject to certain rights (the *dominium directum*) of the superior through the superior's feudal title. For the abolition of the *dominium utile* and its replacement by allodial ownership. *See* **allodial**; **feu**; **feudal tenure**.

dominus litis — the master of the litigation: the effective party to legal proceedings which may be carried on in the name of another. The *dominus litis* may be ordered to pay the expenses involved.

domitae naturae — of a tamed nature, as of tamed or domestic animals as distinguished from animals *ferae naturae* (qv).

donatio inter virum et uxorem — a gift between husband and wife.

donation *inter vivos* — a gift made by one person to another whilst both parties are alive, contrasted with donation *mortis causa* (qv).

donation *mortis causa* — a gift made in contemplation of death and effective only on the donor's death. A gift may be transferred prior to the donor's death, but if the donee predeceases the donor the gift reverts to the donor.

donatory — a person to whom the Crown gives property which has fallen to the Crown by forfeiture or failure of succession.

doom — judgment; sentence.

double distress — two or more competing claims to a fund or to property on separate and hostile grounds, a prerequisite to an action of multiplepoinding.

double jeopardy — prosecution twice for what, in substance, is the same crime or offence, this is prohibited in Scots Law. *See* **thole an assize**.

double ranking — claiming twice against the same estate. No debt may be ranked twice upon a sequestrated estate. Thus if the principal and the cautioner are both bankrupt, a creditor may rank in each estate but the cautioner may not then rank in the principal's estate.

drawback — the amount of customs duties repaid when the goods on which they are charged are exported. **[E]**

droit acquis — acquired right. **[E]**

dubitante — doubting; used of a judge expressing doubt or reservations in his judgment.

Dublin Convention — treaty amongst the member states of the European Union, signed in 1990, in force 1997, determining the state responsible for examining an application for asylum lodged in one of the member states. **[E]**

due —
(1) owed;
(2) (of a debt) now payable; but
(3) a debt is sometimes said to be due if the obligation to pay is constituted even though the debt is not yet payable.

dumping — the introduction of a product from one country into the commerce of another at less than its normal value. **[E]**

durante bene placito — during good pleasure, as of an offence or appointment the holder of which may be dismissed at the pleasure of the person appointing him. Contrast with an appointment *ad vitam aut culpam*.

duress — strictly a term of English law equivalent to force and fear, *vis ac metus*, or extortion in Scots law. It may be relevant as a ground for annulling obligations in the context of civil law or as a mitigating factor in criminal law.

duty solicitor — a solicitor available under the legal aid scheme at the sheriff court of all areas on all court days, whose services are available to persons in custody on charges of murder or culpable homicide, or appearing before the sheriff on petition on solemn procedure, or in custody on their first appearance before the sheriff on summary complaint.

dying declaration — a statement made on his deathbed by a witness which, after his death, may be admissible evidence in a criminal trial.

dying deposition — a dying declaration made on oath.

e

eadem persona cum defuncto — the same person as the deceased. An executor is deemed to stand in the shoes of the deceased and is liable for the debts of the deceased up to the extent of the assets of the deceased.

EAEC. *See* **European Atomic Energy Community**. **[E]**

EAGGF. *See* **European Agricultural Guidance and Guarantee Fund**. **[E]**

earnest — a small sum of money or part of a larger bulk given as a token of the completion of a bargain.

earnings arrestment — a form of diligence against the earnings of a debtor in the hands of his employer to enforce the payment of a debt.

EAT. *See* **Employment Appeal Tribunal**.

eavesdrop *or* **stillicide** — a servitude imposing on a servient tenement the burden of receiving rainwater droppings from the eaves of the dominant tenement.

EC. — **European Community**. **[E]**

ECB. — **European Central Bank**. **[E]**

ECHR — **European Convention on Human Rights** (qv).

ECtHR — **European Court of Human Rights** (qv).

Ecofin — the **Council of the European Union** (qv) meeting in the configuration of ministers of economic and financial affairs. **[E]**

economic development burden — a **personal real burden** (qv) held either by a local authority or Scottish Ministers, which promotes economic development: Title Conditions (Scotland) Act 2003, s 45(1).

economic loss. *See* **pure economic loss**.

ECOSOC — the **Economic and Social Committee** (qv). **[E]**

ECR — European Court Reports, reference prefix for reports of the European Court of Justice and of the Court of First Instance. **[E]**

ECSC. *See* **European Coal and Steel Community**. **[E]**

ECSC Treaty — The Treaty of Paris 1951 (one of the three founding European Community treaties) which established the **European Coal and Steel Community** (qv). **[E]**

EC Treaty — Treaty of Rome (one of two) signed 25 March 1957, which established the European Community; originally the EEC Treaty. **[E]**

economic and monetary union (EMU) — a task of the European Community, adopted in the EC Treaty in 1993 by the Treaty on European Union, seeking to fuse the economic and monetary policies of the member states and the adoption of a single currency. In 2003, 12 of the 15 member states (those other than Denmark, Sweden and the United Kingdom) participate in EMU. **[E]**

Economic and Social Committee (ECOSOC) — an advisory body established by the EC Treaty, comprising representatives of 'the various economic and social components of organised civil society'; must be consulted by the Community institutions prior to the adoption of EC legislation in certain fields. **[E]**

economic entity doctrine — the principle whereby a group of legally distinct **undertakings** (qv) under the same effective control (which is a matter of fact) are deemed to be a single undertaking for purposes of competition law.

EDC — **European Defence Community** (qv). **[E]**

edict *nautae, caupones, stabularii* — the praetorian edict whereby shipmasters, innkeepers and stable keepers were strictly liable, without proof of fault, for the loss of or damage to travellers' property. It was adopted as a principle of Scots law.

edictal citation — the citation of a person subject to the court's jurisdiction but who is furth of Scotland or whose whereabouts are unknown, by delivery to the Keeper of Edictal Citations of a copy of the summons, which is entered in a register.

Edinburgh Gazette — the official periodical government newspaper in Scotland. Numerous statutes require notice of certain events or steps taken in proceedings to be advertised in it. There are also a London Gazette and a Belfast Gazette.

EEA. *See* **European Economic Area**. **[E]**

EEC. *See* **European Economic Community**. **[E]**

EEIG. *See* **European Economic Interest Grouping**. **[E]**

effeiring to — relating to; pertaining to; often applied to ancillary rights transferred along with heritable property.

eik (pronounced 'eek') — an extension of the confirmation of an executor to include property not included in the original inventory.

ejection —

    (1) an action to remove or eject a person who is in possession of heritable property without title (cf **removing**);

    (2) the act of messengers at arms or sheriff officers executing warrant for ejection in a decree of removing against a tenant on termination of the lease or on irritancy or against another person occupying without title;

    (3) a type of **spuilzie** (qv) consisting of the unlawful removal of a person from possession of heritable property. (cf **intrusion**).

ejusdem generis — literally of the same kind or nature: a rule of interpretation of documents, especially of statutes or deeds, where particular classes are specified by name, followed by general words, the meaning of the general words is limited by reference to the particular classes and the general words are taken to apply only to things of the same kind or nature as the particular classes.

Election Petition Court — court which hears petitions relating to the election of Members of the UnitedKingdom, European or Scottish Parliaments. Composed of two judges nominated by the Lord President, the court has the same powers as a judge of the Court of Session presiding at a civil jury trial, cases are rare in contemporary times.

electronic trust service provider — see **trust service provider.**

elide —

    (1) to oust, annul or exclude (Scots legal usage from Latin *elidere*, to crush);

    (2) in English legal usage (rare in Scots law) to join together or merge, eg periods of time.

embezzle — to use money or property fraudulently to one's own advantage after lawfully receiving it for another purpose.

employer and employee — a legal relationship in which one person engages another to perform work or provide services under his direction or control.

Employment Appeal Tribunal — an appellate court comprising, in Scotland, a Court of Session judge and two lay members representing employers and employees, which considers appeals on questions of law from decisions of **employment tribunals** (qv).

employment law — law governing the relationships of employers and employees.

employment tribunal — a statutory tribunal comprising a legally-qualified chairman appointed by the Lord President and two lay members appointed by the Secretary of State for Employment and representing employers and employed persons, with jurisdiction in respect of unfair dismissal, redundancy payments, discrimination and other questions relating to employment. Formerly called an industrial tribunal.

EMS. *See* **European Monetary System**.

emptio venditio — (literally 'purchase sale'), the name for the Roman contract of sale.

EMU. *See* **economic and monetary union**.

encumbrance — a burden, especially a debt or obligation secured over land. A synonym for **real burden** (qv).

endorse. *See* **indorse**.

endowment — a **life assurance policy** (qv) related to a loan designed to pay off the amount originally borrowed at the end of the loan term. An endowment policy will pay out a fixed amount either on a set date or if the insured dies before that date, and so is both a way of saving and life insurance.

enforceable Community right — United Kingdom term for a provision of Community law which has **direct effect** (qv); from the European Communities Act 1972, s 2(1). **[E]**

engross — to produce a fair copy of a deed or other legal instrument in its final form, ready for signature or execution.

enhanced cooperation — formerly 'closer cooperation', the mechanism permitting the member states of the European Union to make use of the institutions, procedures and mechanisms established by the EC Treaty to make rules which are binding only for the participating states. **[E]**

enlargement — the programme for expanding the European Union to include the remaining states of Europe. **[E]**

enorm lesion — serious injury to the estate of a minor child which may entitle him to the reduction, within four years of his majority, of a contract which caused it. Abrogated by the Age of Legal Capacity (Scotland) Act 1991.

enrol the cause — to lodge a cause or case or some related document in court to enable it to be called, usually on a particular date.

entail, tailzie *or* **tailye** — a form of disposition of heritable property on a specified line of successive heirs to keep the property in the family; it often includes special provisions regarding forfeiture, alienation and borrowing. New entails have been prohibited since 1914. Existing entails are abolished by the Abolition of Feudal Tenure etc. (Scotland) Act 2000.

enterprise zone — a designated part of the area of a local authority in which investment in new commercial enterprises is stimulated eg by the simplification of planning procedures.

entitled spouse — in the regime in the Matrimonial Homes (Family Protection) (Scotland) Act 1981 regulating occupancy rights of spouses in the matrimonial home, an entitled spouse is a spouse who is entitled, or permitted by a third party, to occupy their matrimonial home. A non-entitled spouse is not so entitled or permitted.

entry —

    (1) the act of taking possession of land as of right, eg by a purchaser. Title is completed by recording in the General Register of Sasines or the Land Register of Scotland;

    (2) in feudal law, a new vassal whether heir or purchaser had to be entered with his superior;

(3) powers of entry on land are granted by or under statutory provisions to a wide variety of inspectors and other officials.

entry barrier — a condition that imposes higher long-run production costs on an **undertaking** (qv) which wishes to enter or has just entered a new market than those borne by undertakings already established in the market.

environmental law — the law relating to the protection of the environment including the common law of nuisance and water law regimes and increasingly enacted in United Kingdom and European Union legislation designed to control and prevent contamination or degrading of the land, pollution of inland waters and the sea and air, including such matters as protection of flora, fauna, the food chain and water supply; abatement of nuisances; control of radioactive and other dangerous substances; disposal of waste; and sewerage and drainage.

eo die — that day; the same day.

eo nomine — in that name or character.

Equal Opportunities Commission — government agency, established under the Sex Discrimination Act in 1975, as an independent statutory body, to promote gender equality and eliminate discrimination on the grounds of gender or marital status.

equipollent — an equivalent. Thus, if a statute or an agreement prescribes a particular form of procedure, equipollents are inadmissible.

equity —
(1) fairness, the ability of the courts to mitigate the strict letter of the positive law to avoid a perceived injustice. The *nobile officium* (qv). The antithesis of positive law. Scots courts have always held an equitable jurisdiction and there has never been a strict separation between equity and law such as that found in English Law. Equity is not a formal source of law in Scotland. It belongs rather to the same series as 'common sense, expediency, public policy and the public interest';
(2) equity is sometimes seen not as the antithesis but as the essence of positive law; in this sense it has reference to the moral norms which underlie and inform positive law generally or specific doctrines;
(3) judicial discretionary powers;
(4) that part of English law derived from the court of Chancery, as opposed to the common law courts;
(5) share of an investment in an undertaking such as a company or a partnership.

equivalence — a doctrine developed by the **European Court of Justice** (qv) whereby national **technical barriers to trade** (qv) which hinder the free movement of persons or goods cannot be applied where those goods or persons conform in their country of origin to standards of production or training which, although different, are deemed to satisfy the same ends as are sought to be protected by the technical barriers. **[E]**

error — mistaken belief. Error as to an essential fact may render a contract void according to one influential interpretation, or voidable.

error calculi — a mistake in calculation.

errore lapsus — a mistake through error.

ESCB. *See* **European System of Central Banks**. **[E]**

escheat — forfeiture or confiscation: an obsolete penalty affecting a person's estate.

essential facilities doctrine — in competition law, the control by an **undertaking** (qv) of a facility or infrastructure without access to which competitors cannot, or cannot without difficulty, provide complementary or ancillary services in a neighbouring or sub-market, and so the former may be under a duty to allow the competitor access to that facility.

establishment —
(1) the act of founding an organisation;
(2) the act of settling, usually on a permanent basis ;
(3) a fundamental Treaty right in European Community law; *see* **right of establishment**. **[E]**
(4) an organisation, usually of a business nature, such as an agency or bank or a type of

statutory institution such as an educational establishment or residential establishment.

estate — all the property that a person owns, both heritable and moveable. 'Landed estate' is limited to heritable property.

esto — if it be so; a word frequently found in written pleadings to announce an assumption, which is not otherwise admitted, in order to state an alternative or consequential case, eg '*Esto* the pursuer slipped and fell as he avers, which is denied, he negligently failed to keep a good lookout.'

et sequentes paginae — and following pages (abbreviated '*et seq*').

EU. *See* **European Union. [E]**

EU Charter of Fundamental Rights. *See* **Charter of Fundamental Rights. [E]**

Euratom — the **European Atomic Energy Community** (qv). **[E]**

Euratom Treaty — Treaty of Rome (one of two) signed on 25 March 1957, which established the European Atomic Energy Community. **[E]**

eur-lex — official European Union website offering access to many EC and EU legal texts. **[E]**

Euro, the — the common currency of 12 of the 15 member states (in 2003 those other than Denmark, Sweden and the United Kingdom) of the European Community; euro banknotes and coins replaced national banknotes and coins on 1 January 2002. **[E]**

Eurojust — the European Judicial Cooperation Unit, a body of the European Union established in 2002, comprising one member from each member state who is a prosecutor, judge or police officer, and charged with improving coordination and cooperation amongst the competent national authorities in the investigation and prosecution of serious, and especially organised, crime. **[E]**

Europe Agreement — a treaty signed between the European Community on the one hand and a state of central or eastern Europe on the other providing for adoption of the *acquis communautaire* (qv) in, preparatory to accession of, the latter to the European Union. **[E]**

Europe day — proposed public holiday throughout the European Union under the draft **Constitution of the European Union** (qv); being 9 May, the day in 1950 when the **Schuman Plan** (qv) was announced. **[E]**

European Agricultural Guidance and Guarantee Fund (EAGGF) — better known under its French acronym FEOGA, the financial mechanism set up under the **common agricultural policy** (qv) for all intervention support of regulated agricultural markets (the guarantee fund) and direct support for producers (the guidance fund). **[E]**

European anthem — official anthem of the European Union proposed by the draft **Constitution of the European Union** (qv); being the 'Ode to Joy' from Beethoven's ninth symphony, but without Schiller's lyrics. **[E]**

European Anti-Fraud Office (OLAF) — a body created by the European Commission in 1999, based in Brussels, to combat fraud, corruption and any other illegal activity adversely affecting the European Community's financial interests; OLAF is from *Office de lutte antifraude*. **[E]**

European Atomic Energy Community — one of the three (now two) European Communities; came into being on 1 January 1958. **[E]**

European Coal and Steel Community — the first of three European communities, established in 1952 to regulate matters of the production and commercialisation of coal and steel. Because the Coal and Steel Community was, unlike the other communities, established for a 50 year period, it came to an end (and its assets wound up and transferred to the European Community) in 2002. **[E]**

European Central Bank (ECB) — an organ of the European Community, with legal personality, coming into being in 1999 with its seat in Frankfurt (Main). The ECB is responsible for implementing and regulating the Community's economic and monetary union, and so monetary policy, the **euro** (qv) and setting interest rates. **[E]**

European Commission. *See* **Commission of the European Communities** (qv). **[E]**

European Commissioners — the members of the **Commission of the European Communities** (qv). The draft **Constitution of the European Union** (qv) proposes the creation of 'European Commissioners' distinct from non-voting 'Commissioners'. **[E]**

European Community —
(1) one of the three (now two) European communities, came into being on 1 January 1958, and by far and away the most important of the three, charged with the task of creating a **common market** (qv) and **economic and monetary union** (qv) amongst its member states. Originally the **European Economic Community** (qv), it was renamed in 1993 by the **Treaty on European Union** (qv); **[E]**
(2) sometimes shorthand for the three (now two) European communities taken together. **[E]**

European Company — a public limited liability company, called a *Societas Europaea*, or SE, which may be formed in accordance with the Statute for a European Company adopted in 2001 (Council Regulation No 2157/2001 of 8 October 2001) and coming into force in October 2004. **[E]**

European Convention. *See* **constitutional convention.**

European Convention on Human Rights (ECHR) — the Convention for the Protection of Human Rights and Fundamental Freedoms, signed in Rome in 1950, to which all member states of the **Council of Europe** (qv) are party. The convention is separate from European Community law and the Community is not party to the convention, however the rights enumerated in it are deemed to form a part of Community law. Convention rights have been incorporated into United Kingdom law by the Human Rights Act 1998.

European Cooperative Society (SCE) — a form of incorporation, based upon democratic participation and equitable profit sharing amongst its members, comprising natural and/or juridical persons from at least two member states, formed in accordance with, and governed by, the Statute for a European Cooperative Society adopted in 2003 (Council Regulation No 1435/2003 of 22 July 2003). An SCE requires subscribed capital of at least EUR 30,000, has legal personality, and may or may not have limited liability. The regulation applies, and an SCE may be formed, from August 2006. **[E]**

European Council — meetings of the Heads of State or Government of EU member states plus the President of the European Commission. It meets twice every six-monthly period, but may be convened for an extraordinary meeting if required. It enjoys no legal powers but is of supreme political importance in establishing an agenda and guidelines for EC policies and defining principles and guidelines for **common foreign and security policy** (qv) under the **Treaty on European Union** (qv). **[E]**

European Court of Auditors. *See* **Court of Auditors.** **[E]**

European Court of Human Rights (ECtHR) — the court of the **Council of Europe** (qv), competent to make definitive rulings on the **European Convention on Human Rights** (qv). The court is not an EC institution and is based in Strasbourg. Under s 2 of the Human Rights Act 1998 any United Kingdom court or tribunal making a decision concerning convention rights must take the decisions of the ECtHR into account. The court is composed of a number of judges equal to that of the Contracting States (45 in 2003). Judges are elected by the Parliamentary Assembly of the Council of Europe for a term of six years. The court sits in Committees of three judges, in Chambers of seven judges, and in a Grand Chamber of seventeen judges.

European Court of Justice — properly styled the Court of Justice of the European Communities, but known universally as the European Court of Justice; the senior court of the European Communities, consisting of one judge from each member state (15 in 2003), assisted by eight **Advocates-General** (qv), appointed for terms of six years by agreement among the member states. It enjoys jurisdiction in a number of areas, principally: to ensure that measures adopted by the Community institutions comply with the Treaty and with law generally; to ensure that the member states comply with the obligations imposed upon them by Community law; to consider questions of the interpretation or validity of Community law when asked to do so by a national court before which such a matter has arisen; and, now, to hear appeals from a judgment of the **Court of First Instance** (qv). It has some, but very limited, jurisdiction over matters falling under the **Treaty on European Union** (qv). The Court has its seat in Luxembourg. It is not to be confused with the **European Court of Human Rights** (qv) of the **Council of Europe** (qv) or the **International Court of Justice** (qv); consequently the term 'European Court' is ambiguous. **[E]**

European Currency Unit (ECU) — a unit of value based on a basket of European Community national currencies which is used instead of a national currency for Community financial transactions, in particular in the European Monetary System and the financing of the **common agricultural policy** (qv). The ECU was introduced in 1978, replacing the Unit of Account and the European Unit of Account and has itself been replaced by the **Euro** (qv). **[E]**

European Defence Community (EDC) — a Community, based upon the model of the **European Coal and Steel Community** (qv), proposed in 1952 but which never came into being. **[E]**

European Economic Area (EEA) — created by a 1992 agreement, in force in 1994, between the European Community and its member states on the one part, and now, three of the four **European Free Trade Association** (qv) states on the other part (Iceland, Liechtenstein and Norway, but not Switzerland), a free trade regime combined with provisions on the free movement of persons, services and capital throughout the territory of the contracting states. **[E]**

European Economic Community (EEC) — one of the three European communities, established in 1958; re-named the **European Community** (qv) in 1993. **[E]**

European Economic Interest Grouping (EEIG) — a form of association under European Community law, enabling firms in various member states to undertake joint ancillary activities without need for capitalisation; governed by Council Regulation No 2137/85 of 25 July 1985. **[E]**

European Free Trade Association (EFTA) — a **free trade area** (qv) established in 1960 among seven European states (the United Kingdom being a founding member) and in 2003 comprising Iceland, Liechtenstein, Norway, and Switzerland. **[E]**

European governance — a programme of reform of the working of the Community institutions, initiated by a 2001 Commission White Paper. **[E]**

European Institutions. *See* **Community institution**.

European Investment Bank — the European Community's financing institution, it raises funds on the markets which it directs on the most favourable terms towards financing capital projects according with the objectives of the Community. **[E]**

European Monetary Fund — Fund established under the European Monetary System to assist in the stabilisation of exchange rates. **[E]**

European Monetary System — a system of monetary cooperation established in 1978 amongst the member states of the **European Community** (qv) as a precursor to the full **economic and monetary union** (qv). **[E]**

European Monetary Union. *See* **economic and monetary union**. **[E]**

European Ombudsman — an official appointed by and responsible to the European Parliament who investigates instances of maladministration in the activities of the Community institutions or bodies with the exception of the Court of Justice and the Court of First Instance acting in their judicial capacities. **[E]**

European Parliament — an institution, one of the five, created by the EC Treaty; originally known as 'the Assembly'. It consists of representatives (Members of the European Parliament, or MEPs) of the peoples of the Community, since 1979 directly elected, and so the locus of democratic control and accountability of the Community institutions. In 2003 there are 626 MEPs; it is anticipated that their number will settle, post-**enlargement** (qv), at around 732. **[E]**

European Patent Convention — a treaty signed in 1973, open to ratification by all European states, by which 'baskets' of national patents of the signatory states may be applied for, and conferred by, a single office. **[E]**

European Patent Office — the office created by the European Patent Convention; based in Munich. **[E]**

European political cooperation — the former practice, established gradually by the member states of the European Community, and recognised by the **Single European Act** (qv), of consulting in issues of foreign policy with the object of joint formulation and implementation of a common foreign policy. Now replaced by the provisions on **common foreign and security policy** (qv) in the **Treaty on European Union** (qv). **[E]**

European Social Charter — the Community Charter of the Fundamental Social Rights of Workers, adopted by 11 of the then 12 member states of the European Economic Community, the United Kingdom opposing, in 1989. The Charter has no legal force, but is intended to serve as a blueprint for the adoption of Community legislation in the social sphere. Much of its provisions are now written into the EU **Charter of Fundamental Rights** (qv). **[E]**

European System of Central Banks — an organ created by the EC Treaty composed of the **European Central Bank** (qv) and the central banks of the member states participating in **economic and monetary union** (qv), responsible essentially for price stability within the **Eurozone** (qv). **[E]**

European Union (EU) — A transnational organisation created in 1993 by the Treaty on European Union signed at Maastricht. The constitutional structure of the European Union is based upon three so-called 'pillars': the first, or central, pillar is the three (now two) European Communities created in the 1950s; the second and third pillars (alternatively, Title V and Title VI) are, respectively, provisions addressing a **common foreign and security policy** (qv) and provisions addressing **police and judicial cooperation in criminal matters** (qv). The two Community pillars operate under their own long-established legal, quasi-constitutional structure; the second and third pillars do not, rather they operate essentially upon the basis of traditional intergovernmental co-operation between the member states. Community law is therefore a 'subset' of the law of the European Union; and although each comprises the same member states, and the **Community institutions** (qv) govern both, care must be taken not to confuse the European Community and the European Union – especially not to ascribe the principles and practices of the European Community to the whole Union. In 2003 the European Union consists of 15 member states; it is anticipated that 10 more, from central, eastern and southern Europe, will accede to the Union in 2004. The draft **Constitution of the European Union** (qv) proposes the abolition of the pillar structure and the fusion of all Union activities into a single institutional and constitutional system; the proposal will be considered by the 2004 **intergovernmental conference** (qv). **[E]**

Europol — the European Police Office, an organisation to promote police cooperation between EU member states in preventing and combating serious forms of international organised crime, including terrorism and drug trafficking. The convention establishing Europol was signed in July 1995 and Europol has been fully operational since July 1999. It has its seat in the Hague. **[E]**

Eurozone — the territory of those member states of the European Community in which the **Euro** (qv) is the currency. **[E]**

evidents — writs and deeds proving a title to land (obsolete).

ex adverso — opposite to; describing the position of land or buildings.

ex contractu — arising from a contract. The phrase can refer to both a right and an obligation under a contract.

ex deliberatione Dominorum Concilii — after consideration by the Lords of Council: a term of art indicating that a writ can pass the **Signet** (qv) in the Court of Session, thus enabling it to be issued. Formerly all writs required to be read, considered and approved by the Lord Ordinary on the Bills before they could pass the Signet.

ex delicto — arising from a delict.

ex dolo non oritur actio — a right of action does not arise out of fraud. Thus a guilty party may not enforce a fraudulent obligation or contract.

ex facie — on the face of it. Generally something *ex facie* correct is presumed to be so until the contrary is established.

ex facie **absolute disposition** — an apparently absolute disposition of property which was truly granted by the owner as security for a loan and was accompanied by a back letter or explanatory letter making it clear that the disponee (often a building society) did not in fact own the property absolutely but only by way of security. The system was superseded by the standard security in 1970.

ex gratia — gratuitous, done without recognising any legal obligation to do whatever was done. Thus an *ex gratia* payment may be made to settle a claim without any admission as to liability.

ex hypothesi — from the hypothesis; put forward as a theory.

ex lege — according to law. Thus interest on money lent may be due to the creditor *ex lege* from the date of repayment even if there was no specific agreement between the parties as to interest.

ex nobile officio — on account of or by virtue of the **nobile officium** (qv).

ex nudo pacto non oritur actio — no right of action arises from a bare promise or engagement. A promise or bargain without a consideration is an unenforceable obligation: a principle of civil law adopted in England, but not in Scotland where gratuitous obligations are enforceable.

ex officio — by virtue of holding a particular appointment or office.

ex pacto illicito non oritur actio — no right of action may be based on an illicit agreement.

ex parte — from one side; decribes proceedings where only one party has had the opportunity of being heard, eg proceedings for interim interdict. Cf **inter partes**.

ex pietate — from natural affection and duty.

ex post facto — from what is done afterwards; retrospective; effected so as to affect something already done.

ex proprio motu — of his own volition; of his own accord: describes a decision made by a judge without his being requested by a party to take that course.

ex turpi causa non oritur actio — no right of action arises from a disgraceful or immoral consideration.

ex vi aut metu — on grounds of force and fear. A deed granted under coercion may be reduced.

examination — the questioning of a witness, whether by the party calling him (examination-in-chief) or by an opposing party (cross-examination) or, following cross-examination, by the first party again (re-examination).

excambion — the exchange of one piece of immoveable property (land or buildings) for another piece of such property.

exceptio quae firmat legem exponit legem — an exception which confirms a law explains the law: a maxim of interpretation whereby the statement of an exception to a general rule implies the application of the rule in all other circumstances. Thus if the master of a ship is expressly prohibited from doing something otherwise lawful in his home port, that prohibition confirms that he may do it in a foreign port.

exception —
  (1) an objection to a judge's charge in a civil jury trial which may be immediately considered by the judge or form the basis for review by the Inner House of the Court of Session;
  (2) an obsolete term for a defence or defences, which survives in the plea **ope exceptionis** (qv).

exception légale — in competition law, a regime whereby a restrictive agreement or practice which falls within a prohibited field is valid from its formation provided it satisfies certain terms or conditions laid down. To be compared with a scheme whereby such an agreement or practice is valid only if, and upon being, formally exempted by a competent administrative authority. Both EC and United Kingdom competition law adhere to the latter scheme; but in May 2004 the Community is switching to a regime of *exception légale*. **[E]**

Exchequer cause — a revenue matter heard by the Court of Session under jurisdiction derived from the former **Court of Exchequer** (qv).

exclusion — in competition law, the setting aside of defined areas of activity by statute or by the Secretary of State from the prohibitions set out in the Competition Act 1998. Cf **exemption**.

exclusion clause. *See* **exemption clause**.

exclusion order —

(1) an order made by a court on the application of a spouse suspending the other spouse's occupancy rights in the matrimonial home: Matrimonial Homes (Family Protection) (Scotland) Act 1981, s 4;

(2) in the case of an unmarried cohabiting couple (man and woman), a similar order excluding one of the two cohabitants from the house: 1981 Act, s 18;

(3) an order made by the sheriff, on application by a local authority, excluding a person named in the order from a child's family home: Children (Scotland) Act 1995, s 76(1).

Exclusive Economic Zone — maritime zone extending up to 200 nautical miles from the shoreline, within which a coastal state can control fishing, mineral exploration.

execution —

(1) the carrying out or enforcement of an order or decree of court;

(2) the written return or certificate that execution under (1) has been done;

(3) the act of authenticating a deed by signing it in accordance with the appropriate formalities;

(4) the carrying out of a sentence of death.

executor — a legal representative of a deceased person whose duty is to wind up the estate of the deceased.

executor creditor — where others legally entitled to act as executor of a deceased debtor have declined to confirm to his estate, (*see* **confirmation**) a creditor of the deceased holding a liquid ground of debt may be confirmed as an executor creditor on all or part of the debtor's estate in order to pay the debt out of that confirmed estate. The process is a type of diligence.

executor dative — an executor appointed by the sheriff where no executor was nominated by the deceased or has accepted such appointment.

executor nominate — an executor nominated by the testator in his will.

executory — not yet implemented or completed; still to be executed (in contractual and other obligations and in trusts).

executry — the process of winding up the estate of a deceased person in accordance with his will or with the law of intestate succession.

executrix — female **executor** (qv).

exempli gratia — for example; eg.

exemption — in competition law, a declaration from a competent authority (the European Commission or the Office of Fair Trading) that a prohibition against restrictive agreements or practices is not to apply to a particular agreement or practice because of the net competitive benefits it produces. An exemption may be issued upon an individual basis or to pre-determined categories of agreements or practices by means of a **block exemption** (qv). **[E]**

exemption clause *or* **exclusion clause** — a strictly construed clause in a contract providing that failure in performance by one party will not entitle the other to resile or claim damages. The effect of some such clauses was curtailed by the Unfair Contract Terms Act 1977.

exhaustion of rights — the principle whereby certain monopoly rights of commercialisation accruing to an intellectual property right lapse within the **European Community** (qv) and the **European Economic Area** (qv) once the good protected by the right is marketed anywhere within those territories for the first time by the holder of the right or with his consent. **[E]**

exhibition — an action to compel the production of documents.

exoner — to release from further liability. Thus a judicial factor may ask for exoneration and discharge from the court.

expectancy —
  (1) hope of succession to property on owner's death (Latin *spes successionis*);
  (2) life expectancy: the period which a person is likely to live.
expectation interest — in the law on contract damages, the interest of a contracting party in the expectations created by the contract. This interest is protected by law so that the normal objective of an award of damages for breach of contract is to put the pursuer into the position in which he would have been if the contract had been performed. Contrast the **reliance interest** (qv) and the **restitution interest** (qv).
expede — to draw up or complete and issue a document.
expedited procedure — also 'fast-track procedure'; the hearing of a case before the European Court of Justice or the Court of First Instance by special, speedy procedure where the urgency of the case requires judgment with a minimum of delay. **[E]**
expenses — the costs of an action, including legal fees, outlays etc.
explanatory notes — official guidance notes, which accompany Acts of the Scottish Parliament in order to explain the purpose of the act to non-lawyers.
export price — the price actually paid or payable for a commodity sold for export to the European Community. **[E]**
expose — to put up for sale by auction.
expressio (or enumeratio) unius est exclusio alterius — the special mention of one thing implies the exclusion of another: an important principle in the construction of statutes and deeds. Thus if a statute expressly provides for one or more methods of doing something, that provision implies the exclusion of some other method.
extended composition — a formation of a chamber of the Court of First Instance as five judges, rather than the normal three. **[E]**
external trade — trade between the European Community and third countries. **[E]**
extortion —
  (1) the crime or delict of obtaining by means of unlawful threats money or some benefit not otherwise due;
  (2) punitive terms in a contract which (except in certain circumstances relating to interest on loans) do not provide grounds for reduction of the contract.
extra commercium — excluded from commerce; used especially of things which may not be bought and sold, eg public roads and titles of honour.
Extra Division — a temporary division of the **Inner House** (qv) of the **Court of Session** (qv) additional to the two permanent divisions (the First and Second Divisions) constituted from time to time to dispose of proceedings in which the Inner House has jurisdiction.
extra-judicial — not carried out under judicial control; out of court. Thus extra-judicial expenses incurred outwith the normal course of judicial proceedings are not usually recoverable from the opponent by the successful party. A dispute which is being or might be heard by a court may be terminated by an extra-judicial settlement out of court.
extract —
  (1) a formal copy of a decree or other judicial or legal document, duly certified as a true copy;
  (2) to obtain such a formal copy with a view to enforcement.
extract decree — a formal certified copy of a decree which is used to enforce it. Thus to enforce a decree a party must first extract it.
Extractor of the Court of Session — official who prepares and authenticates **extract decrees** (qv) or other judicial proceedings of the **Court of Session** (qv).
extradition — the legal surrender by a state, of a person physically resident in that state, to another state for the purposes of bringing that person before the criminal courts of the transferee state; see the Extradition Act 1989.
extraterritoriality — the application of the law of a state outwith its territorial jurisdiction.
extrinsic — from an external source, used especially of evidence so adduced to construe a statute or document as contrasted with interpretation from the text itself. Cf **intrinsic**.

f

facility and circumvention. *See* **circumvention.**

facility burden — a real burden which regulates the maintenance, management, reinstatement or use of facilities such as the common parts of a tenement, a common recreational area, a private road, private sewerage, or a boundary wall: see the Title Conditions (Scotland) Act 2003, s 122(1), (3).

factor —
(1) a person who manages heritable property on behalf of the owner;
(2) an agent in possession of goods or their title who sells them, sometimes in his own name as apparent owner, for a principal on commission.
See also **judicial factor.**

factoring — the practice of a commercial agent who controls credit and debt collection for a principal or customer on commercial terms.

factory; factory and commission — a deed empowering another to act for the grantor in business transactions, eg buying and selling shares, similar to the English power of attorney.

factum — an act or deed.

factum praestandum. See **ad factum praestandum.**

faculty —
(1) a power which a person can exercise;
(2) a society of lawyers.

Faculty of Advocates — the society comprising the members of the Scottish Bar, ie advocates. The Faculty is a self-regulating professional body and controls its own admissions and discipline. *See also* **advocate, Dean of Faculty.**

fair comment — a defence to an action of defamation: the statement in question must be comment not of fact, fair and in the public interest.

fair hearing and fair trial — a human right under the European Convention on Human Rights, article 6.

fair rent — a rent fixed under the Rent Acts.

fair trading — a way of doing business which is reasonable and does not harm the consumer.

falsa demonstratio non nocet — an erroneous description does not injure. The effectiveness of a provision in a deed is not affected by some error of description so long as there is no doubt as to the identity of the person or thing concerned.

falsehood, fraud and wilful imposition — the crime of obtaining by false pretences.

falsing the doom — questioning a legal decision; appealing.

family law — the law governing personal status, husband and wife; parent and child; cohabiting couples; family life and especially family breakdown, including divorce, judicial separation and nullity of marriage; guardianship and personal welfare of children and of adults with mental disability; parental responsibilities and rights; and residence of and contact with children.

fatal accident inquiry — an inquiry conducted by the sheriff and initiated by the procurator fiscal into any death which was sudden, suspicious or unexplained, or which occurred in circumstances giving rise to serious public concern.

fault — also known as *culpa* (qv), the mental element in delict which in principle involves a continuum beginning at one extreme with malice (deliberate act or omission for the purpose of harming; spite); through intent (deliberate act or omission knowing that harm is certain, or substantially certain, to result but without malice and in the belief that the actor is exercising a right); and ending at the other extreme with negligence (unintentional harm caused by failure to take the reasonable care required in the circumstances to avoid causing it). Distinct from **strict liability** (qv).

feal and divot — a servitude which gives a right to cut turf for building, thatching or fuel.

fee —
(1) the right to and interest in heritable property, in contrast to **liferent** (qv);
(2) the remuneration of a lawyer or other professional person for his professional services.

fee fund — a fund into which court dues were paid by parties to proceedings in the Court of Session, and from which the administration of the court was in part financed.

FEOGA. *See* **European Agricultural Guidance and Guarantee Fund. [E]**

ferae naturae — of a wild nature; describes wild or untamed animals, as distinct from animals *domitae naturae* (qv).

feu — a piece of land held by a feuar or vassal who pays feuduty, a perpetual rent, and who becomes the effective owner provided he observes the conditions of the feu. It is now incompetent to impose feuduties as a condition of granting land, and feuduties may now be redeemed, and must be redeemed upon transfer of the land. Feuduties not extinguished before 28 November 2004 will be extinguished on that day: Abolition of Feudal Tenure etc (Scotland) Act 2000, s 7. *See* **feudal tenure**.

feu farm *or* **feu ferme** — a hereditary **feudal tenure** (qv) under which land was formerly held by a vassal from a superior for a fixed money rent following an initial payment or *grassum*. Originally the vassal might be required to perform personal services (especially agricultural services), or pay rent in the form of cattle or grain. Feu ferme survived other forms of feudal tenure and these words are still used in modern grants in feu.

feuar — vassal. *See* **feu**.

feudal barony. *See* **barony**.

feudal property. *See* **feu**.

feudal real burden — a **real burden** (qv) created before 28 November 2004 in a grant in feu (such as a feu diposition) or in a deed of conditions registered in association with a grant in feu. Feudal real burdens are enforceable by the superior. The **burdened property** (qv) is the **feu** (qv) held by the **vassal** or **feuar** (qv). Some are also enforceable by co-feuars. Compare **non-feudal burdens**.

feudal tenure — land held under a **feu** (qv), the method of land owning in Scotland since the Middle Ages. It will be abolished when the relevant provisions of the Abolition of Feudal Tenure etc. (Scotland) Act 2000 come into force on an appointed day namely 28 November 2004.

feuduty. *See* **feu**.

fiar — the person in whom heritable property is vested (ie who holds the **fee** (qv)), in contrast to the liferenter, whose interest is a burden on that of the fiar.

fiars' prices — the annual prices of grain, until 1973 determined at the Fiars Court, on which some ministers' stipends were fixed. They were also used to fix skat duties in Orkney.

fiat ut petitur — let it be done as asked: a phrase used by a judge or magistrate granting a crave for a warrant.

fideicommissum — a trust to execute a testator's wishes.

fiduciary —
(1) a person who holds something in trust (in contrast to a beneficiary), or who manages the affairs of another person for that person's benefit and who must not use his position to derive an unauthorised profit or advantage for himself, *see* **auctor in rem suam;**
(2) property held in trust;
(3) (adj) of the nature of a trust; held or given in trust;
(4) a special obligation of trust and confidence owed by one person to another.

filiation. *See* **affiliation**.

filius nullius — an illegitimate child.

filum — a line. Thus *usque ad medium filum* means to the middle line of a stream or road.

financial provision — the name given to orders in actions of divorce requiring one party to the marriage on or after decree in the action, to pay to the other party a capital sum or a periodical allowance or to transfer property and includes incidental orders for example for the sale or valuation of property; for regulation of occupation of the matrimonial home; for security for payment of financial provision; and the like. Similar orders are competent in actions of declarator of nullity of marriage.

financial services — services such as banks; building societies; stockbrokers; investment companies and trusts; the provision of pensions; insurance now regulated by the Financial Services Authority acting under the Financial Services and Markets Act 2000.

Financial Services Authority — independent government body that regulates the financial services industry in the United Kingdom.

fine — a financial punishment imposed by court upon a person convicted of a crime or other breach of the law.

fire-raising — setting fire to property. 'Wilful fire-raising' is intentional or deliberate (the equivalent of arson in English law), as distinct from negligent or accidental fire-raising.

firm — a partnership, or other unincorporated group, of persons carrying on a business. Strictly speaking limited company should not be referred to as firms, but they often are.

first generation rights — term for the traditional civil rights such as freedom of expression, the right to vote, presumption of innocence etc as contrast with 'second generation rights' which are socio-economic in content eg minimum wage.

first instance — describes a court before which or judge before whom a case is first heard, as distinct from a court or hearing a case on appeal. A court of first instance will determine issues of fact and law whilst appeals are usually restricted to legal issues.

First Minister — the head of the **Scottish Executive** (qv), ie the equivalent of the Prime Minister within the United Kingdom Government, nominated by the **Scottish Parliament** (qv) and appointed by the **sovereign** (qv).

first offender — a convicted person with no previous convictions.

fiscal — (adj) relating to the national revenue; (noun) shortened form of **procurator fiscal** (qv).

fiscal neutrality —
(1) the principle that taxation should not influence the conduct of business activities and the exercise of the rights and facilities granted under European Community law, which should be influenced only by objective economic factors and considerations of economic efficiency; **[E]**
(2) more specifically, the principle that taxation should not discriminate on grounds of nationality or have a discriminatory effect on cross-frontier transactions. **[E]**

fishing diligence —
(1) the use of **commission and diligence** (qv) for the recovery of documents not for the (legitimate) purpose of obtaining evidence in support of the case stated in his pleadings but rather for the speculative and illegitimate purpose of obtaining disclosure of material which the party hopes will support a case not yet averred on record;
(2) the use of **diligence** (qv) for debt in the off-chance of attaching the debtor's property such as an arrestment used by a creditor in the hands of the arrestee (such as a bank) in order to ascertain whether the arrestee has an arrestable liability to account to the debtor.

fitted account — business accounts which have been drawn up by one party and docqueted as correct by the other, which raise a rebuttable presumption that all claims are settled.

fittings — moveable articles added, connected or attached to heritable property, which can be removed without causing damage (eg light bulbs and curtain rails). Contrast with **fixtures** (qv).

fixed penalty —
(1) under the Road Traffic Offenders Act 1988 the procurator fiscal may send a notice (called a conditional offer) giving an alleged offender the opportunity to pay a fixed pecuniary fine as an alternative to prosecution for certain road traffic offences;
(2) for certain parking offences a police constable or a traffic warden may give a fixed penalty notice to a person on the spot or attach it to a motor vehicle.

fixed security or charge — a security or charge affecting some specific property. Contrast with **floating charge** (qv).

fixtures — moveable articles so added, connected or attached to heritable property that they cannot be removed without damage and so become part of it (eg baths and kitchen sinks). Contrast with **fittings** (qv).

flagranti delicto or flagranti crimine — in the act of committing a wrong or crime. Thus a criminal may be caught in *flagranti delicto.*

floating charge — a security for a debt or other obligation created by an incorporated company in favour of a creditor over all or part of its property, but enabling the company to continue to use the property until the charge becomes fixed. Contrast with **fixed security** (qv).

floating sheriff — a **sheriff** (qv) appointed to sit anywhere in Scotland, as judicial business demands, rather than being based within one particular sheriffdom.

flotation — the offering of shares in a company to the public on the stock market.

fob — free on board; type of maritime contract where the buyer has to arrange for the carriage and insurance of the goods.

forbidden degrees — marriage is prohibited by law where one of the parties is within certain degrees of relationship to the other party (called the forbidden degrees) which are defined by statute (currently the Marriage (Scotland) Act 1977.

force and fear — coercion or duress such as may render an obligation void or voidable.

force majeure — something beyond the control of the parties to a contract, preventing its performance.

foreclosure — a remedy by which the ownership of security subjects is forfeited to the holder of the security by a debtor in default of payment.

forehand rent — rent agreed to be paid in advance, ie before the period of the lease to which it relates, as distinct from **backhand rent** (qv).

foreman — the spokesman for a jury.

forensic — of or used in courts of law, eg forensic medicine or forensic science.

foreseeability — the ability to see or know in advance; hence, the reasonable anticipation that harm or injury is a likely result of acts or omissions.

foreshore — land lying between high and low watermarks of ordinary spring tides.

forfeiture —
(1) in private law, depriving a person of his property as a result of his infringement of a term or condition on which the property is held. The condition may be imposed by an enactment or rule of law or legal instrument such as a will (providing eg for forfeiture of a legacy or of legal rights of succession) or contract (eg conventional irritancy of a lease) provided it does not contravene the rules against penalty clauses. *See* **irritancy**; cf **penalty**. Most forms of feudal forfeiture are abolished;
(2) in criminal proceedings where the accused is convicted, the court may order forfeiture of property which he possessed when apprehended if it was used for the purpose of committing or facilitating a criminal offence;
(3) in modern law **confiscation** (qv) of the *proceeds* of crime must be distinguished from forfeiture of the *means* of committing it.

forgery — the making or alteration of a document so that it falsely appears to be genuine, that is, authenticated by a particular person. The uttering of a forged document is a criminal offence. Forgery by itself is not a crime until the document is uttered, that is,
(1) tendered to a person with the intention to deceive him into thinking that the document is genuine all towards the prejudice of that person or another person; or
(2) put out of the utterer's control.

forisfamiliation — the emancipation of a minor from his family, by attaining majority, by marriage or by setting up an independent household.

formation — the term used in its Rules of Procedure for the composition in which the European Court of Justice sits. **[E]**

forthcoming. *See* **furthcoming**.

fortiori. *See* **a fortiori**.

forum — a court or tribunal appropriate for the exercise of jurisdiction for a particular purpose.

forum non conveniens — a court or tribunal which is not appropriate, even though it may have jurisdiction.

forum-shopping — the practice of commencing proceedings in an inappropriate court usually in order to gain an unfair advantage over the other parties to the proceedings. A non-technical term but one used in modern discourse about private international law issues.

foundation writ — in respect of **Sasine** (qv) titles the ex facie valid title last recorded immediately prior to the commencement of the prescriptive period.

foundations of the Community — originally, the rules of the EEC Treaty governing the free movement of goods, persons, services and capital and the specific rules on agricultural and transport policies. The term was excised from the Treaty in 1993 by the Treaty on European Union, and these matters now fall within general Community policies. The draft **Constitution of the European Union** (qv) proposes they be re-elevated to the status of 'fundamental freedoms'. **[E]**

founding member of the European Communities — one of the six states signatory to the **founding treaties** (qv) establishing the European Communities, as distinct from those which acceded subsequently. See **member states**. **[E]**

founding treaties — the three treaties which founded the European Communities, namely the Treaty establishing the European Coal and Steel Community ('the Treaty of Paris', 1951), the Treaty establishing the European Economic Community and the Treaty establishing the European Atomic Energy Community ('the Treaties of Rome', 1957). **[E]**

four freedoms, the — the four freedoms fundamental to the internal market established by the European Community: the freedom of movement for goods, persons, services and capital. **[E]**

framework decision — under the Treaty on European Union, a measure adopted by the Council of the European Union for the approximation of national laws in the context of police and judicial cooperation in criminal matters. **[E]**

fraud —
(1) in the civil law, something said, done or omitted by one person with the intention of deceiving another to his detriment;
(2) in criminal practice, the crime of false pretences which achieve some practical consequence.

fraudulent preference. See **unfair preference**.

free circulation — the movement of goods within the European Community which is not restricted by customs formalities, tariffs and non-tariff trade barriers. Because the Community is a customs union, it is a regime which applies to all goods, be they domestically produced or imported from a third country provided in the latter case import formalities have been completed and any customs duties and other charges, such as **charges having equivalent effect** (qv), have been levied without there being any total or partial **drawback** (qv). **[E]**

free movement of capital — one of the four freedoms of the internal market in EC law; the complete abolition of restrictions on the movement of capital amongst the member states and between member states and third countries. **[E]**

free movement of persons — one of the four freedoms of the internal market in EC law. Persons fall within one of three categories: workers (natural persons only); natural or juristic persons seeking to establish themselves in another member state; and natural or juristic persons providing or receiving a service in another member state. **[E]**

free movement of services — another of the four freedoms, a fundamental right of natural or juristic persons to travel to another member state unhindered in order to provide or receive any economic consideration, or to provide such consideration to a person situated or established in another member state; becoming more important with the growth of services crossing frontiers, for example, telecommunications and e-commerce. **[E]**

free trade agreement — an agreement between or among states to establish a **free trade area** (qv).

free trade area — the **customs territories** (qv) of two or more states which have granted each other reciprocal trade advantages involving the removal of customs duties and other barriers to trade upon goods produced within the area, each state remaining free to impose autonomous customs duties and other trade restrictions upon goods originating outside the free trade area. **[E]**

free zone — any territorial enclave established by the member states of the European Community in order that goods in it may be considered as being outside the Community **customs territory** (qv). **[E]**

freeing for adoption — a special statutory procedure which enables the court to declare a child to be free for adoption which has the effect of vesting all parental responsibilities and rights in an adoption agency who may thereafter arrange for the child's adoption without either seeking the parents' consent or notifying them of the identity of the adopters.

freight — the charge made by the carrier to the shipper for transporting goods by sea.

frontbench — those members of Parliament (or **MSP**'s (qv)) who are ministers or shadow ministers; derived from the position of the seats where these members sit in parliament.

fructus — fruits; produce grown on land.

fructus civiles — revenue; rents; interests; the produce of capital.

fructus industriales — agricultural produce raised by yearly sowing or planting.

fructus naturales — vegetation which grows naturally without cultivation.

fructus pecudum — produce of a flock (eg wool).

fructus pendentes — hanging or unpicked fruit. Cf *perceptio*.

fructus percepti; *fructus separati* — produce which has been picked or gathered. See *perceptio*.

fructus rei alienae — fruit or produce from another person's property.

fructus separati. See *fructus percepti*.

frustration of contract — the occurrence of an event or events after the formation of a contract, which have the effect of making the contract impossible to perform, or render it illegal, or radically different from its original nature, so that the law treats future performance by either party to the contract as discharged.

FTSE — the Financial Times (FT) and the (London) Stock Exchange, a **share** (qv) index of the 900 largest companies on the London Stock Exchange. The FTSE 100 is an index of the 100 largest companies, by market capitalisation, on the London Stock Exchange.

fugitive offender — a person accused of a crime or offence in one part of the Commonwealth, apprehended in another part and sent back to stand trial.

Full Bench — the High Court of Justiciary sitting with a greater number of judges (eg five, seven or nine) than the normal quorum of three for the hearing of appeals.

functus officio — having discharged one's official duty: the status of a judge or arbiter when he has decided the question brought before him. He may not review his own decision.

fund *in medio*. See **multiplepoinding**.

fungibles — moveables intended for consumption rather than use, and generally estimated by weight, number, volume or measure (eg foodstuffs).

furiosi nulla voluntas est — an insane person has no will.

furth of — out of, beyond the borders or limits of.

furthcoming *or* **forthcoming** — an action raised for the recovery of money or property arrested in the hands of a third person. *See* **arrestment**.

furtum — theft.

future debt — a debt in which payment is to be made in the future or on the occurrence of an event which must occur; the debt is *debitum in presenti solvendum in futuro* that is to say due at present payable in the future. In older usage a future debt was called a 'debt to a day' or *in diem* or *ex die*. Contrast **contingent debt**.

futures — contracts for the future delivery of goods or shares, especially basic commodities such as oil or grain.

g

gable. *See* **mutual gable**.

game — wild animals or birds pursued and killed for sport or food. Different Game Acts regulating the rights of landowners and others to kill and take game define 'game' as including different species of creatures.

gaming — playing games of chance or chance and skill combined for winnings in money or money's worth, formerly illegal but now controlled by statute, and often requiring a licence. Gaming debts are not legally enforceable.

gearing — the ratio of debt to assets, especially of a registered company.

General Assembly — the highest court of the Church of Scotland, sitting annually in Edinburgh and presided over by the Moderator.

general average — rule of **maritime law** (qv) which holds that where it is necessary to dump a cargo to save the vessel and /or other cargo, all the other cargo owners with cargo on board will share the costs of the sacrifice.

general disposition — a deed intended as a conveyance but which, because it lacks a full description of the land or proper feudal clauses, does not of itself constitute sufficient warrant to the disponee to obtain infeftment directly.

General Election — election which chooses the members of the House of Commons, held at least every 5 years.

General Insurance Standards Council — an independent, non-statutory organisation, established in 2000 to supervise the insurance industry.

general legacy — a legacy identified otherwise than by reference to a specific fund or asset. The right to the legacy is enforceable only by a personal action. Compare **special legacy**.

general principles of Community law — a fluid body of law derived from the Community treaties or from sources extraneous to the treaties (in large measure the administrative law of the member states) which is recognised to regulate the manner in which Community law is to be applied; includes, for example, principles such as respect for fundamental rights, proportionality, subsidiarity, legal certainty, legitimate expectation and rules of natural justice. **[E]**

General Register House — main building in Edinburgh housing the National Archives of Scotland

General Register of Sasines — a public register, maintained since the seventeenth century, in which all deeds transferring, creating or extinguishing rights to heritable property require to be recorded in order that they might have effect. The register is being progressively superseded by the **Land Register of Scotland** (qv).

general service. *See* **service** (3).

generalised tariff preferences — the grant of tariff advantages to a range of products or to products from specified countries. *See also* **tariff preference**. **[E]**

gift — a donation; a gratuitous transfer of heritable or moveable property to another.

gilts — common term (an abbreviation for 'gilt-edged securities') for fixed rate **bonds** (qv) issued by the government, and accordingly having a very low risk investment as they are backed by the state. Although the interest rate on the underlying value and the price at maturity are guaranteed, the price will vary during the lifetime of a gilt; so there is some element of risk.

glebe — a portion of land in a landward parish, generally near to the kirk or manse, which a minister has a right to use in addition to his stipend.

good faith. *See* **bona fides**.

goods —
  (1) in Scotland, **corporeal moveables** (qv), the sale of which is governed by eg the Sale of Goods Act 1979;
  (2) in European Community law, corporeal movables falling within those provisions of the EC Treaty regulating the free movement of goods. **[E]**

Grand Chamber —
  (1) a bench of the European Court of Justice consisting of eleven judges, it being quorate with nine judges; a member state or Community institution party to proceedings before the Court may require it to sit in the Grand Chamber; **[E]**
  (2) the largest bench of the **European Court of Human Rights** (qv), consisting of 17 judges. Operates as a court of appeal for decisions by Chambers of the ECtHR. Such appeals will only be considered if they raise a serious question of interpretation or application of the Convention or a serious issue of general importance. **[E]**

grant —
  (1) a deed transferring property;
  (2) to convey or transfer property to another.

grantee — one to whom a grant is made.

granter — one who makes a grant.

grassum — a single payment in addition to or in lieu of periodic payments (such as rent or feuduty), eg key money, or a part payment of rent paid in anticipation of entry.

gratuitous — without payment or other consideration.

gratuitous alienation — a gratuitous disposition of property by the owner to another.

Great Britain — Scotland, England and Wales, but not Northern Ireland. *See also* United Kingdom.

Great Seal, the — the chief **seal** (qv) of the **Crown** (qv), used to show the monarch's approval of important state documents, such as letters patent, royal proclamations, commissions, some writs (such as writs for the election of Members of Parliament), and the documents which give power to sign and ratify treaties. Separate seals exist for England and Wales, Scotland - and for Northern Ireland. Different colours of wax seal are used for different classes of document: dark green seals for **letters patent** (qv) which elevate individuals to the **peerage** (qv); blue seals for documents relating to the close members of the Royal Family; and scarlet red for most other patents.

Great Seal of Scotland, the — name used for the seal which, strictly, should be referred to as 'the seal appointed to be used in place of the Great Seal of Scotland' this seal is now also known by statutory authority as, the **Scottish Seal** (qv). The matrix (mould) of the Great Seal is in two parts, made of silver, and bears a portrait of the sovereign on one side and of the royal arms on the other.

green currency — theoretical values, exchangeable not at market rates but at 'green' or representative rates, for the currencies of the member states of the European Community which are used in the administration of the **common agricultural policy** (qv), now replaced in states which use the **Euro** (qv) by that currency. **[E]**

ground annual — a non-feudal yearly duty chargeable on heritable property, the creation of which has been prohibited since 1974.

GSP — generalised system of preferences. **[E]**

guarantee —
  (1) a cautionary obligation (see **caution**);
  (2) the responsibility of one person for actions of, or the truth of statements made by, another;
  (3) a warranty by a manufacturer or retailer etc as to the quality etc of a product or service;
  (4) to give such a warranty.

guaranteed income bond — a single premium insurance contract providing payments at regular intervals for a fixed period at the end of which the premium is returned.

guardian —
  (1) in relation to a child, guardian incudes:
      (a) a parent exercising parental responsibilities and rights under Part I of the Children (Scotland) Act 1995;
      (b) a person entitled to act as the child's legal representative under the 1995 Act, Pt I: see Age of Legal Capacity (Scotland) Act 1991, s 5(1);
      (c) a person appointed as guardian by a parent or guardian under the Children (Scotland) Act 1995, s 7.

    (2) in relation to the personal wefare, property or financial affairs of an adult suffering from mental disability,

        (a) a guardian is a person appointed as guardian by a guardianship order under the Adults with Incapacity (Scotland) Act 2000, Part 6;

        (b) in relation to such an adult , specified acts or decisions of a guardianship character may be done or made on the adult's behalf by a person authorised to act by an intervention order under the Act of 2000, Part 6.

See also **tutor**; **curator**; **parental responsibilities**; **intervention order**; **safeguarder**.

guide price — the price used in some common organisations of agricultural markets in the European Community as the target price and a trigger for **intervention** (qv) or the imposition of import controls. **[E]**

h

habile — admissible; valid; competent for a legal purpose.

habili modo — in the manner competent. Thus a proof *habili modo* is a proof competent in or appropriate to the circumstances.

habilis causa transferendi dominii — a **habile** or sufficient title for transferring ownership.

habit and repute —

    (1) a form of irregular marriage evidenced by lengthy cohabitation with the reputation of being married;

    (2) in the context of the crime of theft, it formerly implied the reputation of being a thief, and was an aggravation of the crime (now obsolete).

haereditas jacens — idle succession; successsion to the estate of a deceased person which the executor or heir has not yet entered upon or taken up and which, as it still lies in the right of the deceased, is liable to be attached by diligence of creditors for his debts.

Hague Rules — the International Convention for the Unification of Certain Rules of Law relating to Bills of Lading 1924.

Hague-Visby Rules — international convention (1968/1979) governing the carriage of cargo by sea under a bill of lading which amended the **Hague Rules** (qv).

Hamburg Rules — colloquial name for the United Nations Convention of the Carriage of Goods by Sea 1978.

hamesucken — the crime of committing an assault upon a person in his own dwelling-house after breaking into the house for that purpose. It is an aggravated assault, and was formerly a capital offence.

harmonisation of laws — also approximation of laws; the adjustment of the legislative or administrative provisions of the member states of the European Community in a given sector or part thereof so that they are in accord with one another in order that **technical barriers to trade** (qv) are dismantled; invariably by the device of **directives** (qv) adopted by the **Community institutions** (qv). **[E]**

haver (pronounced 'havver') — a person who possesses a document required as evidence in court proceedings.

Health Service Commissioner for Scotland — the health service ombudsman in Scotland.

hearing — a sitting of a court or tribunal at which the parties or their representatives make representations or present arguments which are heard by the judge or members of the tribunal. The term does not generally include a jury trial or a formal proof of disputed facts at which the strict rules of evidence are applied. The term **children's hearing** (qv) has reference to the tribunal itself as well the sitting of the tribunal.

hearsay — evidence by a witness of what he has been told but has not himself seen or heard. It is generally incompetent, since statements made in court by a witness not based on his own knowledge, are not normally admissible. It may, however. be used eg as an explanation or proof of a person's state of mind or in the context of *res gestae* (qv), and under the Civil Evidence (Scotland) Act 1988 and the Criminal Procedure (Scotland) Act 1995, hearsay evidence may be admitted in civil and criminal proceedings respectively in appropriate circumstances.

hedging — method of offsetting investment risk by using **futures** (qv) or **options** (qv).

heir — a person who succeeds to the property of a deceased person.

heir-apparent — one bound to succeed if he or she survives the deceased. CF **apparent heir**.

heir-at-law; heir of line — until 1964 a person entitled to succeed to a deceased's heritable property under the rules of primogeniture, eg the eldest lawful son.

heir-female — the nearest heir of either sex who is related to the deceased only through a female.

heir-*in-mobilibus* — the next of kin or representative entitled to a deceased's moveable property on an intestacy.

heir-male — the nearest male relative who is related to the deceased only through a male.

heir-male of the body — the heir-male in direct line of descent.

heir of entail — a person entitled to succeed to entailed land. The title 'heir of entail' is retained after succession.

heir of line. *See* **heir-at-law**.

heir of provision; heir of tailzie — a person who succeeds by express provisions in eg a settlement.

heir of tailzie. *See* **heir of provision**.

heir of the body — a descendant who is alive at the death of the deceased.

heir-presumptive — the nearest heir at the moment, whose right may be defeated by the birth of a nearer heir.

heirs-portioner — formerly, when there was no male heir to heritage, the females in the same degree of relationship who succeeded in equal portions *pro indiviso*.

heritable property. *See* **heritage**.

heritable security — a voluntary security created over heritable property to secure payment of a debt. The only form currently competent is a standard security.

heritage; heritable property — strictly, property passing to the heir-at-law of a deceased person. The Succession (Scotland) Act 1964 substantially assimilated rights of succession to heritable and moveable property. For historical reasons Scots law generally distinguished between heritable and moveable property, heritage being, in theory at any rate, concerned with the succession to land and its accessories. 'Heritage' and 'heritable property' continue to be used as synonyms for land or immoveable property and its pertinents generally.

heritor — a landowner, especially one formerly liable to contribute to the upkeep of a parish church.

Her Majesty's Advocate. *See* **HMA; Lord Advocate**.

Her Majesty's Inspectorate of Constabulary for Scotland — organisation, independent of all local police forces and authorities which monitor and improve the police services.

Herren der Vertrag — lit. masters (or lords) of the Treaty; the authorities competent to cause amendment or alteration to fundamental treaty texts in European Community and European Union law; essentially the member states acting in concert to that end; *see* **intergovernmental conference**. **[E]**

High Authority — an institution of the European Coal and Steel Community entrusted with ensuring that the objectives of the ECSC Treaty were attained. Its powers and functions were assumed by the single Commission created for all three European Communities in 1967. **[E]**

High Court — the name proposed by the draft **Constitution of the European Union** (qv) for the **Court of First Instance** (qv); in French the *Tribunal de grande instance*. **[E]**

High Court of Justiciary — the superior criminal court in Scotland, comprising the judges of the Court of Session in their capacity as Lords Commissioners of Justiciary, presided over by the Lord Justice-General. The court has original and appellate jurisdiction. At **first instance** (qv) the High Court tries only serious crimes such as murder, culpable homicide, armed robbery, drug trafficking and sexual offences involving children. Cases are tried by a judge and a jury of fifteen men and women. Appeals are heard from the High Court, the Sheriff Court and the District Court by a court of at least three judges. No appeal lies from it to the House of Lords but certain devolution cases under the Scotland Act 1998 may be referred to the **Judicial Committee of the Privy Council** (qv). The court is often referred to simply as 'the High Court' but should not be confused with the English High Court of Justice.

High Representative CFSP — the secretary-general of the Council of European Union, who 'assists' the presidency of the Council in **common foreign and security policy** (qv) matters; increasingly the public face of the European Union on the international stage. **[E]**

High Seas, the — maritime areas beyond the territorial waters or internal waters of any national jurisdiction and open and free for all to use.

Higher Court —
(1) generally, any court exercising an appellate capacity;
(2) for the purposes of **Human Rights Act** (qv) s 4: the **House of Lords** (qv), the **Judicial Committee of the Privy Council** (qv), the Courts-Martial Appeal Court, the High Court of Justiciary sitting otherwise than as a trial **court** (qv), the **Court of Session** (qv) and (in England and Wales or Northern Ireland) the High Court and the Court of Appeal.

highway — a term of art in English law at one time used in Scotland to denote either the heritable property forming a road used by the public or the incorporeal right of passage of the public over a road. The term has been replaced in the Scottish legislation on roads by the term 'road' : Roads (Scotland) Act 1984. *See* **private road; public road.**

hinc inde — on this side; on that side: a term of art meaning 'on either side' or 'on this side and the other'. Thus the claims of parties *hinc inde* are their respective claims against each other.

hire —
(1) a contract (also called 'location' after the Roman contract of *locatio conduction* qv) by which a money prestation is given in exchange for the fruits or use of things or the work of an independent contractor;
(2) the money consideration in such a contract. *See* **lease.**

hire purchase agreement — an agreement whereby goods are hired in return for periodical payments, the ownership of the goods passing to the hirer when specified conditions have been fulfilled.

HMA — Her (His) Majesty's Advocate. All prosecutions on **indictment** (qv) run in the name of 'Her Majesty's Advocate'. By convention, case reports of such decisions are always described as being at the instance of 'Her Majesty's Advocate'. In a civil case where the Lord Advocate is a party, on behalf of the **Crown** (qv), he is always described as 'The Lord Advocate'. Thus one can instantly distinguish criminal from civil cases.

HMCIP — Her (His) Majesty's Chief Inspector of Prisons.

HMIC. *See* **Her Majesty's Inspectorate of Constabulary for Scotland.**

HMP — Her (His) Majesty's Prison.

HMPIS — Her (His) Majesty's Prisons Inspectorate for Scotland.

holder — a person in possession of a **bill of exchange** (qv) or **promissory note** (qv). The person may be a payee, indorsee or bearer. A holder may sue on a bill in his or her own name.

holding —
(1) land held under a lease for commercial agricultural purposes;
(2) feudal tenure (*see* eg **base holding; blench; feu**).

holding out — words or actions whereby a person causes or allows the belief that he has a particular status or authority such as that of an agent or partner. He may thereby be prevented by **personal bar** (qv) from denying that he has that status or authority and so attract to himself personal liability.

holograph — a document in which the essential words were written in the handwriting of the signatory or grantor, this (because of the difficulty of forging it) making it effective without witnesses to the signature. It was possible for a typed deed to be 'adopted as holograph' if these words were written by the signatory in his own hand, but some deeds had to have witnesses. Abolished in respect of documents executed on or after 1 August 1995: see the Requirements of Writing (Scotland) Act 1995, ss 1, 11(3).

Holyrood —

(1) a royal palace in Edinburgh which is the official Scottish residence of the sovereign; originally an abbey and so called because the 'holy rood', ie fragment of the cross upon which Christ was crucified was housed in the abbey;

(2) a colloquial name for the **Scottish Parliament** (qv) derived from the fact that the permanent seat of that parliament will be adjacent to the royal palace of that name.

homeless person — person having no living accommodation which he is entitled to occupy. Some categories of homeless person (eg elderly; infirm; those with dependent children) have a statutory right to be provided with accommodation by the local authority.

homicide — an act which, either directly or indirectly, or by natural consequence, takes away a person's life. *See* **casual homicide**; **culpable homicide**; **justifiable homicide**; **murder.**

homologation — an act approving, confirming, adopting or ratifying a deed or contract which in itself is otherwise defective. This rule was abolished in respect of documents executed on or after 1 August 1995: see the Requirements of Writing (Scotland) Act 1995, s 1.

honorarium — a form of financial gift as an acknowledgment for services. Counsel's fees have been so regarded as counsel may not sue for remuneration for their services.

horizontal agreement — an **agreement** (qv) giving effect to a horizontal arrangement.

horizontal arrangement — an arrangement between **undertakings** (qv) operating at the same economic level (eg production). Cf **vertical arrangement.**

horizontal direct effect. *See* **direct effect. [E]**

horizontal effect — the secondary effect of public law legislation in regulating private law rights. Where an enactment (such as the Human Rights Act 1998) or other legal instrument (such as a Bill of Rights) is construed as in the first place regulating the 'vertical relationship' between the state and its citizens (a matter of public law), it may nevertheless also be construed as in some circumstances regulating the 'horizontal' relationships under private law betweeen citizens among themselves. *See also* **direct horizontal effect.**

horning. *See* **letters of horning.**

House of Commons — one of the two chambers of the United Kingdom Parliament. It consists of democratically elected Members of Parliament. The other chamber is the **House of Lords** (qv). *See also* **Queen-in-Parliament.**

House of Lords — Upper house of the United Kingdom parliament. originally composed of hereditary peers, now largely replaced by Life Peers.

housebreaking — breaking into a building (whether a house or not): an aggravation of the crime of theft. It is not itself criminal unless undertaken for theft or with that intent.

huissier — an official in France and some other civil law countries (similar to a messenger-at-arms or sheriff officer in Scotland) whose functions consist of or include the service of official documents and generally the execution the acts, decrees, warrants and orders of courts.

human rights — fundamental rights, to which all human beings are entitled by reason of their humanity. Most of these are described in the United Nations Universal Declaration of Human Rights (1948) which is not binding in international law. Certain regional conventions on human rights are binding in international law such as the **European Convention on Human Rights** (qv); and domestic law: *see* **Human Rights Act 1998.**

Human Rights Act 1998 — Act which made the provisions of the **European Convention on Human Rights** (qv) justiciable within the domestic courts. All primary and subordinate legislation must be interpreted, as far as possible, in a way which is compatible with the Convention Rights and it is unlawful for a **public authority** (qv) to act in a way which is incompatible with the **Convention rights** (qv).

humani nihil a me alienum puto — I count nothing human unimportant to me: Terence. The motto of the Law Society of Scotland is '*Humani nihil alienum*'.

hypothec — a nonpossessory security; a right in security over the property of a debtor, although (unlike pledge or lien) the creditor does not have possession of the subjects, which remains with the debtor. Thus a landlord has a hypothec for rent over *invecta et illata* (qv). Solicitors have a hypothec, in security of their expenses and outlays incurred on behalf of their client in civil proceedings, over the expenses of the proceedings payable to their client by the adverse party. A maritime lien is a type of hypothec which secures various types of maritime debt such as salvage. *See* **tacit**.

i

ICJ. *See* **International Court of Justice**.

id est — that is (abbreviated 'ie')

IGC. *See* **intergovernmental conference**. [E]

ignorantia juris neminem excusat — ignorance of the law excuses no-one.

IH. *See* **Inner House**.

illegality — a juridical act such as a contract, unilateral promise, conveyance or declaration of trust is illegal if in its constitution, purpose or performance it involves either the commission of a wrong (other than a breach of an obligation created by the juridical act) or conduct which, though not wrongful, is contrary to public policy. *See also* *pactum illicitum*. Views differ on whether an illegal juridical act is wholly void, or valid but unenforceable.

illegitimacy — the status of a child born of a woman who was not married to the father at the time of conception and was never thereafter married to him. Such a child is known as an illegitimate child (the former term 'bastard' is no longer accepted legal usage). Many former disadvantages of illegitimacy were abolished by the Law Reform (Parent and Child) (Scotland) Act 1986 under which the fact that a person's parents are not married to one another is left out of account in establishing the legal relationship between the person and any other person. So any such relationship has effect as if the parents had been married. Illegitimacy however is not entirely abolished and remains relevant for certain purposes including denial of automatic parental rights to some unmarried fathers; the parent's right to appoint a guardian; the child's domicile; and the transmission of titles, coats of arms, honours and dignities.

illiquid — of an amount not yet fixed or ascertained.

immoveable property — land, buildings on land, and land covered by water such as the bed of the sea and of tidal and non-tidal waters. The technical term of art is '**heritable**' (qv).

immunity — an exemption enjoyed by a person (individual or corporate) from the normal operation of the criminal or civil law, eg a legal duty or liability.

impeachment —
(1) a formal allegation by a person accused of crime that another named person is guilty of it; otherwise known as incrimination, it constitutes a **special defence** (qv);
(2) formerly, a prosecution of an offender by the House of Commons, tried before the House of Lords.

imperitia enumeratur culpae — lack of skill is reckoned as a fault. Thus an employer is entitled to rely on an employee as having the ordinary skills of his trade.

impetrate — to obtain by request, especially by fraud or otherwise improperly.

impignorate — to pawn, pledge or mortgage.

implement — to take further action in order to give full effect to a rule of law; often used in European Community law to refer to the process by which Community measures are given effect in the domestic law of the member states. **[E]**

implied — not stated or expressed. Used eg of a trust, an authority, a contract or a term of a contract which, in the particular circumstances, is deemed to exist notwithstanding an absence of express provision.

impotentia excusat legem — inability excuses failure to observe the law. The inability must be absolute and must not arise from the act or omission of the person making the plea.

imprescriptible — a right relating to property or an obligation is imprescriptible if it cannot be extinguished by the operation of the doctrine of the negative prescription by virtue of the Prescription and Limitation (Scotland) Act 1973, ss 7 and 8, Sch 1, para 2(h) and Sch 3 (which contains a list of imprescriptible rights and obligations).

improbation — an action to reduce a deed on the ground that it is forged.

improbative — not **probative** (qv).

improvement area — a declining industrial or commercial area so designated so as to allow the local authority to take measures to secure stable employment there.

improvement notice — a notice served by a health and safety inspector requiring that contraventions of health and safety provisions be remedied. Cf **prohibition notice**.

improvements —
  (1) in the law of leases, meliorations to leased subjects which go beyond mere repairs, which are not removeable from the subjects, and for which a tenant may be entitled to compensation from the landlord;
  (2) in the law of unjustified enrichment, a *bona fide* (qv) possessor of another's property is entitled to claim **recompense** (qv) not only for necessary repairs to that property but also for improvements to the extent that the owner is thereby enriched, provided that they are useful and profitable and not fanciful or luxurious.

in absentia — in absence; undefended. Describes proceedings or a decree where no appearance or defence has been or was entered. Cf *in foro*.

in aemulationem vicini — to the injury or annoyance of a neighbour.

in arbitrio judicis — in the judge's discretion.

in articulo mortis — at the point of death.

in camera — in chambers; describes proceedings heard in the judge's room (and thus in private) as distinct from those heard in open court.

in causa — in the cause or the process.

in diem — as of a debt which is due but not yet prestable.

in dubio — in doubt; in a doubtful case or uncertain circumstances.

in eodem negotio — in the same business; arising out of the same matter or transaction.

in essentialibus — in the essential parts. An error in the essential parts of a deed or contract may render it liable to reduction.

in extenso — in full, at length.

in facie ecclesiae — according to the rules of the church, as of a regular marriage solemnised in church.

in favorem — in favour of.

in flagrante delicto — in the act of committing a crime.

in forma pauperis — as a pauper. Before legal aid became available an indigent person might sue or defend *in forma pauperis* and be excused from paying agent's or counsel's fees and court expenses.

in forma specifica — in the form specified. Thus an equivalent will not suffice.

in foro — in court (a shortened form of *in foro contradictorio* or *in foro contentioso*: in a contested action); describes proceedings or a decree where defences have been lodged. Contrast with *in absentia*.

in fraudem — with fraudulent intention.

in gremio — in the body of, eg any clause or words contained in a deed or document.

in hoc statu — in this position or situation, a phrase which makes it clear that the matter concerned is being considered only in the light of the facts as known at the time, and without prejudice to review if further facts are subsequently disclosed.

in hunc effectum — for this purpose only. *See* **ad hunc effectum**.

in integrum — entirely; to the fullest extent. Thus *restitutio in integrum* is restitution in full to the former state or condition.

in limine — on the threshold; describes a proposition stated at the outset eg of a legal argument or litigation.

in loco parentis — in place of the parent.

in medio — in the middle, eg, in the context of **multiplepoinding** (qv), the fund *in medio*.

in modum probationis — in the form of or by way of proof.

in obligatione — by way of obligation.

in pari casu — in a similar position.

in pari causa potior est conditio possidentis — in an equal case, the possessor is in the better position. Thus any challenger must show a better title than the possessor has.

in pari delicto potior est conditio possidentis — in equal wrongdoing, the possessor or defender is in the better position. Thus a party to an illegal transaction may be unable to enforce a claim for the payment of money or delivery of goods otherwise due under that transaction.

in patiendo — in enduring or permitting. In the law relating to servitudes the servient proprietor is merely obliged to permit the dominant proprietor to exercise his rights, but need not help him as eg in maintaining a path or water pipe.

in personam — against a person; describes a right enforceable against a specific person, as distinct from a right *in rem* (qv) which is enforceable in respect of a thing (*res*) ie specific property. The obligation correlative to this personal right is owed by the specific person and so attaches to him rather than to specific property. *See also* **jus ad rem**; **jus in personam**, **personal right**.

in point — a precedent is in point if it is applicable or relevant to the instant case under consideration.

in praesentia Dominorum — in the presence of the Lords. The initials 'I P D' follow the signature of the presiding judge to an **interlocutor** (qv) or an **Act of Sederunt** (qv) of the **Court of Session** (qv), indicating the presence of the other judges when he signs.

in quantum lucratus est — in so far as he has gained or profited: the measure of payment owed by the defender in a claim in recompense, where there is no claim under contract or implied contract.

in re communi melior est conditio prohibentis — in regard to property held in common, the position of the party prohibiting is the stronger.

in re mercatoria — in a mercantile transaction. Prior to 1 August 1995 writings in mercantile transactions could be valid although lacking the solemnities of ordinary deeds; but see now the Requirements of Writing (Scotland) Act 1995, s 11(3).

in re propria — in one's own affairs.

in rem — regarding a thing; describes a right not against a specific person (*in personam*) but against the whole world in respect of some specific property or some title or status. *See also* **jus in re**; **jus in re aliena**; **real right**; **subordinate real right**.

in rem suam — regarding one's own property; to one's own advantage.

in retentis — among things kept back: describes evidence allowed to be taken and then laid aside until required, because it is in danger of being lost, eg where the witness is in extreme old age or is gravely ill or is about to leave the country.

in rixa — in the course of a quarrel. Words so spoken may not be actionable.

in situ — in its place.

in solidum — for the whole. Several co-obligations bound *in solidum* are each liable to the creditor for full payment or performance, and the creditor may choose which to sue.

in terrorem — as a warning or deterrent.

in toto — wholly; entirely.

in transitu — in transit. The Sale of Goods Act 1979 uses the English words, whereas the Sale of Goods Act 1893 used the Latin. In certain circumstances a creditor has a right to stop goods in transit.

in turpi causa potior est conditio possidentis — in a dispute involving an immoral purpose, the position of the possessor or defender is considered stronger.

in utero — in the womb; unborn. For certain purposes, if it is to the child's advantage, a child as yet unborn is deemed to have been born.

inaedificatum solo cedit solo — anything built on the ground accedes to the ground; more accurately, and subject to many exceptions, it belongs to the owner of the ground.

inalienable — a right which may not be alienated (ie renounced or assigned) or expropriated.

incapax —
(1) (adj) not capable; having legal, mental or physical incapacity;
(2) (n) a person who is *incapax*.

incest — crime of sexual intercourse between persons within specified relationships: see the Criminal Law (Consolidation) (Scotland) Act 1995, ss 1–4.

inchoate — undeveloped or incomplete and therefore in some cases legally ineffectual. Some rights or diligences however – eg an arrestment not followed by decree of furthcoming; or an attachment not followed by sale – are inchoate and yet effectual to create a preference for the arresting or attaching creditor.

incidental application — an application made to the court in the course of proceedings for an order relating to a matter other than the principal subject matter of the proceedings - such as an order granting **commission** (qv) and diligence for recovery of documents or for recall of **arrestment on the dependence** (qv).

incompetent —
(1) describes an action or any procedure which the court does not have power to entertain;
(2) a preliminary plea to the foregoing effect;
(3) describes a witness whose evidence, or evidence which, is not admissible.

incorporation — the formation of individuals or other legal entities into a separate legal entity, distinct in law from its constituent members, eg a public limited company or a local authority.

incorporeal — describes property or rights which are not tangible and which have no physical existence, eg an annuity, copyright, patent or stocks and shares.

incrimination. *See* **impeachment** (1).

incumbrance. *See* **encumbrance**.

indebiti solutio — the payment of something not due. Money paid under the erroneous belief that there is liability to pay it may be recoverable. *See* **condictio indebiti**.

indefeasible — a right or title in property that cannot be made void, defeated or cancelled by reason of any past event, error or omission in the title. For example, a certificate of title issued under a **Torrens** (qv) land titles system is said to be 'indefeasible' because the government warrants that no interest burdens the title other than those on the certificate.

indefinite payment — a payment made to a creditor by a debtor, who owes two or more debts to that creditor, without the debtor specifying to which debt he intends the payment to be ascribed. The rules of **ascription** (qv) of indefinite payments tend to favour the creditor.

indemnity — an undertaking given by one person to protect another from damage or loss that might otherwise have to be suffered.

indenture — a deed made by several parties, now mainly concerned with instruction and apprenticeship. It was so called because the edges of the several copies were cut in a distinct pattern so that each copy corresponded with the others.

independent contractor — a person engaged by another to perform work or services but not as an employee.

indicia — marks, signs.

indictment — a written accusation of serious crime in the name of the Lord Advocate.

Procedure on indictment is called 'solemn procedure', and, whether trial is in the High Court or the sheriff court, the judge sits with a jury of fifteen, whose decision to convict may be reached by a simple majority.

indirect racial discrimination — when members of a racial group are less likely to be able to comply with a requirement or condition, and the requirement cannot be justified on non-racial grounds.

indirect taxation — taxes imposed on or borne by a product.

indistinctly applicable — describing national regulatory rules which apply equally to domestic and imported goods or services. **[E]**

individual concern — describing the quality of a measure adopted by a Community institution which affects a person by reason of certain attributes which are peculiar to him and so differentiates him from persons generally; a natural or juristic person (other than the addressee) must show individual concern in order competently to raise an action of **annulment** (qv) against the measure. **[E]**

indorse *or* **endorse** — to write on the back of a document, eg a cheque or bill of exchange.

induciae — literally a pause; a truce; days of grace allowed in legal proceedings for a person to perform some act, eg for a defender in a civil action to 'enter appearance' or for a debtor to pay before diligence can proceed on a decree.

inducing breach of contract — the delict of intentionally persuading a party to break a contractual obligation owed by him to a third party.

industrial — produced by a person's labour, eg cultivated crops as distinct from crops growing wild.

industrial or commercial property rights — **intellectual property rights** (qv).

industrial tribunal. *See* **employment tribunal**.

inevitably incompatible subordinate legislation — subordinate legislation which is declared incompatible with a **Convention Right** (qv) but where primary legislation prevents the removal of the incompatibility.

infant; *infans* — not strictly a term of art in Scots law, but at one time used in the Roman law sense to indicate a child who has not reached its eighth birthday. Confusion resulted from the application to Scotland of United Kingdom legislation using the term 'infant' in the English sense as comprehending those under the age of majority (now 18 formerly 21). *See also* **minor**.

infanticide — the murder of a baby soon after its birth.

infeftment — investment of title to heritage in a new owner, formerly by symbolically giving him sasine or possession by delivery of earth and stone, now by recording the deed in the **General Register of Sasines** (qv) or registering the title in the **Land Register of Scotland** (qv).

infer — to deduce a fact by reasoning from the existence of one or more other facts.

ingather — to get in money or other property due to eg executors or trustees.

inherent vice — a fault in goods or property that leads to its self-destruction, generally insurance contracts exclude damage arising from such defects.

inheritance tax — a tax payable under the Inheritance Tax Act 1984 on the value of a person's estate on death and on certain gifts made by the person within seven years before death and some other lifetime gifts.

inhibition — an order by the Court of Session, contained in warrants or letters of inhibition, forbidding a debtor to burden or part with heritage to the prejudice of the inhibiting creditor, and giving the creditor (1) a right to reduce *ad hunc effectum* (qv) deeds violating the inhibition and (2) a special type of preference in a competition with the debtor's other creditors.

initial writ — the document by which an ordinary action or summary application is begun in the sheriff court, equivalent to a summons commencing an action or a petition in the Court of Session.

injuria — a legal wrong generally or, more specifically, insult.

injuria non excusat injuriam — one wrong does not excuse another. One is not entitled to take the law into one's own hands.

injuria non praesumitur — wrong is not presumed. Just as guilt of a crime is not presumed, so also a civil wrong must be proved by whoever complains of it.

Inner House — that part of the Court of Session, comprising two permanent **Divisions** (qv), which is primarily concerned with the court's appellate jurisdiction. It may be supplemented from time to time by an Extra Division. Originally the Inner House lay further away from the courthouse entrance than did the **Outer House** (qv). Since 1999 all permanent members of the Inner House have been automatically appointed **Privy Counsellors** (qv) to allow them to sit on devolution appeals before the **Judicial Committee of the Privy Council** (qv).

innominate contract — a contract without a name and so not falling into one of the established nominate categories of contract (eg sale or agency). The requirement that the existence of an innominate and unusual contract could only be proved by a party's writ or oath was abolished by the Requirements of Writing (Scotland) Act 1995.

innuendo — in the law of defamation, an averment that a passage, which *prima facie* is not defamatory, has in fact a particular defamatory meaning.

inquisitorial procedure — a system of civil or criminal procedure found mainly in civil law legal systems in which the judge, rather than the parties, investigates the facts of the case, interrogates witnesses and produces the evidence. Contrast '**adversary**' or '**accusatorial' procedure**.

insider dealing — the criminal offence of the buying or selling of shares whilst in the possession of unpublished price-sensitive information that would affect the value of the shares if that information was known publicly. The improper disclosure of such information or the encouragement of others to deal are also offences.

insolvency — the state of being unable to pay one's debts. *See also* **apparent insolvency**.

insolvency practitioner — in the law of bankruptcy and insolvency, a person qualified to act as a liquidator, administrator or supervisor in relation to a company or an individual: see the Insolvency Act 1986, s 388.

insolvent —
(1) unable to pay one's debts;
(2) a person who is unable to pay his debts.

instance —
(1) in civil procedure the part of a writ or summons which names and designates the parties to the action;
(2) in criminal procedure criminal meaning.

institute (n) —
(1) the person first named in a destination of property, as contrasted with a person named as entitled if the institute fails (the **substitute** (qv));
(2) a comprehensive legal text which aims to cover an entire legal system, following the style and structure of the *Institutes* of Justinian;
(3) an **institutional writing** (qv).

Institutes, the — the *Institutes, 533* was one of the four divisions of the *Corpus Juris Civilis* of Justinian, it was intended as an overview for law students setting out the principles of Roman Law.

institutional writings — legal texts, judicially recognised as authoritative sources of Scots law, which deal comprehensively with Scots civil or criminal law and in civil law generally follow the style and structure of the *Institutes* of Justinian. Examples include works of Stair, Bankton, Erskine and Bell in civil law and Hume and Alison in criminal law.

instruct —
(1) to appoint and authorise a solicitor or advocate to provide professional legal services and provide him with the necessary information on which he is to act;
(2) to supply evidence or documentary proof of a fact.

instrument — a formal legal deed or document. *See also* **statutory instrument**.

insurable interest — a financial or personal loss arising from the occurrence of an event covered by an insurance policy.

insurance — a contract which provides that in return for payment of an agreed sum (the premium) by one party (the insured) the other party (the insurer) will pay the insured a specified sum of money in the event of the occurrence of a specified event; such contracts are ***uberrimae fidei*** (qv).

insured — the party whose risks are covered by an insurance policy.

insurer — the party to the insurance contract who promises to pay losses or benefits, usually a professional insurance company.

integration clause — a provision of the EC Treaty setting out a policy priority and providing that it is to bind, or guide, the Community institutions throughout all of their activities; eg, environmental protection. **[E]**

intellectual property rights — rights such as trade marks, patents, copyright, plant breeders' rights and rights in literary or artistic property. *See* **industrial or commercial property rights**.

intention —
(1) in the interpretation of a document, its meaning is to be found in the intention of its writer or maker as gathered primarily from the words used in it together with other admissible aids to construction;
(2) in delictual liability, generally intention is not limited to the desired consequences of an intentional act. A person is generally taken to intend not only the consequences of his act which he desires to bring about but also the consequences which he knows are certain, or substantially certain, to result from that act. As the probability that the consequences will follow decreases, the act loses its character as intentional and becomes reckless or negligent. Intention differs from motive which is the purpose for which the person acts;
(3) in criminal law, intention (or intent) is a species of **mens rea** (qv) and as such is the most common mental element required for the constitution of a crime, in addition to the criminal conduct (act or omission) or **actus reus** (qv). It suggests design or purpose to do a criminal act (or omission) but connotes a mental state often narrower than desire and often more sharply focused on the criminal conduct than 'motive'. It is the antithesisof 'accident' or 'carelessness' and differs from recklessness.

inter-brand competition — competition between products which form a single product market and are sold under different brands. Cf **intra-brand competition**.

inter partes — between parties; describes proceedings at which each party is present or represented. Cf ***ex parte***.

inter se — between two or more persons or things.

inter vivos — between living persons; describes deeds or legal acts intended to take effect during the granter's lifetime. Cf ***mortis causa***.

interdict —
(1) a judicial remedy granted by a court forbidding the commencement or continuation of an act or activity or the maintenance of a thing or condition infringing or threatening the complainer's rights (in English law, an injunction);
(2) to obtain such a remedy against a person.

interest —
(1) legal concern in a matter, a necessary prerequisite to having the right to raise an action;
(2) money payable for the use of money lent or owed or for forbearance of a debt.

intergovernmental conference (IGC) — a conference of representatives of the governments of the member states of the European Union, convened by the Council for the purpose of amending any or all of the treaties upon which the Union is based. Treaty amendment may be secured only if an IGC unanimously ('by common accord') so recommends, and the agreed text is then ratified by all member states in accordance with their various constitutional procedures. **[E]**

interim — meantime; temporary.

interim Act — an Act of the General Assembly of the Church of Scotland in force only till the next General Assembly.

interim interdict — a temporary **interdict** (qv) granted by the court as a provisional and protective measure usually on an *ex parte* application for a limited period until both sides can be heard and the rights of parties determined on a permanent basis by a perpetual **interdict** (qv) or otherwise.

interim trustee — an **insolvency practitioner** (qv) appointed by the Court of Session or the sheriff to safeguard a debtor's estate and generally administer the sequestration process pending the election of the **permanent trustee** (qv).

interinstitutional agreement — an agreement amongst the European Commission, the Council and the European Parliament for the greater administrative efficiency in matters upon which they must collaborate, especially over, but not restricted to, the Community budgetary procedure. **[E]**

interlocutor — the official document embodying an order or judgment pronounced by the court in the course of a civil action. Interlocutors are signed by the presiding judge and entered on interlocutor sheets which form part of the **process** (qv).

intermeddling — unjustified interference.

internal market — the single, uniform market within the European Community, first defined in the **Single European Act** (qv) as an area without internal frontiers in which the free movement of goods, persons, services and capital is ensured in accordance with the provisions of the EC Treaty. Cf **common market**. **[E]**

internal taxation — a fiscal charge forming part of a general system of taxation which applies systematically to both domestic and imported goods on the basis of the same criteria. **[E]**

International Court of Justice — the principal international law court, created in 1946, and an organ of the United Nations. The court has two roles: (1) the settlement of legal disputes submitted to it by States in accordance with international law, and (2) to give advisory opinions on legal questions referred to it by duly authorized international organs and agencies. The court is based in The Hague (Netherlands) and is composed of 15 judges elected to nine-year terms of office by the United Nations General Assembly and Security Council sitting independently of each other. It may not include more than one judge of any nationality.

International Criminal Court — a permanent international court at The Hague for trying individuals accused of committing genocide, war crimes and crimes against humanity. The ICC will be formally established after 60 countries have ratified the Rome Statute of the International Criminal Court.

International Maritime Organisation (IMO) — UN organisation, based in London, responsible for shipping; promoting and implementing relevant international legislation, especially in the areas of safety and environmental protection.

interpretation clause — a clause in a deed setting forth the special meanings of words for the purposes of that deed.

interprétation conforme. See **uniform interpretation**. **[E]**

interpretation section — a section in an Act of Parliament setting forth the special meanings of words for the purposes of that Act.

interrogatories — written questions, judicially approved, which are put to witnesses examined under a **commission** (qv).

interruption — a step legally required to stop the running of a period of prescription or limitation.

intervention —

(1) the active participation of national public authorities, under the direction of the European **Community institutions** (qv), in the control of markets through the buying in or selling of products within the **common agricultural policy** (qv);

(2) a procedure whereby any member state or Community institution, or a natural or juristic person who can establish sufficient interest in the result, is permitted to make submissions and representations during contentious proceedings before the European Court of Justice or the Court of First Instance in support of or requesting rejection of those of one of the parties;

(3) generally, the participation of the European Commission and appropriate national authorities in the regulation of the common agricultural policy. **[E]**

intervention agency — a body set up by a member state of the European Community to buy in and sell **agricultural products** (qv) at special prices under the common agricultural policy, eg in the United Kingdom the Intervention Board for Agricultural Produce. **[E]**

intervention order — an order granted by the sheriff under the Adults with Incapacity (Scotland) Act 2000, Part 6, which directs or authorises the taking of specified action, or the making of a specified decision, relative to the personal welfare, property or financial affairs of an adult suffering from mental disability.

intervention price — the price at which the producer of an agricultural product may sell it to an intervention agency instead of to another buyer in the market. **[E]**

intestacy. *See* intestate.

intestate —
(1) a person who dies without having left a valid will;
(2) describes such a person or his estate.

intimation — in civil proceedings the giving of notice to a party of some document, application or other step in the proceedings.

intimidation — the use of threats of unlawful acts to compel a person either (1) to abstain from doing something which he is entitled to do or (2) to do something he is entitled to refrain from doing.

intra-brand competition — competition in the marketing of products which are sold under the same brand. Cf **inter-brand competition**. **[E]**

intra-Community trade — trade within the European Community; trade between member states. **[E]**

intra fines commissi — within the limits of the commission or trust. Describes an act within the express or implied authority of eg a servant or agent.

intra vires — within the power. Describes an act which is within the power or authority of the person who does it. Cf *ultra vires*.

intrant — first stage towards qualification as an **advocate** (qv); a person becomes an intrant by the process of **matriculation** (qv).

intrinsic — from an internal source, used especially of evidence of interpretation derived from the text of a deed itself. Cf **extrinsic**.

intromission — the act of handling or dealing with funds or other property of another person. Thus an executor intromits with the property of the deceased. If unauthorised, the intromission is vitious intromission.

intrusion — the delict of entering into possession of heritable property without any title in the person entering, albeit without violence.

invalidity — a plea raised in a reference for a **preliminary ruling** (qv) before the European Court of Justice seeking the Court to consider the lawfulness of a Community measure; if successful, the measure is declared invalid, which technically has a bearing only upon the case in which the national court made the reference; cf **annulment**. **[E]**

invecta et illata — things imported, brought or carried in; the moveable effects of a tenant brought onto leased premises which are subject to the landlord's **hypothec** (qv) as security for rent.

inventory —
(1) a list of the property of a deceased person sworn to and lodged in court by an executor;
(2) a list of the contents of a house etc made up at the beginning of a furnished let;
(3) any account of goods sold or exhibited for sale.

inventory of process — a list of documents in a **process** (qv) which must be lodged in duplicate in court along with them.

inventory of productions — a list of productions in a civil action, which must be lodged in **process** (qv) along with the productions.

investiture. *See* **infeftment**.

invitation to treat — a statement or conduct demonstrating a willingness to negotiate a contract. Cf **offer**.

invoice — a list of goods sold, specifying the prices and other particulars, sent or delivered by the seller to the buyer either along with the goods or separately.

inward processing — customs arrangements by which goods are admitted to the **customs territory** (qv) of the European Community without payment of customs duties so that certain processes can be carried out in relation to the goods, after which they are exported to a third country in the form of **compensating products** (qv). Cf **outward processing**. **[E]**

IOU — a document consisting of the expression 'I owe you' or 'IOU', specifying a sum of money and signed by the debtor. It need not be addressed to the creditor. It is an acknowledgment of debt implying an obligation to pay on demand. It is not a negotiable instrument and so is transferable only by assignation.

Ioannina Compromise — an agreement reached within the European Council in 1994 by which if member states present in the Council representing between 23 votes (the blocking minority threshold provided in the treaties) and 26 votes oppose the adoption of a measure, the Council will 'do all within its power' to accommodate the new threshold. Unlike the **Luxembourg Compromise** (qv), the Ioannina Compromise was codified in a Council decision, and a declaration annexed to the Treaty of Amsterdam extends it until **enlargement** (qv) takes place. **[E]**

I P D. See *in praesentia dominorum*.

ipsissima verba — the very words of a speaker.

ipso facto — by the fact itself.

ipso jure — by operation of law.

irregular marriage — a marriage by parties with requisite legal capacity but without the formalities for a regular marriage. Cohabitation for a material period with the habit and repute of being married constitutes now the only recognised form of irregular marriage, though irregular marriages by other forms prior to 1 July 1940 are recognised.

irretrievable breakdown — under the Divorce (Scotland) Act 1976 the court may grant decree of divorce only if it is established in accordance with the Act that the marriage has broken down irretrievably. The Act describes five ways of establishing irretrievable breakdown namely the defender's (1) adultery; (2) unreasonable behaviour; (3) desertion of the pursuer for two years; (4) no cohabitation between the parties for two years coupled with the defender's consent to divorce; or (5) no cohabitation between the parties for five years.

irritancy — the forfeiture of a right, usually in feudal or leasehold property, through failure to observe, or contravention of, the law (legal irritancy) or an agreement (conventional irritancy). Enforcement requires a court decree.

irritancy clause — a clause in an agreement providing that the agreement will be void if some condition in it is contravened.

irritate —
(1) to make void; to nullify;
(2) to enforce an **irritancy** (qv).

ISA — Individual Savings Account.

ish — issue; the date of termination or expiry of a lease.

issue —
(1) all direct descendants of a person;
(2) the formal question for decision put to a jury in a civil action;
(3) more loosely, a question for decision in a court.

itemised pay statement — a written statement which, under the Employment Rights Act 1996, an employer must provide to every employee working eight or more hours per week on each occasion when wages or salaries are paid.

iter — a rural servitude allowing a person a right of way to pass over the land of another on horse or on foot.

ius. See *jus* (the letters i and j are interchangeable in Latin).

j

JCT — Joint Contracts Tribunal; a trade organisation, which provides standard forms of contract for use in the construction industry.

jedge — a gauge or means of verifying a standard measure.

jedge and warrant — an order given by the Dean of Guild prior to 1975 authorising the repair or rebuilding of dilapidated houses, the expense of which became a real burden on the property.

JHA. *See* **Justice and Home Affairs**. **[E]**

joint action — under the Treaty on European Union, a measure adopted by the Council of the European Union within the framework of common foreign and security policy in order to define the objectives, scope and means of Union action to a specific situation. **[E]**

joint adventure — a partnership confined to one particular transaction, speculation, course of trade or voyage.

joint and several obligation — an obligation resting upon more than one person in which each obligant is liable for performance jointly or collectively with the others but also severally or individually. Thus the creditor in such an obligation may sue all or, alternatively, any one of his debtors.

joint dominant position. *See* **collective dominant position**.

joint obligation — an obligation in which each co-obligant is liable only for his share of the debt.

joint operating agreement — contract governing the rights and duties of the members of a **joint venture** (qv) created for the purpose of the exploration and production of offshore oil and gas.

joint property — property in which ownership is indivisibly vested in two or more persons. Each cannot dispose of any share as there are no shares. Examples include property of the members of a members' **club** (qv) and an estate vested in trustees. The interest of a deceased joint owner passes to the survivors. Cf **common property**.

joint stock company — a business organisation the stock or capital of which was contributed jointly by a number of persons. Since the seventeenth century the liability of those involved could be limited to their contributed capital. In the nineteenth century the joint stock company gradually developed into the modern limited company.

joint venture — an **undertaking** (qv) which is jointly controlled by two or more independent undertakings and which performs all the functions of a business undertaking, or is engaged in the production of goods or the provision of services, but which is expressly not a **partnership** (qv). A joint venture may be created by contract or by establishing a new company jointly controlled by the relevant parties**.**

joint wrongdoers — two or more persons who have contributed either equally or in varying proportions to the commission of a delict. They have a **joint and several obligation** (qv) to make reparation for loss or damage caused thereby. Sometimes called joint delinquents.

JP — **justice of the peace** (qv), in Scotland a judge of the **District Court** (qv).

judex non reddit plus quam quod petens ipse requirit — a judge cannot give more than the petitioner himself asks.

judex tenetur impertiri judicium suum — a judge is bound to give the benefit of his decision. Thus a judge must do his duty and reach a decision on a case properly brought before him.

judge — a person appointed to consider and determine cases brought before the courts.

judge advocate — an officer appointed to advise **courts-martial** (qv) on matters of procedure, law and evidence. He reports the proceedings of courts-martial to the Judge Advocate General, an officer appointed by the Lord Chancellor as adviser to the army and air force in relation to courts-martial and military and air force law. Similar arrangements apply in respect of naval courts-martial, the officer appointed by the Lord Chancellor being the Judge Advocate of the Fleet.

Judge-Rapporteur — in all cases before the European Court of Justice and the Court of First Instance, the sitting judge appointed to draft a preliminary report (*rapport préalable*) on the case to the Court, a report preparatory to the hearing of the parties (*rapport d'audience*) and, eventually, the final judgment. **[E]**

judgment — the final determination in a litigation in which the judge sets forth his decision and, usually, his reasons for reaching it.

judgment roll. *See* **rolls**.

judicia posteriora sunt in lege fortiora — later judgments are stronger in law: a rule on the application of precedents. Thus the latest judgment on a controversial question of law, even though it follows a number of earlier contrary decisions, is binding on judges in inferior courts.

Judicial Appointments Board for Scotland — independent body appointed by the Scottish Executive which will in future make all professional judicial appointments within Scotland.

Judicial Committee of the House of Lords — a committee appointed from among the Lord Chancellor, the Lords of Appeal in Ordinary and legally qualified peers to exercise the jurisdiction of the House of Lords as the highest court of appeal in civil and criminal cases in England and Wales and in Northern Ireland and in civil cases in Scotland.

Judicial Committee of the Privy Council — a tribunal of senior judges appointed to hear appeals competently brought before the sovereign in Council. Those judges eligible to sit in the JCPC consist of the **Lords of Appeal in Ordinary** (qv) and the judges of the **Inner House** (qv) and the **Courts of Appeal** (qv) of England and Wales and Northern Ireland. The JCPC has three areas of jurisdiction: (1) appeals from the courts of certain British colonies, dependencies and commonwealth countries; (2) certain ecclesiastical and admiralty appeals and appeals under certain statutes, eg those relating to the medical and allied professions; and (3) devolution cases relating to the competences and functions of the legislative and executive authorities established in Scotland, Northern Ireland and Wales. Under section 103 of the Scotland Act 1998 membership of the JCPC in devolution issues is restricted to **Lords of Appeal in Ordinary** (qv), or holders of high judicial office under the Appellate Jurisdiction Act 1887.

judicial examination —

(1) formerly the initial interrogation by a magistrate or sheriff of a person charged with serious crime, but latterly the first formal appearance of such a person before a sheriff when the accused may, if he wishes, make a **declaration** (qv);

(2) since 1980 the questions which the procurator fiscal may put to such an accused about the charge at that appearance (Criminal Procedure (Scotland) Act 1995, s 36).

judicial factor — a person appointed by a court to hold or administer property in Scotland where it is in dispute or where there is no one who could properly control or administer it. A judicial factor must find caution, and his work is supervised by the **Accountant of Court** (qv).

judicial knowledge. *See* **judicial notice**.

judicial notice — the doctrine under which some (generally well known) facts and matters are presumed to be within a judge's knowledge and so in court proceedings are admitted and do not require to be proved in accordance with the strict rules of evidence. Other facts averred in parties' pleadings require to be proved though within the judge's actual knowledge as a private person.

judicial panel — a specialist panel of judges 'attached' to the **Court of First Instance** (qv) to hear and determine at first instance certain classes of action; provided for by the Treaty of Nice (in force 2003), none yet created. **[E]**

judicial reference — the reference, with the court's approval, by the parties to an existing litigation of the whole or some part of the matter in dispute to an arbiter or referee.

judicial review — a process available in the Court of Session whereby the Court in the exercise of its supervisory jurisdiction can review the actings or decisions of inferior courts, tribunals and other public officers and authorities, on the ground of illegality, irrationality or procedural impropriety, where no other form of appeal is available. Power is similarly available to compel such bodies to act where they have improperly failed so to do.

judicial sale — the sale of property authorised by a court, eg of goods seized by attachment or arrestment or of a ship subject to an admiralty arrestment, or of land subject to a heritable security.

judicial separation — an order of court, short of divorce (which would permit remarriage), separating spouses *a mensa et thoro* (qv), thus allowing them to live permanently apart. An action for judical separation is usually accompanied by a claim for **aliment** (qv). A decree of judicial separation does not preclude later proceedings for divorce.

judiciary — the collective name for all the professional judges in the country.

judicis est judicare secundum allegata et probata — it is the part or duty of the judge to decide in accordance with what has been alleged and proved. Thus judgment must proceed upon what has been proved in the case.

judicis est jus dicere non jus dare — it is the part or duty of the judge to express the law, not to make it. A judge is required to administer and decide the law. He must not himself purport to legislate.

judicium semper pro veritate accipitur — a judgment is always accepted as true. Thus, subject to any competent appeal, a judgment pronounced by a court upon a matter properly submitted to it for decision is conclusive as between the parties, both on the facts and on the law involved.

junior counsel — an advocate who has not been appointed **Queen's Counsel** (qv).

jural — pertaining to right or doctrines of rights.

juridical — concerning the law or the administration of justice.

juridical act — a generic term for legal transactions or acts-in-the-law such as a unilateral promise, contract, conveyance, assignation, will, trust or donation.

juris et de jure — of law and from law; a presumption *juris et de jure* is irrebuttable.

jurisdiction —
(1) in international law, the power of the state to enact and enforce legislation;
(2) the authority of a court to entertain and determine a particular case, an authority which may be circumscribed by territorial boundaries, the value or type of case or other considerations, and which, in civil proceedings, is now primarily determined by EU rules set forth in the Civil Jurisdiction and Judgments Act 1982;
(3) the territorial area within which a particular court may exercise that authority, eg the Court of Session has jurisdiction over the whole of Scotland.

jurisprudence — (1) the philosophy of law; any studies of the nature of law in general and especially theoretical ones (philosophical and sociological). Legal theory rather than the study of the content of legal doctrine or substantive law. (2) Sometimes however used to denote a body of legal doctrine eg 'contract jurisprudence' or of judicial decisions eg 'Strasbourg case-law jurisprudence'.

jurist — a very learned lawyer. The term is normally applied to well-recognised and respected legal writers, scholars and philosophers.

jurisconsult — a jurist; a professional legal adviser. **[E]**

juristic person — an artificial entity with legal capacity, rights and liabilities (eg a corporation), as distinct from a natural **person** (qv).

juror — a member of a jury.

jury — a group of lay persons chosen from among the local population to hear and consider the evidence in legal proceedings and decide (under the judge's directions on law) the issues of fact. A jury always sits in the more serious criminal cases, which are held under **solemn procedure** (qv). In civil cases a jury is only competent in certain delict cases heard in the **Outer House** (qv) of the **Court of Session** (qv). In Scotland a criminal jury is made up of fifteen persons and can reach a verdict in criminal trials unanimously or, in case of guilt, by a simple majority of at least eight. A civil jury is made up of 12 persons.

jus —
(1) a legal right;
(2) law.

jus accrescendi praefertur oneribus — the right of survivorship is preferred to burdens. Thus one of the proprietors of joint property cannot burden it to the detriment of the survivor or survivors.

jus ad rem — short for *jus ad rem acquirendam* a right to acquire a thing; a personal right (or *jus in personam*) to property under a particular obligation, enforceable against the obligant, contrasted with a real right (or *jus in re*) in the thing or property itself, enforceable against all persons into whose hands the thing may come. For example, the purchaser of a house has a personal right (*jus ad rem*) to it under missives. When he records the disposition in his favour or registers his title, he acquires a real right (*jus in re*) to it.

jus administrationis — right to administer: the former right enjoyed by a husband to administer his wife's property and to validate her acts with his consent.

jus civile — civil law or Roman law. *See* **civil law**.

jus cogens — a statutory or contractual provision stipulating a mandatory legal consequence. Cf *jus dispositivum*.

jus commune — literally 'common law'.
(1) historically the law and legal principles which were common to the European regions prior to the codification movement of the 18th and 19th centuries; literally 'the common law';
(2) the contemporary search for a new core of private law common to all, or a significant majority of, European legal systems upon which, some hope, a common European Civil Code can be built.

jus coronae — the right of the Crown; the right under which the Crown may claim those things said to be under regalia. *See* **regalia**.

jus crediti — the right of credit, ie of a creditor; an enforceable right in property, often contrasted with mere expectancy, eg the right of a beneficiary in property held in trust for his behoof.

jus disponendi — the right of disposing of property.

jus dispositivum — a statutory or contractual provision the stipulated consequences of which may be averted by agreement between the persons concerned. Cf *jus cogens*.

jus dominio proximum — a right of almost, but not quite, absolute property, eg that of one who holds land in feu.

jus exigendi — the right to require immediate fulfilment of an obligation.

jus gentium — the law of nations; international law.

jus in personam — a personal right, contrasted with real right: *see* *jus ad rem*.

jus in re — a real right in a thing a right which can be vindicated and enforced against any person into whose hands the thing comes. *See* *jus in re aliena* and compare *jus ad rem*.

jus in re aliena — right in a thing owned by another which can be vindicated and enforced against any person into whose hands so ever the thing comes including any bona fide purchaser for value; a subordinate real right. The various categories of subordinate real rights (*jura in re aliena*) include rights in security, proper liferents, servitudes and leases.

jus mariti — the right of a husband: the former right under which a husband acquired absolutely the personal property of his wife.

jus non patitur idem bis solvi — the law does not suffer the same debt to be paid twice.

jus pascendi pecoris — the right of pasturing cattle, one of the rural servitudes.

jus pignoris — the right of pledge; the right of a creditor, holding a pledge as security for the performance of an obligation, to keep it until the obligation is fulfilled.

jus possessionis — the right which a possessor has merely by virtue of the fact of his possession, especially the right to bring an action of *spuilzie* to obtain restitution from another person (even the true owner) who has vitiously dispossessed him.

jus possidendi — the right to possess or occupy property held by the owner of the property or by one, such as a tenant, deriving right from the owner.

jus quaesitum tertio — a right acquired by a third party in consequence of a stipulation in his favour expressed in a contract between other parties.

jus relictae — the right of the widow; a widow's right to one-third or one-half of her deceased husband's free moveable property, the proportion depending upon whether or not he leaves children or issue of predeceasing children. The *jus relictae* is calculated after deduction of debts and expenses, and any statutory prior rights if the deceased died intestate. A widower has a similar right, the *jus relicti*.

jus representationis — the right of representation; the right by which a descendant or other relative succeeds to the rights and privileges of a deceased person in accordance with the law of succession.

jus tertii — the right of a third party: a plea against an argument maintained by one who has no title or interest to advance it. The argument belongs to the third party.

jus utendi et abutendi — the right of using and consuming, the essence of ownership. The proprietor can not only use his property; he may destroy it by consuming it. Cf *jus utendi fruendi*.

jus utendi fruendi — the right of using and enjoying, the characteristic of a liferent. The use and enjoyment must be consistent with full preservation of the subject. Cf *jus utendi et abutendi*.

justa causa traditionis — valid legal ground (such as a contractual obligation to convey) underlying a conveyance or transfer of ownership.

jusiurandum — an oath.

Justice and Home Affairs (JHA) — the original name of Title VI of the Treaty on European Union; replaced in 1999 by **Police and Judicial Cooperation in Criminal Matters** (qv). **[E]**

justice of the peace — a lay person appointed by the Secretary of State for Scotland, on the advice of a local committee, to preside as judge in the district court, to administer oaths and to exercise other miscellaneous powers.

Justiciar — the ancient name for the officer of state who became the highest criminal judge in Scotland, now known as the Lord Justice-General.

Justiciary. *See* **High Court of Justiciary**.

Justiciary Cases — series of reports of decisions of the High Court of Justiciary, cited as 2002 JC 100, but physically bound in the same volume as **Session Cases** (qv).

justifiable homicide — killing while exercising a private right, eg of self-defence, or a public duty, eg execution of sentence of death.

justo tempore — in due time; at the right time.

k

KC — short for **King's Counsel**.

Keeper of the Great Seal of Scotland — under the Secretary for Scotland Act 1885 this office is held by the Secretary of State for Scotland.

Keeper of the Records of Scotland — the officer responsible for the Scottish Record Office in which are preserved the public records of Scotland, including records of government departments in Scotland, Scottish courts and other public bodies, and for the Scottish Records Advisory Service, which advises the Secretary of State and the Lord President of the Court of Session on questions relating to Scottish public records.

Keeper of the Registers of Scotland — the officer responsible for the Department of the Registers of Scotland, in which are maintained the General Register of Sasines, the Land Register of Scotland, and registers of a wide range of deeds relating to succession, trusts, family agreements and state appointments.

Keeper of the Rolls — the Principal Clerk of Session in the capacity in which he keeps the rolls of the Court of Session and supervises the listing of all proceedings therein.

Keeper of the Signet — the titular head, appointed by the Crown, of the Society of Writers to the Signet. All summonses in the Court of Session originally required to be prepared and subscribed by clerks in the royal Secretariat of State which controlled the king's personal seal or Signet. All warrants for service of summonses and charges to implement the court's decrees required to be sealed with the Signet, and in that process were said to 'pass the Signet'. The clerks of the Secretariat are now members of the Society of Writers to the Signet. The effective head of the society is the Deputy Keeper of the Signet, a senior member of the society appointed by the Keeper.

kindly tenant — a person who held land under a hereditary lease as distinct from a feudal charter. The tenancy was constituted by entry in the landlord's rent book. For long it has survived only at Lochmaben. On 28 November 2004, kindly tenancies as a type of tenure will be abolished by the Abolition of Feudal Tenure etc (Scotland) Act 2000, s 64 and the interest of a kindly tenancy will be converted into a right of ownership.

kirk session — a church court consisting of the minister and elders of a parish church adhering to the presbyterian form of church government. It is also recognised in regiments such as the Black Watch. It has administrative as well as pastoral functions.

l

label — a physical production, as distinct from a document, in a criminal trial, so-called because there is usually affixed to it a label bearing the signatures of witnesses who have identified it and are expected to identify it again at the trial.

labes realis quae rei inhaeret — a real blemish which inheres in the thing itself: a fundamental defect in the title to property so that no-one may deprive the original owner of his right thereto. Thus the title to stolen property continues to be vested in the original owner and, in the absence of his consent, incapable of lawful **derivative acquisition** (qv) by another even a purchaser in good faith. *See also vitium reale*.

lacuna —
(1) an omission or blank space in a document;
(2) a situation not covered by a statutory provision.

Laeken Declaration — the 2001 **European Council** (qv) 'Declaration on the Future of the European Union' posing a series of questions on the future development of the Union and setting up the **constitutional convention** (qv). **[E]**

laesio enormis. *See* **enorm lesion**.

laird — literally, the Scots version of 'lord'; strictly the term should be restricted to the holder of a **barony** (qv) but in practice it is used colloquially of any large Scottish landowner.

Lammas — a quarter day in Scotland (28 August: Term and Quarter Days (Scotland) Act 1990, s 1).

land agreement — an agreement between **undertakings** (qv) which creates, alters, transfers or terminates an interest in land, or an agreement to enter into such an agreement; a land agreement is excluded from the **Chapter I prohibition** (qv) of the Competition Act 1998.

Land Certificate — document of ownership of land in Scotland; issued by the Registers of Scotland which is proof of ownership and by which the state guarantees that title.

Land Register of Scotland — a map-based public register of title to interests in land in Scotland under the management and control of the Keeper of the Registers of Scotland replacing the recording of deeds in the **General Register of Sasines** (qv). It is being brought progressively into effect under the Land Registration (Scotland) Act 1979. By 2003 all new registrations will be made in the Land Register.

land tenure — the system under which land is held. In Scotland it is mainly feudal in principle, but still **udal** (qv) in parts of Orkney and Shetland, these islands having been formerly under Norwegian rule. Church land and land acquired by compulsory acquisition may be held on **allodial title** (qv).

landfill site — site authorised for the disposal of waste in or on land.

landlord — the party to the contract of lease who grants the lease; the proprietor of heritable property which is the subject of a lease.

Lands Tribunal for Scotland — the tribunal established under the Lands Tribunal Act 1949 to determine referred disputes relating to compensation on compulsory acquisition, the removal or variation of conditions in the title to land and other matters arising out of the use of land in Scotland.

Lands Valuation Appeal Court — a court comprising three judges of the Court of Session determining appeals from local valuation appeal committees. Normally one judge forms a quorum.

landward — until 1975 described that part or area of a county lying outside the boundaries of burghs.

last heir. *See **ultimus haeres***.

lata culpa aequiparatur dolo — gross fault is held to be equivalent to fraud.

lato sensu — in a broad or wide sense.

latent ambiguity — an ambiguity whose existence becomes apparent only in the light of information gathered from outside the document.

law agent — the traditional Scottish term used to describe a solicitor, often abbreviated to 'agent'. The English usage 'solicitor' has been recognised in modern Scottish legislation and is now in general use.

Law Commission. *See **Scottish Law Commission***.

Law Lord — colloquial term for a **Lord of Appeal in Ordinary** (qv); likewise 'law lords' is a colloquial collective term for the **Judicial Committee of the House of Lords** (qv).

Law of the sea — the rules of public international law, contained in custom and international conventions, regulating rights over the seas.

law officers — the Scottish law officers – the Lord Advocate and Solicitor General for Scotland – now act for the Scottish Executive. The law officers of the United Kingdom government are the Attorney General and the Solicitor General (in England and Wales); the Advocate General for Scotland; and the Attorney General for Northern Ireland.

law reports — reports of decisions of the courts published for information and reference. *See also* **precedent**.

Law Society of Scotland — a statutory body created in 1949 comprising all practising solicitors in Scotland. It controls admission to and discipline within the profession. The existing societies of solicitors such as the Writers to the Signet, the Solicitors to the Supreme Court, the Royal Society of Procurators in Glasgow and the Society of Advocates in Aberdeen were not superseded on the institution of the Law Society of Scotland, but their members also belong to the new statutory professional body.

lawburrows — an action by which a person who has good grounds for fearing that another person may damage his person or property may secure a court order requiring that other to find caution or security to keep the complainer harmless from illegal violence.

laytime or **laydays** — the number of days allowed by a **charterparty** (qv) for the loading and discharge of cargo by the charterer.

lead evidence — to call witnesses to give evidence; to adduce evidence.

leader — the senior counsel for a party in a case. He is usually a Queen's Counsel.

leading case — an important judicial precedent.

leading question — a question which suggests the answer. It is not permitted in court except in cross examination.

lease —

(1) the hiring of heritable property (or, more recently, moveable property, especially vehicles and commercial or industrial equipment) by a lessor to a lessee for a specified period and on prescribed conditions, usually for the payment of rent;

(2) the formal document giving effect to such a lease;

(3) to hire on a lease.

leasing-making — the obsolete crime of verbal sedition involving contemptuous defamation of the sovereign or the Prince of Scotland.

legacy — a bequest of money or moveable property to a beneficiary conferred by the will of a deceased person. Legacies are classified into **specific** (qv), **demonstrative** (qv), **general** (qv) and residual, *see* **residuary beneficiary**.

legal (n) — the period of ten years allowed to a debtor to redeem his heritable property after **adjudication** (qv). If he fails to pay the debt within the legal, his right to redeem may be foreclosed by action for declarator of expiry of the legal.

legal aid — professional legal advice or representation provided under a statutory scheme to persons of limited means but who may be required to contribute to its cost.

legal base — also Treaty base; that authority provided in the EC or EU Treaties conferring competence upon the Community institutions to adopt legislative or other acts. The institutions may act only by authority of, and always in accordance with, a legal base. **[E]**

legal capacity — the ability to make legally binding contracts and other juridical acts (active capacity) or to be held liable for one's acts (passive capacity). Only **persons** (qv) have capacity and most persons have capacity but natural persons who are under 18 or insane lack legal capacity.

legal certainty — a general principle of European Community law which requires that the application of the law to a particular situation must be reasonably predictable; embraces principles such as respect for acquired rights and legitimate expectation. **[E]**

legal interest — interest which is, in limited circumstances, due to be paid *ex lege* or according to the law.

legal person — a natural individual person or an artificial entity with legal capacity, rights and duties.

legal professional privilege — the absolute right of confidentiality pertaining to communications (in any form) between a lawyer and his/her client.

legal rights — rights to share in the estate of a deceased person, enjoyed by a surviving spouse and issue, regardless of any will. *See also* **jus relictae**, **legitim** and **prior rights**.

legal tender — cash in which a debt must be paid. A creditor is technically entitled to insist upon payment of a debt in legal tender, which in Scotland includes most current coins and Bank of England notes of a denomination of less than £5. Scottish banknotes are not legal tender. Since the withdrawal of £1 Bank of England notes no notes are now legal tender in Scotland.

legatum per universitatem — a universal legacy; a legacy of the testator's whole estate.

legatum rei alienae — the legacy of a subject not belonging to the testator but to some other person. If the testator mistakenly believed the subject to be his, the bequest is ineffective. If he knew that it was not his, the executors must try to acquire it for the legatee or otherwise satisfy him.

legatum universitatis — a universal legacy; a legacy of the testator's whole estate.

legislation — laws enacted by Parliament (ie the Scots Parliament before 1 May 1707, the Parliament of Great Britain from 1707 to 1800, and the Parliament of the United Kingdom thereafter); and, since 1973, legal acts of the Community institutions. Orders in Council, statutory instruments, regulations and rules made by ministers under the authority of an Act of Parliament are known as subordinate legislation.

legislative competence — those matters over which a parliament may lawfully enact statutes. The United Kingdom Parliament has unlimited legislative competence but the **Scottish Parliament** (qv) may only enact laws on those matters granted or devolved to it by the provisions of the Scotland Act 1998. All matters are within the Scottish Parliament's competence except in so far as they are excluded, notably in the list of 'reserved matters' in Schedule 5, or where legislation would be incompatible with **Convention rights** (qv) or with **European Community** (qv) law.

legitim — a legal right to a share in the moveable estate of a deceased ancestor, which vests in any surviving lawful issue *ipso jure*, sometimes called the 'bairns part'. Illegitimate children are now also entitled to legitim. The legitim fund is either one-third or one-half of the deceased's estate: one-third if there is a surviving spouse entitled to his or her 'legal rights', and one-half if there is no surviving spouse or a surviving spouse has renounced those rights. If the deceased died intestate a surviving spouse is entitled to certain prior rights which rank after claims by creditors of the deceased and are deducted before legal rights such as legitim are calculated.

legitimate expectation — a general principle of European Community law linked to **legal certainty** (qv), creating a legal entitlement to anticipate the occurrence of an event which is induced by the conduct of a public authority. **[E]**

legitimation *per subsequens matrimonium* — the legitimation of a person born out of wedlock by the subsequent marriage of his parents.

lenocinium — pandering to licentiousness: connivance by a husband in his wife's infidelity, affording a defence to an action for divorce brought by the husband and founded on that adultery.

leonina societas — a leonine partnership: a form of partnership in which one partner bears all the loss while another receives all the profit (the lion's share). It is not recognised in Scots law, but the phrase is used generally of a partnership said to be void or otherwise illegal.

lesion — loss or injury. *See* **enorm lesion**.

lessee — a party to whom a lease has been granted; in a lease of heritable property the tenant.

lessor — a party who has granted a lease; in a lease of heritable property the landlord.

letter of credit — a document, issued by a bank under instruction from a buyer of goods, authorising the seller to draw a specified sum of money under specified terms: usually the receipt by the bank of certain documents within a given time.

letter of request — a request to a foreign court or tribunal for the examination of a witness resident abroad or the production or examination of other evidence. The letter may be obtained on application to the Court of Session or the sheriff in civil causes and to the High Court of Justiciary or the sheriff in criminal proceedings.

letters — a writ or warrant by a court. Formerly more common than in current practice.

letters of arrestment — a writ to attach the property of a debtor in the hands of a third person as security against the debtor. *See* **arrestment**.

letters of caption — an obsolete warrant to arrest for debt, finally abolished by the Debtors (Scotland) Act 1987.

letters of horning — an obsolete mode of diligence abolished by the Debtors (Scotland) Act 1987.

letters of inhibition. *See* **inhibition**.

letters of open doors — a warrant authorising the opening of a **lockfast place** (qv) in order to attach subjects held therein.

letters of second diligence — a warrant authorising the apprehension and detention, until he finds caution, of a witness who has failed or, it is reasonably suspected, will fail upon citation to attend court to give evidence.

Letters Patent — a written instrument granting authority from the Crown, not enclosed but open to view, with the seal of the sovereign at the bottom. In Scotland all Letters Patent are entered into the Register of the Great Seal of Scotland, which is held by Registers of Scotland. 'Letters patent' (*litterae patentes*) were so called, because they were open (or 'patent') for all to read, as distinct from 'letters close' (*litterae clausae*), which were sealed closed so that only the recipient could read them (since the seal had to be broken to get at the text).

leviora delicta — the lighter delicts: petty crimes and offences which may be tried summarily, as distinguished from the more serious crimes which are tried before a jury under **solemn procedure** (qv).

Lex Aquilia — an important Roman law which, as developed by the later civilians, provided the basis for the fundamental principle of liability for damage to the person or to property. It is the basis of much of the Scots law of delict.

lex contractus — the law of the contract. This may include stipulations which differ from the provisions of the common law or statute law but which are not illegal or immoral and which the law will therefore enforce.

lex domicilii — the law of the domicile. The personal law of an individual may be governed by the law of his domicile or the law of his nationality. *See also* **domicile**.

lex fori — the law of the court; the law of the country in which litigation takes place, and which regulates matters such as evidence, court procedure and diligence.

lex loci actus — the law of the place where the act was performed.

lex loci contractus — the law of the place where the contract was made or concluded. This law may be relevant in determining the proper law of the contract, its formal validity and the capacity of the parties. Cf *lex loci solutionis*.

lex loci deliciti — the law of the place where a crime was committed.

lex loci rei sitae — the law of the place where the subject (usually heritable) is situated.

lex loci solutionis — the law of the place of payment; the law of the place where the contract is to be performed. Cf *lex loci contractus*.

lex mercatoria — literally 'the Law Merchant'; the customary mercantile law of medieval Europe. Some scholars believe that certain trans-national trade usages, commercial customs and international conventions constitute a contemporary *lex mercatoria* recognized and enforced especially in international commercial arbitration proceedings.

lex nil frustra facit — the law does nothing in vain. Thus the court will not pronounce a useless or impractical decree, for example it will refuse a simple declarator of an abstract inconsequential fact or an interdict where no wrong has been committed or threatened.

lex non cogit ad impossibilia — the law does not compel the performance of what is impossible.

lex non requirit verificari quod apparet curiae — the law does not require proof of what is apparent to the court. For example, the court can see for itself whether a deed has been stamped.

lex posterior derogat priori — a later statute derogates from a prior one: a maxim of interpretation that the later of two mutually inconsistent enactments prevails.

lex semper dabit remedium — the law will always afford a remedy for every wrong of which it can or does take notice.

lex talionis — the law of retaliation; the rule of Mosaic law that punishment be analogous to the crime, ie an eye for an eye and a tooth for a tooth (*Deut* 19:21). It has never been part of the law of Scotland.

lexis — an on-line searchable directory of case law, legislation and certain other legal materials.

liability — subjection to a legal obligation.

libel —
(1) a written defamatory statement (an English term now loosely used in Scotland, though Scots law does not distinguish between libel and slander in defamation, as does English law and the expression is therefore not a term of art in Scotland);
(2) a statement of a criminal charge detailing the alleged offence(s);
(3) to defame in writing;
(4) to set forth a criminal charge.

liberalisation — the removal of restrictions. **[E]**

liberation — release from custody, detention or imprisonment.

liberis nascituris — to children yet to be born. Certain legal rights may be conferred, especially in marriage contracts, on children yet unborn.

licence —
(1) a permit, granted by the state or other public body, to do what otherwise could not lawfully be done (eg drive a vehicle on a road, sell intoxicating liquor, take and kill game or possess firearms) or that which may only be done by explicit permission of the state (eg extract oil or gas from the ground);

(2) the document constituting that permit;

(3) a contractual right, falling short of what is recognised as a legal tenancy, to use or occupy the heritable property of another;

(4) to grant such a permit, document or right.

licensee — a party to whom a licence has been granted.

licensing board — a board, comprising members of a local authority, established under the Licensing (Scotland) Act 1976 to consider and determine applications for licences to sell alcoholic liquor.

liege —

(1) (adj) bound by feudal tenure;

(2) (n) a subject of the reigning monarch; sometimes used as a synonym for citizen, especially in the criminal law.

liege poustie (n) (perhaps derived from *legitima potestas*) — the state of sufficient health in which a person can validly and effectively dispose, *mortis causa* or otherwise, of heritable property (an obsolete phrase).

lien (pronounced 'lee-en') —

(1) a right to retain a debtor's moveable property until he has paid his debt. The right arises by operation of law and is triggered by some event (such as the repair of property), particularly in commercial situations. In Scotland all liens are possessory in the sense that they depend on the lien-holder having and retaining possession of the property;

(2) in English legal usage the name lien is also given to the non-possessory equivalent in English law to the Scottish tacit **hypothec** (qv), and this usage is sometimes found in Scotland eg maritime liens.

liferent (pronounced 'life rent') — the right to use and enjoy during a lifetime the property of another, without consuming its substance. 'Proper liferents', which are rare in modern practice, involve only liferenter and fiar, and the right enjoyed by the liferenter is of the nature of a personal servitude. When the fee is vested in trustees and the liferenter has only a trust liferent, the liferent is described as an 'improper liferent'. Liferents may be created by reservation, as where the granter gives the fee while retaining the liferent; or by constitution, when he grants a liferent while retaining the fee or disposing of it to another.

light — a servitude, which must be constituted in writing, which restrains the proprietor of the servient tenement, by building or otherwise, from obstructing the light of the dominant tenement.

limitation period — the period within which an action or claim must be raised in court. If an action is raised out of time the claim will normally be barred.

limited company — a publicly registered corporation, with separate legal personality, which may be either a private limited company or a public limited company but where the shares are held privately rather than being listed in the stock market.

limited liability — the principle whereby the liability of the contributors of capital to a commercial undertaking for losses incurred by that undertaking is limited, for each individual contributor, to the actual amount of the capital introduced by him. The principle forms the fundamental basis for the development of the **joint stock company** (qv) and the limited company.

limited liability partnership — a publicly registered corporation, with separate legal personality. Each LLP must have at least two members and the liability of the members of the United Kingdom LLP is limited to any agreed capital contribution.

limited partnership — a partnership where one or more general partners are liable for all the partnership debts and obligations, and one or more limited partners are liable for those debts and obligations only to the extent of their contribution to the partnership assets: see the Limited Partnership Act 1907, s 4(2).

lining — the measuring or tracing out of the boundaries of holdings of land, especially in burghs. A decree of lining was an order of the Dean of Guild authorising building works within the burgh in conformity with statutory or customary requirements.

linking system — a scheme by which a benefit granted by the European Community (eg the suspension of an export levy) is subject to a condition (eg that goods be purchased from an **intervention agency** (qv)). **[E]**

liquid (adj) — of a certain, fixed and ascertained or instantly ascertainable amount.

liquidate damages — damages provided for in a contract as the parties' estimate of the loss which will result from breach. These are consequently recoverable in the event of breach without proof of actual loss. Cf **unliquidate damages**.

liquidation — the procedure for winding up and dissolving a limited company. It may be voluntary, if agreed upon by the shareholders, or judicial, if ordered by a court. See the Insolvency Act 1986.

liquidator — the person appointed in a **liquidation** (qv) to ingather the assets of a company and settle and adjust the claims of its creditors.

lis alibi pendens — a suit pending elsewhere: a defence, constituting a preliminary defence, that the same question as that raised in the action is already the subject of litigation depending between the parties in another court of competent jurisdiction. If that court is outside Scotland, the court may at its discretion sist the action in Scotland until the other action is determined.

lis est finita or lis est sopita — the case is finished. Not only is the action ended but its subject matter is finally determined. Where, for example, a case has been referred to the defender's oath and he commits perjury in denying liability, he may be prosecuted for the perjury but, as regards the civil action, *lis est sopita*.

lis pendens — a pending action or petition. See *pendente lite*.

litem suam facere — to make the suit his own. A judge was said to make the suit his own where, through corruption, malice, fear or favour or even, sometimes, through ignorance of the law, he made the wrong judgment. However, acts done by a judge, including a sheriff in his judicial capacity, are absolutely privileged and cannot be made the subject of an action for damages.

litigant — a party engaged in a legal (court) action.

litigation — the process of raising and engaging in a legal action.

litigiosity — the implied prohibition of the alienation of heritable property which defeats an action or diligence to acquire the property. Land is rendered litigious on inhibition or on the service of a summons in certain proceedings relating to land.

litiscontestation — the stage of an action at which issue is joined by the lodging of defences, and at which, consequently, the action becomes contested.

LJ-C. *See* **Lord Justice-Clerk**.

LL.B. — bachelor of laws, the usual academic qualification of Scots lawyers.

LL.D. — doctor of laws, highest law degree. Mostly commonly awarded on honorary grounds to distinguished persons who may or may not be lawyers. May also be awarded on academic merit for distinguished published legal scholarship.

LL.M. — master of laws, a higher degree in law, which may be earned by examination or by research.

Lloyd's — major provider of insurance, especially maritime, based in London.

loan — a contract whereby the lender gives money or moveable property to the borrower for his temporary use. Species of loan include *commodatum* (qv) and *mutuum* (qv).

local authority — a statutory body of councillors, elected as a council by local voters, with extensive statutory administrative powers, functions and duties, especially over services within its area. In Scotland local authorities comprise councils constituted under s 2 of the Local Government etc (Scotland) Act 1994.

local valuation appeal committee — a committee, comprising members of a local valuation panel, constituted for a valuation area to hear and determine appeals and complaints under the Acts relating to the valuation of land.

locatio; **location** — hire of premises, goods or services; derived fom Roman law *locatio conductio*, the categories of which are adopted into the terminology of Scots law: see the entries which follow.

locatio custodiae — the hire of the custody of a thing, ie the contract of deposit.

locatio operarum — the hire of service, ie the contract of employment.

locatio operis faciendi — the hire of services, ie a contract to do a particular piece of work.

locatio rei — the hire of a thing.

locator — a lessor.

lockfast place — a place (other than a building) which is secured by a lock (eg a room, drawer, box or car), the key not being in the lock. The opening of a lockfast place is an aggravation of the crime of theft.

loco parentis — in the place of a parent.

loco tutoris — in the place of a tutor. A factor *loco tutoris* may be appointed by the Court of Session where a pupil has no tutor.

locum tenens — a person who acts as substitute or depute for another.

locus — the place.

locus delicti — the place where the delict or crime was committed.

locus poenitentiae — place for repentance: an opportunity for reconsideration, that is, the right of a party to resile from an imperfectly constituted contract, obligation or trust unless he is prevented by personal bar under either common law or the Requirements of Writing (Scotland) Act 1995, s 1(3) and (4).

locus solutionis — the place of payment or performance of an obligation.

locus standi — lit. a place to stand: the right to be heard by a court or tribunal.

lodge — to deposit pleadings or other documents with the clerk of court.

Lomé Conventions — a series of **association agreements** (qv) renewed every five years between the European Community on the one hand and a number of developing **ACP countries** (qv) on the other; now replaced by the **Cotonou Agreement** (qv). **[E]**

loosing of arrestment — the taking off or removal of an arrestment, eg on finding caution or making **consignation** (qv).

Lord —

(1) a title of honour given to a **peer** (qv) of the realm of the rank of lord of parliament (in England baron), viscount, earl, or marquess. and also as a courtesy title to the sons of a duke or the eldest son of an earl;

(2) a title accorded generally to judges of the Court of Session (who are Lords of Council and Session) and, within their own courts, to sheriffs;

(3) a title incorporated in the titles of certain other honourable offices though the holders are not necessarily peers, eg the Lord President, the Lord Justice-Clerk, the Lord Justice-General, the Lord Advocate, the Lord Lyon and a Lord Provost.

Lord Advocate — the senior law officer of the **Crown** (qv) in Scotland. Prior to **devolution** (qv) he/she was a member of the United Kingdom government advising it on legal matters affecting Scotland; post devolution a member of the Scottish Executive. Government minister in charge of the prosecution of all crime and the investigation of deaths. The Scotland Act 1998 protects the independent position and role of the Lord Advocate in connection with criminal prosecutions.

Lord Advocate's Reference — an appeal on a point of law by the **Crown** (qv) against a decision of the High Court of Justiciary; if the appeal is successful the law will be clarified or changed but the acquittal of the accused stands unchanged.

Lord of Appeal in Ordinary — formal style of a judge who sits as a full time member of the **Judicial Committee of the House of Lords** (qv) but more commonly referred to by the colloquial expression 'law lord'.

Lord Clerk Register — official formerly responsible for the administration of the registers of Scotland, these duties were transferred to the Keeper of the Registers and Records of Scotland in 1928.

Lord Commissioner of Justiciary — A judge of the High Court of Justiciary (qv).

Lord High Commissioner — the Queen's representative at the General Assembly of the Church of Scotland.

Lord Justice-Clerk — the second in rank of the Scottish judges who constitute the Court of Session and the High Court of Justiciary. He presides over the Second Division of the Inner House of the Court of Session.

Lord Justice-General — the senior judge of the High Court of Justiciary. In 1823 the office was combined with that of Lord President of the Court of Session.

Lord Lieutenant — the official representative of the sovereign in each county, the duties are now primarily ceremonial.

Lord Lyon King-of-Arms — an officer (who takes his title of Lyon from the armorial bearings of the kings and queens regnant of Scotland, the lion rampant) who has wide jurisdiction in the Court of the Lord Lyon in all heraldic matters and who is responsible for the ordering of state ceremonies. His functions correspond to those discharged in England by the Earl Marshal and Garter King of Arms.

Lord of Council and Session — A judge of the **Court of Session** (qv). The title derives from the origins of the Court of Session in the king's council in Scotland a body which combined political and judicial functions in the fifteenth century. *See also* **Senator of the College of Justice**.

Lords of the Articles — a committee of the pre-union Scots Parliament appointed by the Crown to which the Scots Parliament delegated most of its powers in the sixteenth and early seventeenth century.

Lord Ordinary — a single judge of the **Court of Session** (qv) sitting at **first instance** (qv) in the **Outer House** (qv).

Lord President — the first in rank of the Scottish judges who constitute the Court of Session and the High Court of Justiciary. He is the presiding judge of the First Division of the Inner House of the Court of Session. *See also* **Lord Justice-General**.

Lord Provost — the convenor of the city councils of Aberdeen, Dundee, Edinburgh and Glasgow. Every Lord Provost is *ex officio* **Lord Lieutenant** (qv) of their city.

loss of society award — in the law of damages for death caused by personal injuries, an award of damages to a relative within the deceased's immediate family by way of compensation for the loss of such non-patrimonial benefit as the relative might have been expected to derive from the deceased's society and guidance if the deceased had not died. Sometimes taken to include the closely associated heads of damages for distress and anxiety from contemplating the deceased's suffering and for grief and sorrow caused by the death.

lost property — in property law, property the ownership of which is temporarily uncertain.

loyalty rebate — also fidelity rebate; discount made conditional upon a buyer using only, or principally, a particular supplier; normally an **abuse of a dominant position** (qv) in competition law.

L P. *See* **Lord President**.

L S — *locus sigilli* (the place of the seal): the letters may be found printed within a circle on documents to indicate the place where a personal seal used to be affixed.

lucratus — enriched; frequently relevant in the context of that aspect of unjustified enrichment called recompense. A person who has benefited by the work or services of another which were not rendered in implement of contract may be obliged to remunerate the party who has provided the benefit, not for all that party's expenditure but to the extent of benefit enjoyed *quantum lucratus*, ie in so far as he is enriched.

lucrum cessans aut damnum emergens — gain ceasing or damage arising. Either kind of loss attracts the liability of the person who wrongfully caused it.

Lugano Convention — international agreement governing the allocation of jurisdiction and recognition and enforcement of judgments as between the member states of the European Community and those of the **European Free Trade Association** (qv). **[E]**

Luxembourg Compromise — a compromise solution reached to resolve a 1965/66 crisis in European Community affairs. Alarmed at the ambition of the Community institutions, the French government refused to take its seat in the Council, leading to paralysis of the Community machinery; it was coaxed back only with a promise from the other five member states that where a member state was to declare its 'very important interests' to be at issue, the Council would act only by unanimity – creating, in effect, a right of veto. This 'agreement to disagree' had no legal status, but was to cripple Council procedures for the next 20 years. **[E]**

Lyon Court — the court of the **Lord Lyon King-of-Arms** (qv).

m

Maastricht Treaty. *See* **Treaty on European Union**. **[E]**

mace — an ornamental staff of authority, which was originally a weapon in the form of a club, borne by a **macer** (qv) before a judge of the Court of Session or of the High Court of Justiciary and displayed in his court when the court is sitting. Ceremonial maces are also used by the Scottish and United Kingdom parliaments, and by some local councils and universities.

macer — is the term for an usher in the Court of Session, so called because of the **mace** (qv) he bears before the judge at the beginning of a court. Macers were recognised as members of the College of Justice on its formation in 1532, but their functions are less important in modern practice than formerly.

magistrate — generally, any person with judicial powers. The term is now applied to provosts and bailies of burghs, as previously constituted, and also to stipendiary magistrates presiding in the district court, but not (as in England) to justices of the peace.

mail *or* **maill** — an obsolete term for rent. Thus blackmail is illegal rent. The action of maills and duties still exists as a form of diligence enabling a heritable creditor to receive payment of rent directly.

main proceedings — the case pending before a national court or tribunal which has made an order for reference to the European Court of Justice for a **preliminary ruling** (qv). **[E]**

maintenance — order for financial support for children to be paid by a parent, governed by the Child Support Act. A term of English law broadly equivalent to the Scottish concept of **aliment** (qv).

majori minus inest or majus includit minus — the greater includes the less. Thus a conveyance of heritage includes not only the land itself but also all the ancillary rights attached to it.

majority — the status of a person of full age (eighteen since 1969 but formerly twenty-one) and capacity. Cf **minor**. See Age of Majority (Scotland) Act 1969, s 1.

mala fide — in bad faith; lacking good faith; *mala fides* (nominative) bad faith.

mala grammatica non vitiat chartam — grammatical error does not vitiate a deed if the meaning is clear and intelligible.

male appretiata — wrongly valued. **Confirmation** (qv) *ad omissa vel male appretiata* is competent where any estate was originally omitted or undervalued.

malice — the preconceived intention to cause mischief or injury to another. Reckless or culpable disregard for common justice may, as with evidence of personal ill will, be sufficient to constitute malice.

malicious mischief — the crime of maliciously destroying or damaging the property of another.

malitia supplet aetatem — malice supplies the place of age. Formerly the presumption that a child in pupillarity was incapable of forming criminal intent was rebuttable if such intention could be proved.

malum in se — an intrinsic evil; an act which is inherently wicked. Cf *malum prohibitum*.

malum prohibitum — a forbidden evil: an act which is wrongful because it is prohibited, although in itself it is not necessarily morally wrong, eg exceeding the speed limit.

malum regimen — bad or unskilful medical treatment. It may be pled as a defence to a charge of homicide when the victim of an assault dies following defective medical treatment.

malus animus — dole, or evil intention: the state of mind required to make conduct criminal in general or in relation to a particular crime. In English law, and now generally in Scotland, *mens rea*.

malversation — corrupt behaviour in an office of trust.

man of skill — an expert to whom a court may remit a matter before it for investigation and report.

mandant — a person who authorises another to act for him under a contract of **mandate** (qv).

mandatary. *See* **mandatory**.

mandate —
(1) *mandatum*: a contract whereby a person (the mandatory) is authorised by another (the mandant) to act gratuitously on his behalf, eg a power of attorney;
(2) the actual authority conferred under the contract of mandate.

mandatory —
(1) (n) or **mandatary** a person who is authorised to act under a contract of **mandate** (qv);
(2) (adj) describes a requirement which must be complied with (as contrasted with a merely directory requirement) or a statutory requirement which cannot be altered by a court.

mandatory requirements — certain fields of public interest the national regulation of which may create impediment to the free movement of goods within the European Community, but is permissible if the national rules are **indistinctly applicable** (qv) and they legitimately and proportionately serve those ends; including, for example, consumer protection, cultural protection, protection of the environment; also known as the rule of reason or the *Cassis de Dijon* rule. **[E]**

mandatum. *See* **mandate**.

manse — a dwellinghouse provided for a parish minister.

mansuetae naturae — of a tame nature. *See* ***domitae naturae***.

manu aliena — by the hand of another.

manu propria — by one's own hand.

march — a boundary, especially that between one farm or estate and another. The land on the border between Scotland and England was called 'marches'.

margin of appreciation — a central interpretive principle used by the **European Court of Human Rights** (qv) when interpreting the **European Convention on Human Rights** (qv). Because the Convention applies to many different states the ECtHR developed this doctrine to allow the domestic courts of each state a degree of discretion in interpreting Convention rights having regard to local needs and conditions.

mark —
(1) an old Scots coin: *see* **merk**;
(2) an old Scots weight;
(3) a cross or other sign by which deeds were formerly subscribed by those who were blind, but now incompetent as **notarial execution** (qv) is now provided for those who are thus disabled;
(4) to enter or give notice of an appeal in a litigation.

market power — in competition law the ability of a buyer or seller of particular goods or services to obtain a price that is lower or higher, as the case may be, than would be the case were the normal competitive forces to prevail.

market share — part of the total market for particular goods or services which is held by an **undertaking** (qv) or group of undertakings.

market sharing — the division of the market for particular goods or services between competing **undertakings** (qv); prohibited by competition law and, if dishonest, may constitute a **cartel offence** (qv).

marking — a system, abolished in 1933, by which the pursuer in an action raised in the Court of Session could select the Lord Ordinary to hear the cause or the Division of the Inner House to hear it on review.

maritime law — law governing shipping and the transport of goods by sea.

marriage —
(1) a contract entered into between a male and a female of marriageable age by which they become related to each other as husband and wife and acquire the legal status of married persons in a union dissoluble only by decree of divorce or by death;

(2) marriage is not merely a contract but a legal institution or status which carries with it certain legal consequences which are not alterable by contract;

(3) a marriage is either regular or irregular depending on its mode of constitution. *See also* **forbidden degrees**; **habit and repute**; **regular marriage**; **irregular marriage**.

marriage contract — an ante-nuptial or post-nuptial contract which regulates property rights to be enjoyed by the spouses and their issue. The English term 'marriage settlement' is sometimes substituted.

martial law — rule by the armed services of a country normally at the instance of its government in time of war or civil unrest or insurrection. No specific constitutional provision is made in the United Kingdom enabling the Government to introduce martial law by declaration or otherwise. Not to be confused with **military law** (qv).

Martinmas — a quarter day in Scotland (28 November: Term and Quarter Days (Scotland) Act 1990, s 1), a term day for the payment of rent, (the name is derived from St Martin's Mass).

master and servant — an obsolescent term for 'employer and employee'.

materiality — the importance or significance of some question, factor or particular which may be at issue in a dispute. For example, in the law of contract a material (ie significant) departure from one of the terms of the contract might entitle a party to resile or recover damages.

maternity rights — statutory rights which a woman employee has against her employer when she is absent from work wholly or partly because of her pregnancy or confinement.

matriculation —

(1) as an **intrant** (qv) is the submission of references and the presentation of a petition to the **Court of Session** (qv) as the first stage in qualifying as an **advocate** (qv);

(2) of arms – a grant of a coat of arms by the **Lord Lyon** (qv);

(3) the process of formally registering as a student at a university.

matrimonium ipsum — marriage itself. Consent at the time the marriage is constituted is essential to the contract. Consent or agreement to marry in the future does not constitute the contract, although such a promise, if followed by intercourse, might formerly have constituted an irregular marriage.

maxim — a phrase or sentence comprising a short, succinct statement of legal principle, and usually, in Scots law, derived from Roman law and expressed in Latin. It is sometimes called a **brocard** (qv).

measure — any legislative, judicial or administrative act adopted by a European **Community institution** (qv) or national authority. Where a **legal base** (qv) under which an institution acts authorises the adoption of 'measures', the institution may choose amongst the various types of Community legislation. **[E]**

measure having equivalent effect to a quantitative restriction (meqr) — :

(1) an encumbrance to trade which, whatever its form or description or the technique employed, has the same effect as a direct restraint, whether partial or total, on imports, exports or goods in transit;

(2) a trading rule adopted by a member state of the European Community which is capable of hindering intra-Community trade directly or indirectly, actually or potentially. **[E]**

measure of constraint — an act adopted by a judicial or administrative body in a member state of the European Community which constitutes an intervention in the sphere of interest of a Community institution. **[E]**

measure of instruction. *See* **preparatory inquiry**. **[E]**

media concludendi — the grounds of action; the basis on which the pursuer seeks a decree.

mediation — form of **ADR** (qv) in which a third party, called a mediator, assists parties, who are involved in a dispute, to settle it through negotiation but does not himself adjudicate in the dispute.

medio tempore — in the meantime.

meditatio fugae — the intention of absconding. A warrant in *meditatione fugae* by which a debtor intending to abscond abroad might be apprehended and imprisoned was formerly in frequent use but has been incompetent since 1880.

medium filum fluminis — the middle line of a river, which often forms the boundary between properties on opposite banks.

melior est conditio possidentis vel defendentis — the condition of a possessor or of a defender is better. Thus in a dispute the onus is on the challenger or pursuer.

meliorations — improvements to property made by a liferenter or tenant, the costs of which are irrecoverable from the fiar or landlord.

member states —
(1) generally, those states party to a treaty which founds an international organisation;
(2) the states party to the treaties establishing the European Communities and the European Union. In 2003 they consist of 15 member states, being the six **founding members** (qv) signatory to the original Community treaties (Belgium, Germany, France, Italy, Luxembourg and the Netherlands) plus other states which acceded subsequently: Denmark, Ireland and the United Kingdom (1973); Greece (1981); Spain and Portugal (1986); and Austria, Finland and Sweden (1995). Ten further states from central, eastern and southern Europe (the Czech Republic, Estonia, Cyprus, Latvia, Lithuania, Hungary, Malta, Poland, Slovakia and Slovenia) signed a **Treaty of Accession** (qv) in 2003 and are expected to accede in 2004. **[E]**

members — the member of a company are its shareholders.

members' club — a club the assets and property of which belong to the members. *See* **club**.

memorandum of association — a document subscribed by persons seeking the registration of a limited company, setting out the name, capital, objects and powers of the company. Cf **articles of association**.

memorial — a document, usually prepared for counsel by an instructing solicitor, setting out the relevant facts and circumstances and specifying the matters on which counsel's opinion is required.

mens rea — guilty purpose or criminal intent. Cf *actus non facit reum,* and *malus animus.*

mens testatoris in testamentis spectanda est — in the construction of a will the testator's intention is to be regarded. If the words of the will are clear, they will be held to express that intention. If there is doubt, his presumed intention derived from the rest of the will prevails as a construction.

mental disorder — means mental illness or **mental handicap** (qv) however caused or manifested: Mental Health (Scotland) Act 1984, s 1(2).

mental handicap — includes
(1) 'mental impairment' which means a state of arrested or incomplete development of mind not amounting to severe mental impairment but which includes *significant* impairment of intelligence and social functioning, and is associated with abnormally aggressive or seriously irresponsible conduct on the part of the person concerned; and
(2) 'severe mental impairment' which is defined in the same terms except that for 'significant' there is substituted 'severe'. See Mental Health (Scotland) Act 1984, s 1(2).

mental impairment. *See* **mental handicap**.

MEP — member of the **European Parliament** (qv).

meqr. *See* **measure having equivalent effect to a quantitative restriction**. **[E]**

mercantile law — slightly old fashioned expression for that branch of the law which is concerned with the legal principles and customs affecting business, commerce and trade. The term 'commercial' law is now more commonly used.

mercy — the royal prerogative of clemency whereby the sovereign might pardon a convicted offender or reprieve and commute a sentence imposed upon him.

merger — a transaction between two or more **undertakings** (qv) as a result of which either a new single undertaking is formed in their place or one or more of them transfers all or part of its business to the other or others.

Merger Regulation — a 1989 Council regulation (Regulation No 4064/89 of 21 December 1989) which provides for the administrative regulation of mergers and other concentrations within the European Community. **[E]**

Merger Treaty — a 1965 treaty, in force 1967, by which the three Councils created by the Community treaties were fused into a single Council and the ECSC High Authority and two remaining Commissions fused into a single Commission. **[E]**

merits — that part of a claim or defence which is concerned with the rights or wrongs or the essence of the dispute or litigation between parties, as distinct from technical or ancillary considerations.

merk *or* **mark** —
> (1) an old Scots coin of the value of thirteen shillings and four pence Scots (*see* pound Scots);
> (2) a measure in udal law.

messengers-at-arms — officers of court appointed by the Lord Lyon to serve and execute writs and warrants of the Court of Session and the High Court of Justiciary. They are also **sheriff officers** (qv) and as such discharge similar functions for the sheriff court.

messis sementem sequitur — the crop follows the sowing. The person who in good faith sows crops on land possessed by him is entitled to reap those crops.

metus causa — through fear. Deeds executed or contracts entered into through fear may be reduced.

midcouples — statutes, decrees or deeds used or referred to as links, tracing an entitlement to heritable property, in what is called a deduction of title.

migrant worker. *See* **worker**. **[E]**

Military law — the law regulating the armed forces of the Crown.

minerals — fossils, fuels and other materials below the surface of heritable property which pass with the conveyance of the heritage or which may be reserved. At common law gold and silver belong to the Crown, and by statute oil is vested in the Crown and coal in British Coal (formerly the National Coal Board).

minister —
> (1) a senior member of the government or the Scottish Executive, responsible for one or more government/executive departments;
> (2) an ordained clergyman in a protestant church.

minor — a person under the age of eighteen; or, more precisely, a person who had ceased to be a **pupil** (qv) but who had not reached the age of eighteen. A minor had legal personality but limited active legal capacity. See now the Age of Legal Capacity (Scotland) Act 1991, s 1.

minor agreement — also agreement of minor importance; in competition law, an anti-competitive agreement between **undertakings** (qv) which is not regarded as infringing the competition rules because of the low market shares of the parties to it and so its inconsequential effect on the market.

minority — the status of a **minor** (qv). When he reaches the age of eighteen he attains **majority** (qv).

minority and lesion. *See* **enorm lesion**.

minus solvit qui tardius solvit — he pays too little who pays late: the principle under which interest may be exigible in respect of a debt where due payment is delayed.

minute — a document which forms part of the **process** (qv) of a civil litigation. In it a party (or both parties jointly) may state a position on some aspect of the case or make a procedural application.

minute book —
> (1) a book containing in succinct form particulars of the acts and decrees pronounced by the Court of Session;
> (2) a book kept at the office of the **General Register of Sasines** (qv) containing brief particulars of details of deeds presented for registration.

minute of wakening. *See* **sleep**.

miscarriage of justice — a serious injustice in the course of a criminal trial which usually leads to the conviction being quashed.

misdirection — a mistake in law made by a judge in the course of his charge or directions to the jury.

misfeasance — the wrongful or unlawful performance of official duty: a term of English law often used now in Scotland in relation to company law.

misprision of treason — the crime of simply knowing, without any participation, of treason and failing to report it forthwith to the proper authorities.

misrepresentation — an untrue statement which is successfully designed to induce someone to enter into a contract. It may render the contract void or voidable and, if fraudulent or negligent, may found a claim for damages.

missives — in the sale of heritable property, the probative letters exchanged by the parties which constitute a binding contract and set forth its terms and conditions in detail.

misuse of powers — action by a Community institution ostensibly within its proper competence, but in fact for purposes other than for which the power was conferred; drawn from the French principle *détournement de pouvoir*; a ground for **annulment** (qv) of a Commnunity measure. **[E]**

Mitbestimmung — **worker(s') participation** (qv). **[E]**

mitigation — alleviation or amelioration. A plea in mitigation normally follows conviction at a criminal trial in an attempt to lessen the severity of the sentence to follow.

mixed agreement — an international agreement covering matters which fall partly within the competence of the European Community and partly within the competence of the member states. **[E]**

mixed legal system — comparative lawyers classify the world's legal systems into various 'families', eg civilian, common law, Islamic. Any system, which shows strong influences from more than one of these traditions, is known as a 'mixed legal system'. The term is most commonly used to refer to a system which is a mixture of civil and common law; Scots law is one such system.

mob — a group of persons acting together in riotous violence or intimidation for a common illegal purpose. *See* **mobbing**; **rioting**; **stouthrief**.

mobbing — the crime of participating in a **mob** (qv).

mobilia sequuntur personam — moveables follow the person. Moveable property is transferred or dealt with (eg in the law of sale or succession) in accordance with the personal law of its proprietor.

moderator — presiding officer a body, especially of the presbyteries and the **General Assembly of the Church of Scotland** (qv).

modify — to restrict eg expenses or a penalty.

modus — manner or method.

modus habilis — a competent method. *See* **habile modo**.

modus operandi — the method of operation or the manner of doing something.

modus tenendi — the manner of holding, eg the tenure by which land is held.

modus transferendi dominii — the actual form by which the transfer of the ownership of property is expressed and effected, as opposed to *titulus transferendi*, which is merely the will or intention to do so.

moiety — one of two equal parts or shares; more loosely, one of two or three not necessarily equal parts.

molestation —
  (1) an action of molestation is a **possessory action** (qv) now obsolete the object of which was to determine to which of two conterminous tenements a **part and pertinent** (qv) belongs in order to prevent the pursuer from being further molested in his possession of his lands;
  (2) personal molestation is a delict of modern origin by which a person is harassed, inconvenienced or annoyed by such acts as unsolicited telephone calls, home visits, threats of injury or harassment and the like. The usual remedy is interdict against continuation or repetition in the future.

monarch — a reigning king or queen, a hereditary head of state.

money laundering — methods by which criminals disguise the source of their illegal funds by passing the funds through legitimate businesses.

money of account — is the currency in which an obligation is measured. It tells the debtor how much he has to pay.

money of payment — is the currency in which an obligation is to be discharged. It tells the debtor by what means he is to pay.

monetary compensation amount — a subsidy or levy applied to intra-Community exports or imports of an **agricultural product** (qv) in order to compensate for divergences in the exchange rates of the currencies of the member states. **[E]**

moorburn. *See* **muirburn**.

Moorov doctrine — in the law of evidence, the rule which provides that where an accused is tried on two or more criminal charges alleging similar acts which are so connected in time, character and circumstances as to raise an inference that they are instances of a course of similar conduct systematically pursued by him, the evidence of a single witness in relation to one charge may be corroborated by the evidence of another single witness in relation to another. The rule was affirmed in *Moorov v HM Advocate* 1930 JC 68.

mora — delay.

mora **taciturnity and acquiescence** — a plea in litigation to the effect that delay now bars any entitlement to assert a claim or right.

morte legatarii perit legatum — a legacy lapses on the death of the legatee prior to the testator's death.

morte madatoris perit mandatum — a **mandate** (qv) falls on the death of the mandant.

mortgage — an English term for the grant of a loan secured on moveable or immoveable property, commonly now used in Scotland to describe a loan to assist in the purchase of heritable property and secured by a **standard security** (qv) over the property itself.

mortis causa — in contemplation of death. *See* **donation** *mortis causa*.

motion — an oral or written application to the court in the course of civil or criminal proceedings.

motion roll. *See* **rolls**.

Motor Insurers' Bureau — an institution established by insurance companies in agreement with the Department of Transport to satisfy established claims for damages in respect of losses arising from road traffic accidents which should by statute have been, but were not, insured against.

mournings — the reasonable expenses incurred by a widow on attire etc appropriate for mourning on the death of her husband, constituting a privileged debt, akin to funeral expenses, chargeable against the estate of the deceased.

moveable property; **moveables** — all property not classed as **heritage** (qv). Corporeal moveable property, such as furniture, vehicles and animals, can be handled or moved. Moveable property which has a legal but not actual physical existence, such as debts and company shares, is classed as incorporeal moveable property.

MSP — member of the **Scottish Parliament** (qv).

muirburn *or* **moorburn** — the burning of heath or moorland (including the heather or grass on it) which is subject to statutory regulation under the Hill Farming Act 1946. The exercise of the right is called 'making muirburn'.

multiplepoinding (pronounced 'multiplepinding') — an action in which the court is asked to adjudicate upon conflicting claims made to property or money (called the 'fund *in medio*') held by a person who is called either the 'real raiser' where he brings the action or the 'nominal raiser' where a claimant brings the action.

multures (pronounced 'mooters') — the proportion of grain formerly required to be given to the miller for grinding it. Dry multures were duties in grain or money paid whether grain was ground or not. *See* **thirlage**.

munus publicum — a public office, such as that of a judge, formerly held *ad vitam aut culpam* (qv), and involving duties to the public.

murder — the crime of homicide committed intentionally or with wicked disregard for the consequences of one's actions.

murmur — to defame a judge, whether in writing or orally, by imputing to him corruption, partiality, oppression or failure of duty in his office.

mutatis mutandis — changing that which has to be changed; making the necessary alterations. Thus a deed or writ which is used as a style in another similar situation will be adapted *mutatis mutandis*, the particulars special to the circumstances being appropriately altered.

mutual gable — a wall between two buildings and forming a gable to each. Each adjacent owner has a right of property in his own share of the wall and both have a common interest in the whole.

mutuality in contract — in the law of contract, the principle of mutuality arises in circumstances where a contract creates mutual (ie reciprocal) obligations. In the event of breach of contract, the contract-breaker is not entitled to enforce the innocent party's reciprocal counter-obligation; and the innocent party may suspend performance of that reciprocal counter-obligation for so long as the contract-breaker remains in breach of contract.

mutual settlement. *See* **mutual wills**.

mutual wills — where wills by two (or more) testators are contained in the same deed which is construed as being a mutual settlement, then the wills are treated as mutual with the effect that each testator is taken bound by the settlement not to alter his or her will without the other testator's consent, and in particular the surviving testator cannot alter his or her will after the death of the predeceasing testator.

mutuum — equal return: a species of loan; a contract under which **fungibles** (qv) are lent for consumption without payment on the basis that an equal amount of the same commodity will be returned to the lender by an agreed date.

n

name and arms clause — a clause in a deed by which a benefit under the deed is made conditional on the beneficiary assuming the grantor's name and arms.

names — members of a syndicate who authorise a syndicate member to underwrite insurance policies in their names.

narrative — the clause, usually the opening clause, in a deed which sets forth the names and designations of the parties, the consideration and, where appropriate, the circumstances giving rise to the deed.

nasciturus — yet to be born. Rights may be conferred by law or by **destination** (qv) on those to be born in the future.

national insurance — a state scheme of insurance which finances medical care and various social security benefits. National insurance contributions are paid into the scheme by employers as well as by workers.

national law —
(1) the domestic law of a member state as distinct from European Community and European Union law **[E]**;
(2) the domestic law of a state as distinct from international law.

natural justice — the equitable principles of fairness governing the conduct of a litigation, arbitration or hearing to determine an application or dispute. These include the principles that no man can be judge in his own cause, that each party is entitled to be heard and that justice be not only done but also be seen to be done.

natural law — the law written by the finger of God in men's hearts; a synonym for equity (qv) or the moral law; regarded by some as the basis of **positive law** (qv) and by others as its antithesis; a theory of justice emphasising the moral basis of positive law.

natural person — a human individual as contrasted with a juristic or legal **person** (qv).

natural possession — possession through an act of one's own (as distinct from **civil possession** (qv) ie possession through another's act).

naturalisation — the procedure of conferring nationality or citizenship of a country upon an alien of that country.

nautae, caupones, stabularii. *See* **edict nautae, caupones, stabularii**.

necessitate juris — by necessity of law; necessarily arising from the effect of the law.

negative burden — in the law of property a **real burden** (qv) which imposes an obligation to refrain from doing something. Contrast **affirmative real burden**. Title Conditions (Scotland) Act 2003.

negative clearance — a declaration by the European Commission that, on the basis of the facts in its possession, a particular agreement does not infringe the Community **competition rules** (qv). **[E]**

negative prescription. *See* **prescription**.

negative resolution — a method of imposing a measure of parliamentary control on **subordinate legislation** (qv) under which a **statutory instrument** (qv) is required to be laid before Parliament and is liable during a prescribed period to be annulled following (1) in the case of control by the United Kingdom Parliament, a resolution of either House of Parliament or in some cases a resolution of the House of Commons or (2) in the case of control by the Scottish Parliament, a resolution of the Parliament.

negative servitude. *See* **servitude**.

negligence — failure to exercise a duty required by law to show reasonable care to avoid loss or harm to the person or property of another. Cf **contributory negligence** and **delict**.

negotiable instrument — a document constituting evidence of the right to a sum of money, transferable simply by delivery or indorsement and delivery without the need for a formal transfer. An exception to the general rule that nobody can pass a better title than he himself has.. Examples include banknotes, cheques (unless marked 'not negotiable'), bills of exchange and promissory notes.

negotiorum gestio — the management of another's affairs. See *animus negotia aliena gerendi; negotiorum gestor*.

negotiorum gestor — the manager of another's affairs; a person who acts with reasonable care but gratuitously and without express authority on behalf of another (the *dominus negotii*) who is unable to act on his own account (eg through absence or incapacity). The *gestor* is entitled to be relieved of liability and expense reasonably incurred.

neighbour burden — a new non-statutory term for a **real burden** (qv) in which the **benefited property** (qv) is itself free from burden. Enforcement is therefore non-reciprocal in the sense that the owner of the benefited property can enforce against the owner of the **burdened property** (qv), but not vice versa. Compare **community burden**.

nemine contradicente — without a dissenter: describes a proposition accepted without contradiction; sometimes abbreviated '*nem con*'.

nemo contra factum suum venire potest — no one can go against his own act; having agreed to a course of action or maintained in pleading a particular position, one cannot do or maintain something different.

nemo dat quod non habet — no one can give what he has not got. One cannot acquire title from a person who is not the owner or his agent.

nemo debet bis vexari — no one ought to be troubled twice; one may not be called upon to answer a second time for the same offence, ie when one has '**tholed an assize**' (qv).

nemo debet esse judex in propria causa — a rule of natural justice that no one ought to be judge in his own cause.

nemo debet locupletari ex aliena jactura — no one should be enriched out of another's loss; the principle underlying the law of **unjustified enrichment** (qv).

nemo ex proprio dolo consequitur actionem — no one can pursue an action based on his own fraud or wrongdoing. *See ex dolo non oritur actio*.

*nemo judex in parte sua. See **nemo debet esse judex in propria causa.***

nemo patriam in qua natus est exuere nec ligeantiae debitum ejurare possit — no one may abandon his native country or forswear the obligation of allegiance, unless, of course, he become a national of another country.

nemo plus juris ad alium transferre potest quam ipse habet — no one can transfer to another a greater right than he has himself. Thus the *bona fide* purchaser of stolen property acquires no better right to it than the thief had.

nemo praesumitur malus — no one is presumed to be bad. This maxim embodies the principle of the presumption of innocence.

nemo tenetur ad impossibilia — no one is bound to perform impossibilities, ie an impossible contract is unenforceable.

nemo tenetur se ipsum accusare — no one can be forced to testify against themselves.

nervous shock — psychiatric illness caused by shock. Those (called primary victims) directly involved in an accident caused by negligence may be entitled to **reparation** (qv) for nervous shock. Others, such as relatives coming on the scene later, called secondary victims, have very limited rights to reparation.

next of kin — before 1964, relatives entitled at common law to succeed to moveables on the death of the owner. Strictly a spouse is not next of kin, and an ancestor is not necessarily so. The phrase is also used loosely in other contexts to mean a person's nearest relative or relatives, including a spouse.

nexus — bond, tie, fetter or connection. Thus an arrestment is said to create or attach a *nexus* to the property or fund arrested.

nihil agitur si quid agendum superest or *nihil perfectum est dum aliquid restat agendum* — nothing is done, or effectually performed, if anything still remains to be done.

nimious — excessive, as in the phrase 'nimious and oppressive'.

no case to answer — a submission which may be made on behalf of the accused at the close of the Crown case in a criminal trial to the effect that there is insufficient evidence in law at that stage to justify a conviction. If the submission is successful, the accused is there and then acquitted of that charge.

nobile officium — noble office or power. The High Court of Justiciary or the Court of Session may use this ultimate equitable power, as distinct from its *officium ordinarium*, within strict limits to modify the rigorous application of the common law or to give proper relief in a situation for which the law has made no provision.

nomen juris — legal term: any word having a particular technical legal meaning, eg 'heritage' and 'sale'.

nomen universitatis — the name of the whole together, a term describing a right which incorporates a variety of different or supplementary rights, eg a barony, which includes title to the land and also other related and subsidiary rights.

nomina debitorum — personal debts (literally, names of debtors).

nominal damages — a token sum of damages awarded by a court to mark the commission of a wrong suffered by a party who has not thereby suffered loss. Decree of **declarator** (qv) may be a more appropriate remedy. Nominal damages awards were invented by the English courts before they acquired power to grant declarations in 1854.

nominal raiser. See **multiplepoinding**.

nominate contract — a contract possessing a *nomen juris* (qv), such as sale, from which the legal rules and consequences are implied and readily understood. Innominate contracts, by contrast, are unusual agreements creating no rights and obligations other than those expressly agreed between the parties.

nominatim — by name, as when a testator expressly names beneficiaries rather than describing them as a class, eg grandchildren.

non bis idem — not the same thing twice. *See **nemo debet bis vexari**.*

non compos mentis — of unsound mind.

non constat — it does not hold; it may or must not be assumed from one fact, admitted or proved, that another fact is true. The phrase refers to unwarranted assumptions of fact. Cf *non sequitur*.

non-contributory pension — a pension paid for by the employer and not by the employee pensioners.

non decipitur qui scit se decepi — he is not deceived who knows that he is being deceived. One cannot plead fraud, deception or misrepresentation in seeking to reduce or avoid the consequences of a contract if one knew all along of the fraud, deception or misrepresentation.

non entia — things having no existence; nonentities. Thus documents which require by law to be stamped may not be looked at by the court.

non est factum — it is not his deed.

non exemplis sed legibus judicandum — things are to be judged not by examples but by laws. Thus disputes must be determined on principles of law, not on precedents based on particular instances.

non memini — I do not remember. Where a party to an action to whose oath the case has been referred swears '*non memini*', he is entitled to absolvitor unless what he says that he cannot remember is so recent that he is disbelieved and can, in those circumstances, be said to have confessed.

non obstante — notwithstanding; not opposing.

non officiendi luminibus vel prospectui — of not obstructing the lights or prospects; the servitude of light or prospect, a negative servitude which may be constituted only by express grant.

non remota sed proxima causa spectatur. *See causa proxima, et non remota, spectatur.*

non sequitur — it does not follow, ie it does not follow from an assumed state of fact or argument that a particular conclusion can be drawn. The phrase refers to an illogical inference. Cf *non constat*.

non utendo — by non-usage. Rights that may be acquired by long usage may similarly be lost by long non-usage. Cf *res merae facultatis*.

non valens agere — not able to act. Prior to 1924 if and whilst a person was not able legally to act by reason of minority or some other disability, prescription did not run against him.

non videntur qui errant consentire — those who are in error are not to be taken to consent. Thus voluntary obligations entered into in essential error may be rescinded.

nonage — the state of not being of full age, ie the state of being in **minority** (qv) or (formerly) **pupillarity** (qv). See now the Age of Legal Capacity (Scotland) Act 1991.

non-entitled spouse. *See* **entitled spouse**.

non-parentage — an action of declarator of non-parentage is an action to have it declared that a person is not or was not the parent, or is not or was not the child, of another person. Cf **parentage**

non-tariff barrier — a measure or practice, other than a customs tariff, which has the effect, whether direct or indirect, either of hindering the importation of goods or the sale of imported goods or of favouring the sale of domestic goods. **[E]**

not guilty —
  (1) a plea by a person accused of a criminal charge whereby he denies his guilt and requires the Crown to attempt to prove the charge at the trial;
  (2) a verdict of acquittal in a criminal trial which is appropriate where the judge or jury is satisfied of the innocence of the accused or where the Crown has failed to prove his guilt beyond reasonable doubt.

not proven — an alternative verdict of acquittal in a criminal trial, appropriate where the judge or jury is seriously suspicious but is not satisfied that the accused has been proved to have committed the alleged offence.

notarial execution — a procedure whereby a deed may be subscribed by a notary on behalf of a blind or illiterate person: see the Requirements of Writing (Scotland) Act 1995, s 9, Sch 3.

notarial instrument — any instrument drawn up and executed by a notary; more especially such an instrument, introduced in 1858, used and recorded for the purpose of infeftment where the direct recording of a conveyance itself was inconvenient, insufficient or impossible. It was superseded by the **notice of title** (qv).

notary public — a solicitor, admitted as a notary public by the Court of Session, before whom affidavits and other documents may be sworn.

note —
(1) an incidental application in the Inner House of the Court of Session or in certain proceedings in the sheriff court;
(2) a statement appended to an interlocutor in sheriff court proceedings setting out the grounds upon when the sheriff has proceeded.

notice —
(1) official document giving information; eg notice of appearance; notice of intention to defend;
(2) a type of legal deed or instrument eg **notice of title** (qv);
(3) a step in a legal procedure eg **notice to quit** (qv); **notice to admit** (qv) and notice of non-admission;
(4) knowledge of a fact whether actual or constructive (that is deemed or imputed by law);
(5) **judicial notice** (qv).

notice of title — an instrument superseding the **notarial instrument** (qv) setting out the right of a person to heritable property which, when recorded in the General Register of Sasines or registered in the Land Register of Scotland, completes the person's title to the property.

notice to admit — a notice by one party in a court action calling on another party to admit such facts averred in the pleadings or the authenticity of such documents as are specified in the notice. The recipient may respond by intimating a notice of non-admission.

notice to quit — a notice given by either party to a lease intimating an intention to bring the contract to an end.

notification — in EC competition law, the procedure whereby parties to a restrictive agreement or practice inform the European Commission of its detail in the hope of securing an **exemption** (qv) or **negative clearance** (qv). There is no legal obligation to notify such an agreement or practice, but notification is necessary if exemption is to be obtained (unless the agreement or practice falls within the terms of a **block exemption** (qv)). In May 2004 the competition rules are to change, abolishing the need for notification. **[E]**

notour bankruptcy — formerly a state of insolvency which had become 'notorious'. The circumstances in which the state arose were prescribed by statute. It was a prerequisite to the initiation of sequestration proceedings by creditors. It has been replaced by **apparent insolvency** (qv).

novatio non praesumitur — **novation** (qv) is not presumed: the new obligation must be shown to replace the old one completely, failing which it may be regarded as corroborative of the old or as constituting a separate and additional obligation.

novation — the extinction of a contractual obligation and its replacement by a new obligation with the consent of all the parties concerned. The parties remain the same. Contrast **assignation** (change of creditor) (qv) and **delegation of debt** (change of debtor) (qv).

Novels or *Novellae*, the — that part of the *Corpus Juris Civilis* (qv) which consists of compilations issued between 535 and 565 AD, of imperial legislation going back to the second century AD.

novodamus — we give of new: a charter by which a superior renewed a feudal grant of heritable property already made. It was granted in order to enlarge, alter, replace or correct the previous title.

novus actus interveniens — something new intervening: a fresh circumstance which may or may not break the connection between cause and effect or consequence.

nudum pactum — a mere paction; an unenforceable understanding or engagement.

nudus cum nuda in loco suspecto non paternoster dicere praesumuntur — an unclothed man and woman found together in a suspicious place are presumed not to be praying together: a presumption of consistorial law which is difficult to rebut even in modern conditions. *See also* ***solus cum sola in loco suspecti***.

nuisance — an act or omission at common law or under statute, usually connected with the occupation of heritable property, which causes annoyance, damage or inconvenience to others.

nulla crimen sine lege — no crime without law, ie the principle that behaviour should not be retrospectively criminalised.

nulla poena sine lege — no punishment without law, ie the principle that retroactive criminal punishments are forbidden.

nullity — non-existent, lacking legal force etc when used of ineffective acts or writs which are null and void. *See also* **nullity of marriage**.

nullity of marriage — an action for declarator, competent in the Court of Session. The contract of marriage is void when it has, from the start, suffered from an inherent defect such as the existence of a prior marriage, relationship within prohibited degrees or want of consent. Divorce, followed by habit and repute, may cure the first defect. The contract of marriage is voidable on grounds of impotency of either party.

numerus clausus — a closed number – the types of **real right** (qv) recognised by Scots law form a closed list. A creditor and debtor are not free to create new types of real right by agreement because real rights affect the rights of third parties and therefore their existence and nature must be publicly known. There is no 'freedom of property' akin to freedom of contract.

nunc – now; *ex nunc* from now; cf *tunc*.

nuncupative — oral, not written, especially of a legacy which, if proved by parole evidence, is valid in the case of moveables to a value of £100 Scots (£8:33p).

nuptias non concubitus sed consensus facit — consent, not cohabitation, constitutes a marriage.

O

oath — a solemn undertaking, with a formal reference to God, that what is asserted is in fact true or what is promised will be performed, used especially of the pledge made by a witness promising to speak the truth in giving evidence. A person without religious belief may solemnly affirm instead of taking an oath.

oath of allegiance — a promise to obey and uphold the authority of the lawful **sovereign** (qv); all MPs, MSPs, judges, advocates, members of the armed services, the police and certain other officials are required to take the oath of allegiance on being returned as a member. The form of the oath is set out in the Promissory Oaths Act 1868, and the corresponding affirmation, which may be taken instead, is set out in the Oaths Act 1978.

oath of calumny — an oath formerly required from the pursuer in a divorce action to the effect that his averments were true and that there had been no agreement to advance a false case or withhold a proper defence. The purpose was to prevent collusion.

oath on reference, *or* **reference to oath** — obsolete form of proceedings, derived from romano-canonical procedure and competent only in civil causes, under which a litigant was entitled to require his opponent to answer on oath questions as to the truth of his case or some specific part of it. Abolished by s 11 of the Requirements of Writing (Scotland) Act 1995.

ob contingentiam — on account of connection or similarity. *See* **contingency**.

ob majorem cautelam — for greater security or **caution** (qv).

ob non solutum canonem — on account of unpaid canon or feuduty. A ground of forfeiture in feudal tenure.

ob pias causas — on account of religious reasons or natural or dutiful considerations.

obediential — of an obligation or duty imposed by law rather than by contract.

obiter dictum — an incidental pronouncement; an opinion expressed by a judge, in giving judgment, on a point which is not essential to the decision. Cf *ratio decidendi*.

objection —
(1) in court a protest against the admissibility of a piece of evidence;
(2) in the **Scottish Parliament** (qv) a formal statement lodged by any person or body who considers that their interests would be adversely affected by a **Private Bill** (qv).

objection period — in the **Scottish Parliament** (qv) the period of (normally) 60 days from the introduction of a **Private Bill** (qv), during which objections to the Bill can be lodged.

obligant — the debtor or obligor bound by an obligation; the person who is liable to perform what has to be done. The creditor is the obligee.

obligation — a legal connection or relationship between two persons arising from unilateral promise, agreement, by force of law or by order of a court, whereby an obligee is endowed with enforceable rights and duties. The law of obligations, based primarily upon Roman concepts, forms a substantial branch of the modern law of Scotland. Its main divisions include obligations arising from unilateral promise, from contract, from delict, from rules to avoid unjustified enrichment, from fiduciary relationships, from the requirements of statute and from the judgments of courts.

obligationes literis — a contract which must be constituted in writing, eg one for the sale of heritable property. The common law category abolished: see now the Requirements of Writing (Scotland) Act 1995, ss 1(2), 11(3)(a).

obligee, obligor. *See* **obligant**.

obreption — obtaining gifts by telling falsehood. Cf **subreption** (qv).

observations — written or oral submissions made to the European Court of Justice where the party making them is not seeking a remedy or the vindication of a right. **[E]**

obtemper — to obey, comply with or fulfil, used especially of a court order.

occupancy *(occupatio)* *or* **occupation** —
(1) the physical possession and use of heritable property;
(2) the acquisition, with a view to appropriation, of things which have no owner, eg catching salmon or finding pearls.

occupier's liability — the duty of care required of the occupier of premises to those coming on to the premises. It is regulated by the Occupier's Liability (Scotland) Act 1960, which abolished the conceptual categories of invitee, licensee and trespasser introduced from England and applied to Scots law by the House of Lords in 1929.

odal tenure. *See* **udal tenure**. — Etymologically 'odal' is the more correct form, but 'udal' has been accepted generally by Scots lawyers and jurists and by custom.

OECD — Organisation for Economic Co-operation and Development.

offence — an act or omission which is contrary to and punishable by the criminal law. A crime. As a matter of usage acts and omissions prohibited by statute are generally termed 'offences', those offending against common law being called 'crimes', but usage varies. The expression 'criminal offence' also applies to statutory and common law offences.

offensive weapon — an article made or adapted or carried with the intention of using it for the purpose of causing injury to the person: see the Prevention of Crime Act 1953, s 1.

offer — a statement of terms which a party (the offeror) proposes to another party (the offeree) as the basis of a contract between them, coupled with a promise, express or implied, that the offeror will adhere to these terms if the offer is accepted. An offer contemplates the constitution of binding contractual obligations as from the moment when it is met by an unqualified acceptance. Cf **invitation to treat**.

Office for Harmonisation in the Internal Market (Trade Marks and Designs) (OHIM) — a European Community **agency** (qv), based in Alicante, competent to award **Community Trade Marks** (qv) and industrial designs. **[E]**

Office of Fair Trading — a body corporate acting on behalf of the Crown, responsible for consumer protection and competition law.

Office of the Public Guardian — senior official in the Scottish Court Service appointed to supervise and advise guardians or other authorised person in the exercise of their functions relating to the property and financial affairs of adults with incapacity

official. See court of the official.

official —
(1) a permanent employee of a state body or institution;
(2) within the **Community institutions** (qv) a permanent employee in an established post; **[E]**
(3) in pre-reformation Scotland a judge appointed by the bishop of a diocese to decide matters of canon law.

Official Journal — Official Journal of the European Union (formerly Official Journal of the European Communities), a daily publication in two 'series': the L series (for legislation), containing the texts of regulations, directives, decisions, recommendations, agreements and other measures adopted by the Community institutions; and the C series (for *communications*; in English, information and notices), containing daily Euro exchange rates, notices, drafts of proposed measures, particulars of cases brought before the European Court of Justice (with the operative part of the judgment or order) and other information. A Supplement (also known as the S series) contains notices of public contracts. **[E]**

Official print — The official archived copy of an **Act of the Scottish Parliament** (qv) signed by the **Clerk of the Parliament** (qv) after **Royal assent** (qv) and deposited in the National Archives of Scotland.

Official Report — the authoritative report of the proceedings of the **Scottish Parliament** (qv) (including committees and written answers).

officium nemini debet esse damnosum — an office should inflict damage upon no one. Thus nobody should incur loss in the discharge of an office or duty. A tutor, curator, mandatory and *negotiorum gestor* (qv) are all entitled to recover expenses reasonably incurred by them.

offshore — in the context of the exploitation of the United Kingdom's oil and gas reserves a colloquial term for the **UKCS** (qv).

offshore funds — collective investment funds that are based overseas, often in 'tax havens' or other locations with particular tax advantages.

Ofgem — the Office of the Gas and Electricity Markets, the state regulator of the gas and electricity industries in Great Britain.

OFT — *See* **Office of Fair Trading**.

Oftel — the Office of Telecommunications, the state regulator for the United Kingdom telecommunications industry, set up under the Telecommunications Act 1984.

OH. *See* **Outer House**.

OHIM — *See* **Office for Harmonisation in the Internal Market (Trade Marks and Designs)**.

OLAF — the **European Anti-Fraud Office** (qv). **[E]**

oligopoly — a market structure characterised by effective control, or dominance, of the market being shared out amongst a small number of **undertakings** (qv); also an oligopsony, which describes similar control on the demand side. **[E]**

ombudsman —
(1) the colloquial designation, derived from Scandinavian sources, of the Parliamentary Commissioner for Administration, the Commissioner for Local Administration in Scotland and the **Health Service Commissioner for Scotland** (qv) who, in their respective spheres, investigate complaints by citizens of bureaucratic maladministration, ineptitude or injustice;
(2) an official of the Community institutions; *see* **European Ombudsman. [E]**

omissa (vel male appretiata) — items which have been omitted from (or undervalued in) the inventory of the estate of the deceased in the confirmation of an executor. An additional confirmation *ad omissa (vel male appretiata)* or an **eik** (qv) to the original confirmation may require to be obtained.

omne majus continet in se minus — the greater includes the lesser.

omne verbum de ore fideli cadit in debitum — every word sincerely spoken will constitute an obligation: a rule of Canon law adopted by Scots law whereby verbal undertakings or promises given in earnest can constitute enforceable obligations.

omni exceptione major — beyond all exception, as of a witness whose status or character renders his evidence unimpeachable.

omnia praesumuntur contra spoliatorem — all things are presumed against a wrongdoer. The maxim has no application in criminal law but arises in civil litigation. Thus if one party hides or destroys a document the terms of which are in dispute, it will be presumed to have been in the terms alleged by the other party or, at least, in terms disadvantageous to the loser or destroyer.

omnia praesumuntur rite et solemniter acta esse (or omnia rite acta praesumuntur) — all things are presumed to have been solemnly done and with the usual ceremony: the rebuttable presumption of compliance with the appropriate formalities.

omnis definitio in jure periculosa est — all definition in law is dangerous. For a judge to define or limit the meaning or application of the law too nicely is dangerous, because he cannot foresee all the circumstances or cases to which the law may be applied and the inconvenience and injustice which might ensue.

omnis ratihabitio retrotrahitur et mandato priori aequiparatur — every ratification operates retrospectively and is equivalent to a prior authority. To ratify or **homologate** (qv) what has been done without authority has the same effect as if the act had been authorised at the time of its performance, in other words the homologation has retrospective effect.

onera realia — real burdens; encumbrances affecting heritable property and binding singular successors of the owner. Singular – **onus reale**.

oneris ferendi — bearing a weight or burden: an urban servitude by which the dominant proprietor may rest the weight of his building on the wall or property of the servient proprietor.

onerous — given for value, payment or services, as opposed to gratuitous.

onus probandi. *See* **onus of proof**.

onus of proof — the burden of proving each disputed issue of fact arising in a litigation. This rests upon one party or the other. If that burden is not discharged by the party on whom it rests, he usually fails on that issue. Procedural considerations and sometimes statute regulate the incidence of burden of proof, but it generally rests on the prosecutor or pursuer on the principle that he who asserts something must prove it.

ope et consilio — by aid and counsel; aiding and abetting; art and part.

ope exceptionis — by force of **exception** (qv); a plea by way of peremptory and preliminary objection in a civil cause that a document which is founded on, and which concerns the parties to the cause alone, should be set aside as null and void. It is particularly useful in the sheriff court where the alternative action of reduction is not competent.

open court — public court proceedings (cf **chambers**).

open doors — in the law of **diligence** (qv), a warrant to open doors authorises a messenger-at-arms or sheriff officer to open shut and lockfast places.

open exclusivity — the quality of an agreement, such as a licence or assignation of an industrial or commercial property right, by which one party agrees:
(1) to supply goods for resale in a particular geographical area to the other party and to no other person; and
(2) not to compete directly with the other party in that area; but where there is no agreement between the parties to prevent other persons from competing in the area in question. Cf **absolute exclusivity**. **[E]**

open record — a document comprising the written pleadings of the parties to a civil action, prepared at a stage when the pleadings are incomplete and capable of adjustment. Cf **closed record**.

operative part — the *dispositif*; that part of a judgment or order of the **European Court of Justice** (qv) or of the **Court of First Instance** (qv) which contains the decision. This part follows the part of the judgment or order which sets out the reasons given for the decision. **[E]**

OPG — **Office of the Public Guardian** (qv).

opinion —

(1) written expression of views, made by counsel or by another person learned in the law such as a law professor, on the law applicable, in a particular set of circumstances, (*see* **memorial**);

(2) a statement by a judge of the Court of Session or the House of Lords setting forth the reasons for his judgment;

(3) the reasoned submissions (in French, *conclusions*) made by an **Advocate–General** (qv) of the European Court of Justice to the Court prior to the judges reaching a decision in a case; **[E]**

(4) an advice (*avis*) given by the European Court of Justice, at the request of a Community institution or of a member state, on the compatibility with the EC Treaty of a proposed agreement between the Community and a third state, group of states or international organisation. **[E]**

(5) a measure adopted by a Community institution, which lacks binding force. **[E]**

opinion evidence — a form of evidence given by an expert and constituting his views, arising from his knowledge and experience, on some aspect of a litigation.

opinion of the court — a judgment agreed by all the judges of the court (such as a division of the Inner House of the Court of Session) and delivered by one of them speaking for all.

oppression — vindictiveness or disregard of the essentials of justice, formerly a ground of appeal against sentence in summary criminal proceedings.

option — a right to do or not to do something often within a specified time.

option to buy — a right to compel the owner of property to sell it on agreed terms to the holder of the option.

options hearing — a preliminary stage in a defended ordinary action in the sheriff court at which the sheriff seeks to secure the expeditious progress of the case by ascertaining from parties the matters in dispute and certain other information.

opus manufactum — artificial work, eg earthworks to prevent flooding, in contrast with what is natural.

OR. *See* **Official Report**.

Order in Council — an order made by the Queen in session with her **Privy Council** (qv), either by virtue of the royal prerogative or under statutory authority. Orders in Council are generally issued in the statutory instruments series.

order for reference — an order made by a court or tribunal in a member state of the European Community in the course of proceedings pending before it, sisting those proceedings before judgment and referring to the **European Court of Justice** (qv) one or more questions of Community law arising on which a decision is necessary to enable the national court or tribunal to give judgment. *See also* **preliminary ruling. [E]**

ordinary —

(1) a judge who exercises original jurisdiction to hear and determine causes;

(2) see **Lord Ordinary**;

(3) the sheriff is judge ordinary of the bounds.

ordinary cause or action — the main form of civil proceedings in the sheriff court, other than a summary cause, summary application, statutory application or other proceedings for which a special procedure is provided. Ordinary causes are regulated by the Ordinary Cause Rules.

origin principle — a system under which goods are taxed only in the country of production: the tax burden is the same whether the product is manufactured for domestic consumption or for export, and no tax is imposed on goods originating in another country which are imported into the country in question. **[E]**

original acquisition of property — one of the two main modes of acquiring ownership of property, the other mode being **derivative acquisition** (qv); applies where a title to property comes into being for the first time and also where the property has been subject to prior ownership but ownership is then acquired otherwise than by a transfer from the previous owner. The main modes of original acquisition are

occupation (qv); **accession** (qv); *specificatio* (qv); *confusio* and **commixtion** (qv); and **positive prescription** (qv).

ostensible — describes that which is apparent or seems to be so. Thus an agent may have ostensible authority, creating the impression that he has power to do something when in fact he may not have that power.

Outer House — that part of the Court of Session in which **Lords Ordinary** (qv), sitting alone, try cases at **first instance** (qv), so-called because the court was originally situated closer to the courthouse entrance than the **Inner House** (qv).

outward processing — a customs arrangement under which goods may be exported temporarily from the **customs territory** (qv) of the European Community for purposes of undergoing processing operations and, when re-imported, are valued for customs purposes only upon the basis of the value added. **[E]**

outwith — outside; beyond; away from.

overdraft — an unauthorised sum of money which has been withdrawn from a bank account by the customer, in these circumstances the account is said to be 'overdrawn' and the unauthorized sum is called the 'overdraft'.

overriding interest — a temporary or permanent restriction or other right over heritable property (eg a lease or servitude) which binds the proprietor whether or not it is recorded in the General Register of Sasines or registered in the Land Register of Scotland. See the Land Registration (Scotland) Act 1979, s 28(1).

overrule — to reverse or correct the decision of an inferior court in the same or in separate and later proceedings.

oversman — an umpire upon whom a decision in an arbitration is to devolve where the arbiters fail to reach agreement.

overt — open; public; not concealed.

own resources — the system initiated in 1970, whereby the financial resources of the European Community and subsequently European Union, derived from its own revenue (agricultural levies, CCT duties, a portion of VAT and payments derived from rates of national GNP) and not from contributions made by the member states. **[E]**

p

PC —
(1) Privy Council;
(2) Privy Counsellor;
(3) police constable;
(4) personal computer.

P&I Club — Protection and Indemnity Club. An association of ship owners to provide insurance to their cargo, crew, as well as spill/pollution matters etc.

pacta dant legem contractui — the stipulations of the parties constitute the law of the contract. These stipulations may differ from the common law or statute, but will be enforced if not illegal or immoral.

pacta sunt servanda — agreements should be kept; a basic principle of contract law.

paction — an agreement or bargain.

pactum — a bargain, agreement or paction.

pactum de non petendo — an agreement not to seek; an agreement, absolute or temporary, not to require performance of an obligation.

pactum de quota litis — an agreement for a share of the subject of a law suit. Such an agreement by a lawyer for a 'contingency fee', ie to accept a share of what may be recovered by legal action in place of a fee, is illegal and void in Scotland but is permitted in certain foreign jurisdictions.

pactum de retrovendendo — an agreement to sell back. The most common modern example is an agreement that a seller of heritable property is to have a right of pre-emption upon any resale.

pactum donationis — an agreement to give in donation. It creates a *jus ad rem* or personal obligation on which the donee may sue the donor for performance or for damages for breach of the agreement.

pactum illicitum — an illegal contract or agreement. *See* **illegality**.

palinode — the remedy of judicial recantation of defamatory words which was competent in actions of defamation in the Commissary Courts but fell into disuse in the early nineteenth century after the abolition of those courts and the transfer of their jurisdiction in defamation to the Court of Session and sheriff court.

panel, pannel — a person appearing in court upon an indictment charged with a crime or offence.

Pandects — another name for the *Digest* (qv) in the *Corpus Juris Civilis* (qv) of Justinian.

par in parem non habet imperium — an equal has no power over an equal. Thus a judge is not bound to follow or regard as a precedent the decision of another judge of equal jurisdiction and, conversely, the one has no power to review or alter the decision of the other.

parallel import — goods imported into a member state of the European Community other than through a distribution system set up by the manufacturer or an authorised distributor. **[E]**

paraphernalia — an obsolete term for a woman's personal possessions, including her clothes and jewellery, which remained her property notwithstanding marriage and never became her husband's property.

pardon — the withdrawal by the Sovereign of a criminal sentence or punishment; a bar to prosecution or punishment.

parentage — an action of declarator of parentage is an action to have it declared that a person is or was the parent, or is or was the child, of another person.

parental responsibilities — legal responsibilities of parents to their children, including the responsibility to safeguard and promote a child's health, development and welfare; to provide appropriate direction and guidance; to act as the child's legal representative; and, if not living with the child, to maintain personal relations and direct contact on a regular basis. See Children (Scotland) Act 1995, s 1.

parental responsibilities order — sheriff court order transferring parental responsibilities to a local authority.

parental rights — the right of a parent over a child to decide such matters as the child's residence, education and upbringing and to act as the child's legal representative, see Children (Scotland) Act 1995, s 2.

pari passu — a form of the ranking of the general body of the unsecured creditors of an insolvent debtor on a common fund for example in a **multiplepoinding** (qv), or **sequestration** (qv) or the like whereby the creditors rank rateably in proportion to the amounts of their debts.

parking offence — a criminal offence relating to the parking of a motor vehicle.

Parliament —
(1) generally an assembly of representatives of the citizens of a state with the power to make law by means of statutes and which also scrutinizes the actions of the executive and representation of people and their interests;
(2) the United Kingdom parliament created by the **Treaty of Union** 1707 (qv), see the **Queen-in-Parliament** (qv);
(3) the **Scottish Parliament** (qv) created by the **Scotland Act** (qv);
(4) the **European Parliament** (qv).

Parliament House — the building in Edinburgh comprising the Court of Session, the High Court of Justiciary and their attendant offices. It also contains the hall where the Parliament of Scotland sat until the Union of 1707.

Parliamentary Commissioner for Administration — an officer, popularly called the 'ombudsman', who investigates complaints of injustice arising from alleged maladministration by government departments.

Parliamentary papers — papers published by the authority of either House of Parliament.

parole —
(1) the conditional release of a prisoner before he had served his full sentence;
(2) spoken, as opposed to written evidence.

Parole Board for Scotland — statutory body which advises the Scottish Executive on prisoners' suitability for **parole** (qv).

parole evidence — oral evidence given *viva voce* by witnesses, as distinct from real or documentary evidence.

parricide — the murder of a parent by his or her child.

pars contractus — part of the contract. If it is agreed that a contract should be reduced to writing, that agreement being *pars contractus*, the contract does not become binding until that is done.

pars judicis — the part or duty of the judge; that which a judge must notice and act upon, irrespective of the wishes of the parties, eg his duty to dismiss proceedings which it is not competent for him to determine.

parte inaudita — one party being unheard, as of an *ex parte* (qv) application in court, eg for interim interdict, or a decree pronounced *in absentia*.

partial loss — in marine insurance ; the damage to the thing insured is less than an actual or constructive total loss.

particeps criminis — partner in crime; accomplice.

particeps fraudis — partner in fraud.

partner — a person carrying on a business in common with another or others with a view to profit.

partnership —
(1) a contract between two or more persons made for the purpose of carrying on a business in common with a view to profit;
(2) a firm comprising partners.
See **limited partnership**; **limited liability partnership**.

partnership and cooperation agreement — a type of association agreement between the European Community and several of the former republics of the Soviet Union. **[E]**

parts and pertinents — everything which passes with the actual land on its transfer or disposition, eg minerals, servitudes and fishing rights.

partus sequitur ventrem — the offspring follows the mother — a rule of natural accession whereby the young of animals belong to the owner of the mother at the time of their birth.

party — any legal actor; may be used of both **natural persons** (qv) and **legal persons** (qv), especially in the context of **litigation** (qv) or participation in a **contract** (qv).

party litigant — a litigant in civil proceedings who conducts his own case.

passing off — an actionable wrong comprising the misrepresentation of a business or goods with the purpose or effect of misleading the public into thinking that the business or the goods are those of another.

pasturage — a servitude entitling the dominant proprietor to graze his cattle, sheep and horses on the servient tenement.

patent — a monopoly right or exclusive privilege over an invention granted for a specified period by letters patent by the Crown through the Patent Office, an executive agency of a government department. Patents are now regulated by statute. The **European Patent Office** (qv) in Munich can grant patents which are valid throughout all or part of the territory of the contracting parties to the **European Patent Convention** (qv).

patent ambiguity — an ambiguity in a document which is obvious to anyone looking at the document.

pater est quem nuptiae demonstrant — he is the father whom the marriage indicates to be so. Thus children born to a married woman are rebuttably presumed to have been fathered by her husband.

patria potestas — paternal power; the power which a parent has as guardian of a child.

patrial — in immigration law, a person lacking full citizenship who by virtue of blood-line has the right of abode in the United Kingdom.

patriality — the status adhering to a **patrial** (qv).

patrimonial — pertaining to one's patrimony in the broadest sense of one's economic estate or property.

patrimonial loss — strictly, loss sustained by one's estate, now a term of art in reparation claims for the loss of money or any property which can be assessed in monetary terms, as distinct from pain and suffering arising from physical injury or injury to feelings.

patrimony —
(1) an estate or property inherited from an ancestor;
(2) a person's whole estate or property.

pawn — to deliver an article of moveable property to another as security for a debt or other obligation. Cf **pledge**. At common law 'pawn' and 'pledge' were synonymous.

PAYE — Pay As You Earn, a form of income tax calculation and collection used for employees.

peer —
(1) an equal;
(2) a member of the nobility (Duke, Marquis, Earl, Viscount or Baron); a peerage may be hereditary or for life only. The House of Lords Act 1999 abolished the right of hereditary peers to sit in the House of Lords but gives the hereditary peers the right to elect 90 of their number to sit in the Lords.

peerage — the collective body of **peers** (qv).

penal — of punishment; attracting punishment as a penalty; punitive.

penal damages — punitive or exemplary damages. Such damages by way of reparation are not recoverable in Scotland.

pendente lite — during the dependence of a litigation; so long as an action is pending before the court.

pendicle — a small piece of land, subsidiary to a larger estate, or something attached to another thing. In older conveyancing practice the phrase 'parts, pendicles and pertinents' was sometimes used. *See* **parts and pertinents**.

pension — income from the state (retirement pension) payable on reaching the state retirement age or payable by a company or personal occupational pension scheme.

penuria testium — scarcity of witnesses. Formerly this justified calling as witnesses those otherwise disqualified because of relationship or interest.

per aversionem — by bulk or aggregate quantity, as of the sale of a particular unquantified crop or cellarful of wine.

per capita — by heads. In succession, where an estate is to be divided among beneficiaries (eg grandchildren) *per capita*, it is divided equally among them, and the right of representation (eg of their parents) *per stirpes* (qv) is excluded.

per curiam — by the whole court; a term of English law referring to a dictum expressed unanimously by judges participating in a decision.

per incuriam — through mistake or error, describing eg a judgment delivered in ignorance of a decisive precedent or statutory provision.

per modum exceptionis — by way of exception: a defence admitting the relevancy of a claim, but denying the conclusion on grounds eg of force or fear.

per se — by itself or by himself or herself.

per stirpes — according to the stems or stocks (*stirpes*) of the family instead of *per capita* among individual members of the family. In succession, where the estate is to be divided among beneficiaries *per stirpes*, it is not just the survivors who benefit; the share of a predeceasing beneficiary is divided among his children or remoter issue. Called succession by right of representation. Cf *per capita*.

per subsequens matrimonium — by subsequent marriage. Children born out of wedlock are legitimated by their parents' subsequent marriage.

perceptio — a gathering in. A person in possession of land in good faith who gathers in the fruits of that land thereby becomes their owner. If the land really belongs to another, ungathered fruits *(fructus pendentes)* remain the property of the true owner.

peremptory —
(1) admitting no denial, absolutely fixed, as of a **diet** (qv) at which the case must proceed;
(2) a peremptory defence enters into the merits of the cause and either takes away the pursuer's ground of action or extinguishes its effects; examples are the defences of payment; **set-off** (qv); and *res judicata* (qv). Contrast **preliminary plea**.

perficere susceptum munus — to perform the duties of an office undertaken. Anyone who undertakes an office or duty must perform the obligations thereby incumbent upon him and, until he has done so, he may not capriciously resign.

performance bond — a bond giving security for the performance of a contractual or other legal obligation.

performers' rights — the rights of performers, such as musicians, in the live performance of their works entitling them to prevent recording or broadcasting without consent.

periculo petentis — at the risk of the petitioner. All judicial warrants obtained *ex parte* (qv) are granted at this risk. Thus if the operation of an interim interdict, obtained groundlessly, causes loss, the petitioner will be liable in damages.

periculum rei venditae nondum traditae est emptoris — the risk of a subject sold, but not yet delivered, lies with the purchaser. This rule of the common law was an exception to the general rule *res perit suo domino* (qv). Since the Sale of Goods Act 1893, s 20 (now the Sale of Goods Act 1979, s 20), the risk normally transfers to the buyer when the 'property' in the goods passes, whether or not the goods have been delivered.

periodical allowance — a regular maintenance payment ordered by the court in its discretion and payable by one spouse to another following their divorce. It is technically distinct from aliment which is an obligation arising between spouses during their marriage.

perjury — a common law crime committed by a person who, under oath or affirmation, wilfully gives evidence in judicial proceedings which he knows to be untrue.

permanent trustee — an **insolvency practitioner** (qv) elected by the creditors or appointed by the court to administer a **sequestration** (qv). Cf **interim trustee**.

perpetual interdict — an interdict (sometimes called permanent interdict) contained in a final decree and intended to regulate the rights of parties on a permanent basis as opposed to an interim interdict granted by the court as a temporary, provisional and protective measure.

perpetual succession — doctrine that a limited company does not die but continues to exist until its name is struck off the register of companies or it is dissolved through a winding up or liquidation even if there are no directors, members or employees.

person — the law recognises two types of person: the natural (a human being) and the juristic or artificial person (corporation); only persons may hold and exercise **rights** (qv).

personal bar — the rule precluding a person from maintaining that which he has previously denied.

personal bond — a written undertaking, without security, to pay a debt or perform an obligation.

personal estate, personal property or personalty — English legal term for moveable property.

personal real burden — a real burden in favour of a person. Compare **praedial real burden** (qv). In a personal real burden there is a **burdened property** but no **benefited property**. Eight types are recognised by the Title Conditions (Scotland) Act 2003, including a **conservation burden** (qv) and an **economic development burden** (qv).

personal right. *See jus in personam.*

personation — pretending to be somebody else. Personation of a policeman, or of a voter at an election, is criminal under statute. If fraudulently undertaken, personation is criminal at common law.

pertinents. *See* **parts and pertinents**.

perverse verdict —
- (1) a verdict where the jury has deliberately declined to obey the judge's direction on a matter of law;
- (2) loosely, a verdict which, in the judge's opinion, flies in the face of common sense.

perverting the course of justice — a common phrase used in formal charges to describe the purport of a number of common law crimes involving interference with witnesses, fabrication of evidence, escaping from custody and the like.

petition —
- (1) a special or 'extraordinary' form of civil proceedings in the Court of Session (in which the originating writ is itself called a petition). The element unifying petitions is that the subject matter is deemed inappropriate for the normal form of process namely an action commenced by summons. Petition procedure is less closely regulated by rules of court and more at the discretion of the court than procedure in an action. Often a petition is non-contentious and lacks a proper contradictor. It is often unsuitable for enforcing rights and its distinctive functions are to request the court in its discretion to grant authority for the petitioner to do some act which he could not otherwise do; or to order another to do some act which the petitioner cannot himself require that person to do. Petitions may also request the remedy of suspension or interdict. The equivalent form of process in the sheriff court is a summary application;
- (2) loosely, an application to a court;
- (3) to present a petition to the court;
- (4) the tabling of a request or a grievance by a citizen or group of citizens before the United Kingdom, Scottish or European parliaments.

petition and complaint — an application to the Court of Session, made with the concurrence of the Lord Advocate, for the exercise of the court's criminal or quasi-criminal jurisdiction. In the Inner House such an application is appropriate for **malversation** (qv), misconduct or neglect of duty by a judicial officer, and in the Outer House for breach of interdict or contempt of court.

petitioner — a person who presents a petition to the court.

petitory action — an action in which the court is asked to order the defender to do something to fulfil an obligation to the pursuer, eg to pay a debt, or to abstain from doing a prohibited act.

Phare — EU aid programme for states in central and eastern Europe launched in 1989 following the collapse of the communist regimes in those states. **[E]**

PICC — Permanent International Criminal Court, alternative name for the **International Criminal Court** (qv).

picketing — attendance by employees, trade union representatives and others near a place of work for the purpose of persuading other employees to cease working in furtherance of a trade dispute. They may have immunity from civil legal action for inducing others to break contracts. Secondary picketing is directed at the premises of another employer (such as a supplier or customer of the employer involved in the dispute) who is not an immediate party to the trade dispute. It is not normally covered by immunity.

pignus — a pledge; the contract of pledge.

pillars of the European Union — the three so-called 'pillars' which comprise the constitutional structure of the European Union; *see* **European Union**. **[E]**

PIN — personal identification number.

plaintiff — former English law term for a person raising an action (equivalent to the Scots 'pursuer') replaced from the 26th April 1999 by the term 'claimant'.

plagium — the crime of stealing a human being. In modern practice it is restricted to child stealing.

PLC — public limited company.

plea in bar of trial — a plea in criminal proceedings that the trial cannot proceed for want of jurisdiction or because the accused is insane.

plea in mitigation — a plea made to the judge before sentence by or on behalf of a convicted person seeking to show cause why a lenient sentence should be imposed.

plea of illegality — also the 'exception' or 'objection' of illegality (*exception d'illégalité*); in an action before the **European Court of Justice** (qv) or the **Court of First Instance** (qv), an ancillary plea that a decision competently challenged by the pursuer should be annulled because the general measure from which it derives its legal authority is invalid. **[E]**

plea of irrelevancy — a defence that an action is not **relevant** (qv).

plead —
(1) to present and argue a case in court;
(2) to present a case in writing.

pleadings — the formal written presentation of his case in court by a party to a civil action.

pleas-in-law — in civil procedure concise legal propositions which link the factual grounds of action or of defences with the remedy sought and by which the pursuer and the defender conclude their written pleadings and upon which they found their respective cases. Peremptory pleas-in-law are directed to the merits of the case and preliminary pleas-in-law raise issues which require to be disposed of before the merits are considered. Pleas-in-law are always required in actions in the Court of Session or in all sheriff court initial writs including summary applications; and in petitions for judicial review. They may be required by the judge in Court of Session petitions especially if opposed.

pleas of the Crown — the crimes of murder, robbery, rape and willful fireraising reserved to the High Court of Justiciary. Formerly all four offences were capital offences, the concept now has no practical significance.

plenary session — a sitting of the **European Court of Justice** (qv) which includes all the judges, the quorum being eleven judges (the '*petit plenum*'). **[E]**

pled — pleaded.

pledge —
(1) an item of moveable property delivered as security for an obligation, usually a debt;
(2) the contract (*pignus*) constituted by delivery of such property;
(3) to deliver moveable property as a pledge.
Cf **pawn**. At common law 'pledge' and 'pawn' were synonymous.

plenishing — furniture, equipment, stock or gear; moveable property brought on or into heritable property, especially to furnish it.

pleno jure — with full right. The transfer of property *pleno jure* carries the property with all the profits or advantages pertaining to it.

plenum dominium — the full right of property, including both the *dominium directum* and the *dominium utile* (qv). See also **allodial**; **feu**; **feudal tenure**.

pluris petitio — a claim for more than is due. Such a claim may affect expenses. To seek a larger random sum of damages than that which is ultimately awarded is not *pluris petitio*.

plus enim valet quod agitur, quam quod simulare concipitur — that which is done is of more avail than that which is pretended to be done. The law will have regard to the real character of a transaction rather than the form in which it was effected. Thus a debtor is entitled to insist upon a reconveyance of property conveyed by an *ex facie* absolute disposition when it was truly granted in security.

plus petendo tempore — where a creditor sues for a debt prematurely, he is seeking it *plus petendo tempore*. He renders himself liable to pay the expenses of defending his claim.

plus quam tolerabile — more than can reasonably be endured. The phrase is used eg:
(1) as of extraordinary damage to crops or temporary partial damage to subjects let which might entitle a tenant to some abatement of rent, or
(2) to describe the degree of interference with rights of property (eg noise) which constitutes an actionable nuisance.

poaching — the crime of taking game or fish without legal right or authority.

poind (pronounced 'pind') — an older form of diligence used to impound a debtor's corporeal moveables in his own hands in execution of diligence as a preliminary to a warrant sale or adjudment to the creditor in satisfaction of a decree. Now abolished and replaced by **attachment** (qv).

poinding the ground — a form of diligence available to heritable creditors whereby moveables on the land over which the debt is secured are impounded as a preliminary to their public sale in satisfaction of the creditor's decree.

police —
(1) the body of officers responsible for the enforcement of law and order in a particular defined area;
(2) an obsolete term for the civil domestic administration of the country and for the municipal regulations on such matters as watching, lighting, cleansing, abatement of nuisances, public health and punishing minor delinquencies within burghs.

Police and Judicial Cooperation in Criminal Matters — originally 'Justice and Home Affairs', and still indicated by the shorthand JHA, provision for the adoption by the member states of the European Union of common action in the field of police and judicial cooperation in order to prevent and combat serious crime, organised and otherwise, and particularly terrorism; created and governed by Title VI of the Treaty on European Union. **[E]**

policies — enclosed grounds of a substantial residence; park.

policy of insurance — a document which contains all the terms and conditions of an insurance contract together with details of the perils covered and excluded.

pollicitation — from the *pollicitatio* of Roman law; a (unilateral) **promise** (qv).

political groups — the transnational groupings in which members of the European Parliament sit. **[E]**

pondere, numero et mensura — by weight, number and measure. The tests apply to ascertain whether goods are **fungibles** (qv).

poor's roll — the roll of litigants who, by reason of poverty and having *probabilis causa litigandi* (qv), were formerly entitled to sue or defend *in forma pauperis* (qv). The legal profession provided counsel and solicitors who were prepared to act in such circumstances without fee. The roll has now been superseded by the provision of legal aid in civil and criminal causes.

Porteous Clerk — an officer who formerly travelled from place to place to hear evidence of crimes.

Porteous Roll — a list of offenders' names and file of indictments in early criminal procedure.

portio legitima — legal portion; **legitim** (qv).

positive law — laws enacted by appropriate authority, ie by **statute** (qv) or **precedent** (qv).

positive prescription. *See* **prescription**.

positive servitude. *See* **servitude**.

positivism — belief that only positive law is real law and that morals should be kept strictly separate from law; is the opposing school to that of **natural law** (qv).

posse comitatus — the power or force of the county; the police or officers of court whom the sheriff has a right to require to assist in the enforcement of court orders.

possessio bona fide — possession in good faith in the belief that the possessor is entitled to possession and knows of no other person with a better right. Such possession carries the right to the fruits of the property which the possessor has gathered.

possessio mala fide — possession in bad faith, in the belief that another is the true proprietor. A person possessing property in bad faith is liable to that other person for all the fruits of the property and for **violent profits** (qv).

possession — physically detaining a corporeal moveable or physically occupying heritable property with the intention of keeping it as one's own property or for one's own use. *See also* **animus possidendi**; **civil possession**; **detention**; **natural possession**.

possessory action —
(1) an action (eg for delivery, interdict or removing) to retain or recover possession of property which another has wrongfully claimed or acquired;

(2) an action to recover lost possession raised by a dispossessed bare possessor (whether or not he has title to possess) against the dispossessor who may even be the true owner. In such an action the point of right is not directly concerned but only restoration of the pursuer's previous bare possession.

See **detention**; *jus possessionis*; **spuilzie**.

post hoc ergo propter hoc — after this therefore because of this: illogically ascribing the cause of a result to an event simply because the event preceded the result.

post litem motam — after an action has been raised. The subject of a pending litigation cannot effectively be altered to the detriment of either party.

post tantum temporis — after so long a time.

posteriora derogant prioribus — later enactments repeal earlier ones. Even if it is not expressly stated therein (though it usually is), a provision in an Act of Parliament inconsistent with or opposed to a provision in an earlier Act operates to repeal it.

postponed debt — a debt which is payable in a sequestration only after all other claims have been satisfied, eg a loan made by the debtor's spouse or partner.

potior est conditio possidentis vel defendentis — the condition of a possessor is stronger. *See melior est conditio possidentis vel defendentis*.

pound Scots — the unit of Scots currency in general use in Scotland before and for some time after the Union of 1707. Its value was one-twelfth of a pound sterling; thus one pound Scots was worth one shilling and eightpence sterling (in decimal currency 8.5p). The pound Scots was divided into twenty shillings Scots, each of which was divided into twelve pence Scots. Six pence were one bawbee. See also **merk**.

power of appointment (*or* **apportionment**) — an authority conferred by deed or will to a person to distribute or divide the property of the grantor or testator, usually in accordance with general guidelines prescribed in the deed or will.

power of attorney — a deed conferring authority granted by one person to another (called the 'attorney' or 'factor') to act on his behalf. Originally a term of English law, it is now widely used in Scotland instead of the Scots term 'factory and commission'.

practicks — (1) the earliest practicks were collections of notes on decisions of the Court of Session formerly compiled by members of the court. Sometimes called 'decision practicks' they were the precursers of the law reports, and were originally recorded chronologically. (2) Some of the later practicks (now called 'digest practicks') contained also abstracts of statutes and other sources as well as notes of decisions and were arranged under subject headings as digests of Scots law.

praeceptio haereditatis — taking an inheritance in advance. To avoid the possibility of an heir otherwise entitled to succeed receiving his inheritance from the testator gratuitously before the testator died, thus avoiding responsibility for the testator's debts, the law describes the heir's title to the property as a 'passive' title incurring liability for the debts unless the heir can prove that the transfer was onerous.

praecipuum — taken before others; that part of a testator's estate which is not subject to division and so formerly passed to the eldest of heirs-portioners, eg titles of honour and the mansion house of the estate.

praedial — affecting land, especially of servitudes.

praedial real burden — a non-statutory term for a real burden on one plot of land in favour of another plot of land (or *praedium*) (qv). So a praedial real burden requires a benefited property as well as a burdened property. After 28 November 2004 most real burdens are praedial (under the Title Conditions (Scotland) Act 2003, s 1(1)) but a new category of **personal real burden** (qv) is also introduced.

praedium — land; heritable property.

praepositura — the power conferred by a principal upon an agent or servant to execute the principal's business and thereby bind him; the presumption that a wife was placed by her husband in charge of the household, so that he was liable for contracts entered into by her within the scope of her ostensible authority. That presumption was abolished in 1984. Ordinary principles of agency are now considered to suffice.

praepositus negotiis — entrusted with the charge of certain affairs, ie vested with the *praepositura* (qv). The principal is liable for obligations thus incurred.

praepositus negotiis societatis — placed over the affairs of business of the partnership. The contract of partnership implies that each party is entrusted with the partnership business and may thus bind the firm.

praescriptio longissimi temporis — the prescription of the longest period. The period of forty years during which certain rights were either acquired or extinguished was reduced to twenty in 1973.

praeses or **preses** — the elected chairman of a meeting, especially a meeting of creditors.

praesumendum est pro libertate — the presumption is in favour of liberty. There is such a presumption against any restrictions upon the full and unrestrained enjoyment of property, and servitudes are thus strictly construed.

praesumitur pro legitimatione — the presumption is in favour of legitimacy. Thus all children born in wedlock are presumed to be the children of the spouses.

praesumptio hominis vel judicis — the presumption of the man or judge, the judge's opinion arising from the circumstances of the particular case laid before him.

praesumptio juris — a legal presumption which may be rebutted. Thus ownership of moveables is presumed from possession, and debtors are presumed not to make gifts to creditors.

praesumptio juris et de jure — a legal presumption amounting to a legal rule, which may not be rebutted.

praesumptione — by presumption; according to the *praesumptio juris* (qv).

precarium — a form of the contract of **commodatum** (qv) where the subject is lent not for a particular time or occasion but indefinitely, and is returnable at the will of the lender.

precatory — praying; describes words in a will which pray or express the desire that a thing be done, without positively directing it. Whether their effect is precatory or mandatory is a question of construction.

precedent —
(1) a court decision regarded as authoritative in deciding later cases;
(2) an English term for a style or model form of a legal document used as a pattern or in drafting other documents.
See also **condition**.

precept — a warrant or order.

precognition — a preliminary written statement of the evidence which a witness may be expected to give. It is usually paraphrased after interview with the witness and prepared in the first person. It is not signed, and is not binding.

predatory pricing — selling goods or services at less than their real value in order to drive competitors from the market; prohibited by competition law.

pre-emption — a right to buy before another has the opportunity to do so.

preferred debt — a debt which is payable on bankruptcy, or the winding-up of a company, before other debts (eg taxes, social security contributions and employees' wages).

preliminary plea — a **plea in law** (qv) by either party in a civil action that is purely technical and does not go to the merits but which, if sustained, results in the dismissal of the action or its defence. Examples are pleas that the pursuer has no title to sue, that the court has no jurisdiction to hear the case, that the action is incompetent or that the pleadings for the pursuer or the defender are irrelevant.

preliminary reference — the order seeking a **preliminary ruling** (qv) from the European Court of Justice. **[E]**

preliminary ruling — a decision of the European Court of Justice on a point of Community law referred to it by a court or tribunal of a member state. *See also* **order for reference**. **[E]**

preparatory inquiry — an investigation, in proceedings before the European Court of Justice, into disputed matters of fact carried out after the end of the written procedure and before judgment, and involving one or more measures of instruction, such as the examination of a witness. **[E]**

prerogative —
(1) the common law royal superiority of the **Sovereign** (qv) involving powers, privileges and dignities most of which are now subject to the authority of Parliament

(the prerogative of mercy is now exercised in Scotland upon the advice of the Scottish Ministers);

(2) a right or dignity attached to an office;

(3) the place of a Community institution or body within the legislative process set out in the treaties; in some circumstances a Community body may raise contentious proceedings before the European Court of Justice but only for the purpose of protecting its prerogatives. **[E]**

presbytery —

(1) a court of the Church of Scotland comprising ministers and elders largely from congregations within the presbytery (as defined in (2)), the functions of which include superintending kirk sessions within the presbytery and electing members to the General Assembly of the Church of Scotland;

(2) the area which is under the jurisdiction of a presbytery (as defined in (1)), the numbers and boundaries of such areas being designated by the General Assembly.

prescription — rules of law by which on the elapse of specified periods of time certain rights and obligations are established or extinguished, or the modes of proving them are limited; examples include:

(1) the grant of a right arising from long usage and enjoyment of the right (positive prescription: 10 years, or 20 years in certain cases), or

(2) the extinction of a right arising from abandonment or long neglect to exercise or enforce the right (negative prescription: 5 years, or 20 years in certain cases).

The rules are now regulated by the Prescription and Limitation (Scotland) Acts.

presents — the use of the words 'these presents' within a document means the document itself.

preses — the elected chairman of a meeting, particularly a meeting of creditors.

Presidency of the European Union — misnomer, more correctly presidency of the Council of the European Union; held by each member state rotating at six-monthly intervals, during which time ministers from the member state will chair all meetings of the European Council and the Council and represent the Union in its **common foreign and security policy** (qv). With 15 members a state holds the Presidency every seven and a half years. Significant change to the present system is proposed by the draft **Constitution of the European Union** (qv). **[E]**

Presiding Officer — the convener of the Scottish Parliament, the Presiding Officer, is an MSP elected by the Parliament at its first meeting following a general election, or if there is a vacancy in the office. The Presiding Officer is supported by two Deputy Presiding Officers.

prestable — capable of being executed or enforced; payable; exigible.

prestation — what requires to be done under an obligation or duty.

presumption — an inference as to the existence of one fact drawn from the admission or proof of the existence of another fact. The inference may amount to a legal conclusion, rebuttable or otherwise, arising by law from a given set of facts. Alternatively it may be a practical conclusion inferred from the facts held to be proved.

presumption of death — the presumption under the Presumption of Death (Scotland) Act 1977 that a person who has disappeared and either is thought to be dead, or has not been known to be alive for more than seven years, is dead. A declarator to that effect may be sought from the court.

presumption of innocence — a fundamental rule of criminal law that a person charged with a crime or offence is presumed to be innocent unless and until he is proved at a trial and beyond reasonable doubt to be guilty. The onus of proving the charge therefore remains upon the Crown, as prosecutor, throughout the trial. *See also* **burden of proof**.

presumption of life — the presumption at common law that a person known to have been alive at a particular time continues to be alive for a reasonable period thereafter, probably at least eight years.

pretium affectionis — the price of regard; sentimental value; the value of a thing due to the owner's regard for it, irrespective of intrinsic value, as with heirlooms, gifts from deceased relatives etc.

pretium periculi — the price of the risk; an insurance premium.

prevarication — concealment or misrepresentation of the truth by giving evasive or equivocating evidence. It is usually demonstrated by a witness avoiding giving proper answers to legitimate questions, and is punishable summarily as a contempt of court.

price competition — rivalry between different goods or services based on price.

price fixing — an **agreement** (qv) or other restrictive practice whereby **undertakings** (qv) agree (or otherwise) not to compete on price in the supply of goods or services; prices may be fixed in both horizontal and vertical arrangements; prohibited by competition law and, if dishonest, may constitute a **cartel offence** (qv).

prima facie — at first appearance or sight. A *prima facie* case is one in which, at first sight, appears compelling and calls for an answer.

primacy —
(1) generally, the prevailing effect of one system of law over another;
(2) in the European Community the principle that Community law prevails over any rule of national law of a member state when there is inconsistency between the two; also the 'supremacy' of Community law. **[E]**

primary legislation — statutes enacted by a parliament, such as Acts of Parliament, and Acts of the Scottish Parliament (and, rarely, Prerogative Orders in Council).

primo loco — in the first place. *Secundo loco* means in the second place, and so forth.

primo venienti — to the person who comes first; first come, first served. If six months after a death the estate of the deceased appears solvent, the executor must pay all creditors known to him, and if any others appear while the estate is still undistributed then he will pay *primo venienti*.

primogeniture — first born. The former rule that the eldest male descendant was entitled to succeed to the heritable property of an intestate parent as heir at law. It is now obsolete except in respect of transmissible titles, honours and dignities.

Prince and Great Steward of Scotland — one of the titles of the eldest living son of the Sovereign.

principal — a person for whom another (the **agent** (qv)) acts, or purports to act, under a contract of **agency** (qv).

Principality of Scotland — the lands of the Stewartry of Scotland and certain other lands constituting an appanage of the **Prince of Scotland** (qv).

prior rights — rights of the surviving spouse of a person dying intestate to the dwelling-house, with furniture and plenishings, and financial provision out of the estate. The rights rank after those of creditors but before those of all other beneficiaries.

prior tempore potior jure — prior in date, preferable in right. Thus in a competition the conveyance first recorded gives a preferable right to one recorded subsequently, irrespective of the dates of the actual conveyances.

prison breaking — the crime of escaping or attempting to escape from local custody in prison.

private Act of Parliament — a local or personal statute which grants special powers or rights to an individual, a local authority, a public corporation or a limited company. If solely applicable to Scotland the procedure is usually regulated by the Private Legislation Procedure (Scotland) Act 1936.

private key — a confidential algorithm, held by the user, which can decipher a computer document 'locked' (encrypted) with the **public key** (qv) to provide security; a document encrypted with a public key can only be decrypted with the relevant private key.

private limited company — a registered company which is not a public limited company; the shares being held privately rather than being publicly listed on the stock exchange. Subject to certain exceptions, the name of a private limited company must have 'limited' (often abbreviated to 'ltd') as its last word.

private road — a road other than a **public road** (qv) and therefore not required to be maintained by a roads authority. The public may have a right of passage over a private road.

privative jurisdiction — jurisdiction exclusive to a particular court.

privilege — the legal right in particular circumstances to do or not to do something free from normal restriction. Thus it may afford a defence to an action for defamation. Privileged statements in such cases may be either absolute (eg statements in Parliament or in judicial proceedings) or qualified (where the statement was made under a duty to someone with an interest to receive it). In the latter case the defence fails if malice is proved. Privilege in evidence may allow a witness to withhold from disclosure certain communications (eg between a party and his legal advisers).

privileged debts — debts owed by the estate of a deceased person (eg expenses of confirmation, funeral and deathbed expenses, mournings and taxes), which are payable before debts of unsecured creditors.

Privy Council — at one time (before cabinet government developed) the principal council of the Sovereign, now made up of past and present **cabinet** (qv) ministers, Lords of Appeal in Ordinary, judges of the Inner House and the English Court of Appeal, commonwealth leaders and certain others. The membership of the Privy Council is over 1,000 but it rarely meets. The active Privy Council consists of the sovereign together with three other Privy counsellors and by this means orders in council are made. The Privy Council also exercises a judicial function in certain appeals through the **Judicial Committee of the Privy Council** (qv).

Privy Council terms — information provided, on a strictly confidential basis, by the government to senior members of Opposition parties on matters of the national interest.

Privy Counsellor —— a member of the **Privy Council** (qv); counsellors are appointed for life by the sovereign and hold the title of 'Right Honourable'.

pro bono publico — for the public good; for the advantage of the public generally.

pro confesso — as having confessed. Thus a person is generally held *pro confesso*, ie to have admitted a claim, if he does not appear to answer or defend a civil action raised against him.

pro forma — as a matter of form; as of proceedings which are purely formal or a partly printed formal document which requires completion by insertion of particulars.

pro hac vice — for this turn; for this occasion, as of an appointment to an office or duty to effect one particular task.

pro indiviso — in common; in an undivided manner; as of one person's right in property owned in common by two or more persons. *See* **common property** and contrast **joint property**.

pro loco et tempore — for the place and time. Thus a prosecutor may desert criminal proceedings *pro loco et tempore*, while reserving the right to renew the prosecution at a later date.

pro non scripto — as not written; matters in a deed that are ignored, eg illegal or impossible conditions in a will.

pro possessore habetur qui dolo desiit possidere — he is held to be the possessor who, for a fraudulent purpose, has ceased to possess. All the liabilities of a possessor must be borne by such a person.

pro privato commodo — for private convenience. Contrast *pro bono publico*.

pro rata — proportionately. Joint debtors or creditors are only bound by or entitled to the shares of the debt due *pro rata*. Joint and several debtors are each indebted to the creditor *in solidum* but only *pro rata* in a question with each other.

pro re nata — in an emergency; out of the ordinary course, as of a meeting or proceedings necessarily called or taken to consider or meet a sudden emergency.

pro tanto — for so much; to account of. When a defender consigns a sum admitted but the pursuer obtains decree for the whole sum claimed, the pursuer may uplift the amount consigned and apply it *pro tanto* in satisfaction of his decree.

pro tempore — for the time being; temporary.

pro veritate — as if true.

probabilis causa litigandi — a probable or plausible ground of action. Thus an applicant for legal aid must demonstrate that he has a reasonable case for taking or defending the proceedings in question.

probate — the certificate, granted by the High Court in England, that a will has been proved, constituting the title of the executors to the testator's estate and evidence of their right to administer it.

probatio probata — a proved proof. Where there is no provision for an appeal on the facts (as distinct from matters of law), the facts found to be established by a jury or by a judge at first instance may not be contradicted.

probation —

    (1) proof in civil proceedings. *See also* **conjunct probation or proof**;

    (2) a requirement imposed by order on a person found guilty of a crime or offence that he submit, subject to conditions, to the supervision of a social worker for a specified period (the order constitutes a final disposal of the criminal proceedings but does not constitute a conviction).

probatis extremis praesumuntur media — the extremes being proved, what falls within or between them is presumed.

probative — self-proving, as of a deed which, when executed in accordance with the prescribed formalities (eg as to subscription and attestation), itself constitutes proof that it is authentic and is unchallengeable except in proceedings for its reduction. See the Requirements of Writing (Scotland) Act 1995, s 3.

procedure roll. *See* **rolls**.

process —

    (1) the court file containing the collection of documents relating to a case; all the formal collected documents and papers relating to a civil action, petition or summary application;

    (2) a civil action, petition or summary application.

process caption — a summary warrant to imprison a person who has removed or borrowed a process from the court and failed to return it.

procuration — agency, commonly applied to agency to sign a bill of exchange.

pro-curator — a person who acted as curator without having been legally appointed as such. Obsolete now that curatory is abolished.

procurator —

    (1) a general term for a person who acts for another and under his authority.

    (2) At one time law agents (solicitors) practising before the inferior courts were called procurators a usage now found only in the term **procurator fiscal** (qv) and in the titles of certain regional associations of solicitors eg the Royal Faculty of Procurators in Glasgow.

    (3) an advocate appointed as official legal adviser to the General Assembly of the Church of Scotland.

procurator fiscal (*plural* procurators fiscal) — an officer appointed by the Lord Advocate as his agent to act within a sheriffdom as public prosecutor in the sheriff court and the district court, to investigate and report serious crime to the Crown Office, to investigate sudden or suspicious deaths and to initiate fatal accident inquiries. At one time all inferior courts had procurators fiscal so called because their functions included the recovery of fines imposed by the court and payable to the 'fisc' or public purse.

procurator *in rem suam* — an agent or **mandatory** (qv) acting under his mandate or procuratory 'on his own behalf' (*in rem suam*). At one time personal debts were not assignable and to get round this restriction, resort was had to the device of a *procuratory in rem suam*. In that device the procurator *in rem suam* was in form a procurator or agent but in substance an assignee. That device is now rarely used because in the modern law personal debts are freely assignable.

procuratorio nomine. *See* ***proprio nomine***.

procuratory — an authority, mandate or commission to a person to act for another.

production — a document or article produced as evidence in court (in English law called an exhibit).

progress of titles — the series of successive and linking recorded sasine title deeds, extending over at least ten years, which, prior to registration under the Land Registration (Scotland) Act 1979, constitutes evidence of a secure title to heritable property.

prohibition notice — a notice served by a health and safety inspector prohibiting activities which the inspector considers will involve risk of serious personal injury. Cf **improvement notice**.

promise — (or unilateral promise) an undertaking by one party, the promisor, constituting an obligation to be performed by him in favour of another, called the promisee, being an undertaking which does not require an acceptance by the promisee in order to bind the promisor. The obligation is enforceable against the promisor at the promisee's instance. Unilateral promises form a branch of the law on voluntary obligations co-eval with the law of contract although unilateral promises are much less common in practice than contracts.

promissory note — an unconditional promise to pay money made in writing by one person to another, eg a cheque.

proof —

    (1) the formal hearing at first instance in a civil case by a judge (either a **Lord Ordinary** (qv) or **sheriff** (qv) as appropriate) sitting alone, ie without a **jury** (qv) to decide matters of fact;

    (2) the establishment of a fact by evidence;

    (3) loosely, evidence itself;

    (4) in England, a written statement by a witness of his evidence in a case.

proof before answer — in civil procedure, the formal hearing of evidence as to the facts before the court decides the questions of law raised by a **preliminary plea** (qv).

proof in replication — the hearing of evidence which, with leave, may be led by the pursuer after the defender has completed his evidence, if some unforeseen matter has come to light.

property —

    (1) ownership;

    (2) things which are owned or capable of being owned.

property law — the body of legal doctrine governing **real rights** (qv). *See also jus in re aliena.*

propone — to put forward, submit or propound.

proportionality — a general principle of **Community law** (qv) and of the **European Convention on Human Rights** (qv) that there must be a reasonable relationship between the aim to be achieved and the means used. **[E]**

proprietary club. *See* **club**.

proprietor — the person having right to property (usually heritable property), even though his title is not complete.

proprio jure — by one's own proper right.

proprio nomine — in one's own name. When one sues for oneself, one sues in one's own name and character. If a trustee or a factor or the like sues in that capacity, he sues *procuratorio nomine*.

propter commodum curiae — for the advantage of the court.

propter eminentiam masculini sexus — on account of the superiority of the male sex: a justification which, with its feminine counterpart *propter fragilitatem sexus* (on account of the weakness of their sex), formerly explained privileges extended respectively to men or women. They must now be regarded as discredited.

propter fragilitatem sexus. See propter eminentiam masculini sexus.

prorogate —

    (1) to confer on a court, by consent of the parties, jurisdiction to hear a case by waiving objections to it;

    (2) to extend a time limit, as of a procedural order in the course of a litigation.

prorogation of parliament — the termination of a parliamentary session, made by Royal proclamation.

prosecution — a proceeding in which the Lord Advocate, or the procurator fiscal on his behalf, institutes and pursues a criminal charge before a court.

prosecutor — lawyer appointed by the state to raise and insist in criminal proceedings against alleged offenders, *see* **Lord Advocate**, **Crown Office** and **procurator fiscal**.

prospectus — a document which must be issued by any company, before it issues shares to the public, giving details about its business and financial state.

protective measure — a measure taken to protect the economy of a member state of the European Community from economic difficulties usually arising from external sources, such as low-priced imports. **[E]**

protest — a procedure for establishing proof of dishonour of a bill of exchange or promissory note, whereby a notary public presents or 'protests' the bill or note to the drawer or acceptor for payment, failing which the notary 'notes' the date and fact of the dishonour on the bill or note and declares the fact in a certificate or 'protest'. Once registered in the Books of Council and Session or the Sheriff Court Books the protest may be extracted and diligence can proceed.

protestation — a procedure by which the defender in a civil action may in certain circumstances compel a pursuer either to proceed with or abandon his action.

protocol —
(1) an original;
(2) a record of a diplomatic transaction; also used to refer to additional agreements made to supplement an international treaty;
(3) an entry in a protocol book kept by a notary recording an instrument or act;
(4) an ancillary document, attached to a treaty, and in particular the EC and EU Treaties, and forming an integral part thereof. **[E]**

pro-tutor — a person who has acted as tutor without having been legally appointed as such. Obsolete since the abolition of the office of tutor.

prout de jure — according to law. A general proof according to law is thus called in contrast to a proof restricted to the writ or oath of a party.

proving the tenor — an action in which the pursuer seeks, by proving from drafts, copies or otherwise the contents of a lost or destroyed document, to replace it by a decree to the same effect.

provisio hominis non tollit provisionem legis — a provision made by an individual does not abrogate the provisions of the law. Thus no one by will or settlement can circumvent legal rights.

provisional and protective measures — measures such as diligence (inhibition or arrestment) on the dependence; an admiralty arrestment *in rem* and dismantling of a ship; orders under the Administration of Justice (Scotland) Act 1972, s 1, for the detention, custody, preservation or inspection of property which is the subject of current or prospective civil proceedings; and interim interdict. The expression was introduced into Scots law by the European Convention on Jurisdiction and Enforcement of Judgments of 27 September 1968, article 24 and provisions of the Civil Jurisdiction and Judgments Act 1982.

provisional order — an order issued by the Secretary of State at the request of its promoters as part of the preliminary procedure for the enactment of a private **Act of Parliament** (qv).

provocation — words or actions which have the effect of exciting or inspiring the commission of a crime of violence. If proved it may have the effect of reducing murder to culpable homicide. It is not otherwise a defence but may be a mitigating factor in the assessment of the appropriate sentence.

Provost — the chief magistrate and chairman of a Scottish town or burgh council prior to 1975, equivalent to the English Mayor. The title is now held by the conveners of some councils. *See also* **Lord Provost**.

proximate cause — in delict, the closest effect or factor causing loss or harm. *See causa proxima, et non remota, spectatur.*

proxy —
(1) a person appointed to vote for and in the absence of another person at an election or meeting, eg a shareholders' meeting;
(2) a document appointing such a person.

puberes — **minors** (qv).

public authority —
(1) a person or body invested with power to act of a public or state (as opposed to a private) nature;
(2) a power to act of a public or state nature;
(3) under s 6 of the **Human Rights Act 1998** (qv) a public authority must not act incompatibly with any **Convention right** (qv). A public authority is defined by s 6 as 'any person certain of whose functions are functions of a public nature'; courts and tribunals are specifically included and the United Kingdom parliament specifically excluded.

public analyst — an analyst appointed by a local authority under the food and drugs legislation to act as analyst for its area.

public burdens — public taxes and assessments imposed in respect of the ownership or occupation of heritable property.

public general Act — a statute of general application, as contrasted with a **private Act of Parliament** (qv).

Public Guardian — an office introduced by the Adults with Incapacity (Scotland) Act 2000 and held *ex officio* by the **Accountant of Court** (qv).

public key — a complex algorithm, held by the **Certification Authority** (qv) and available to all as part of the provison of a secure sytem of e-commerce.

Public Key Infrastructure — system to provide secure e-Commerce based round a **public key** (qv), a **private key** (qv) and a **digital certificate** (qv).

public law — branch of law dealing with the legal relationships between the state and individuals and between governmental agencies.

public limited company — a company is public (as opposed to private) after it issues ownership of itself, in the form of shares, to the public. It is a legal requirement that the words public limited company or plc must follow the company's name and only plcs can be listed on the London Stock Exchange.

public policy — general well being of the order of the state (*ordre public*), in the legitimate interests of which a member state of the European Community may derogate from even fundamental rules of Community law. **[E]**

public road — a road which a roads authority has a duty to maintain. Cf **private road**.

public roup — a public auction.

punctum temporis — point of time.

pupil — formerly a boy under the age of fourteen, or a girl under the age of twelve. A pupil had passive legal capacity to acquire rights but was incapable of acting or consenting in legal transactions. A tutor acted or consented for a pupil. See now the Age of Legal Capacity (Scotland) Act 1991, section 1. Cf **minor**.

pupillarity — the status of a **pupil** (qv).

pure; **purify** — obligations are either *pure* or *in diem* (to a day). Performance of the former can be required at once, because there are no conditions attached to them. Performance of the latter can only be insisted upon when that day arrives, ie when the conditions have been fulfilled or 'purified'.

pure economic loss — financial loss sustained as a result of an act or omission, which does not cause physical injury or damage, to the victim or his property.

purge an irritancy — to clear an **irritancy** (qv) by remedying the default which led to it before decree or declarator that the irritancy exists is granted. Legal but not conventional irritancies may be purged.

pursuer — a person raising or insisting in a civil action as distinct from a **petition** (qv) (in English law, a claimant).

putative — believed; reputed, as of the alleged father of an illegitimate child.

q

QC — **Queen's Counsel** (qv).

QMV. *See* **qualified majority voting**. **[E]**

qua — as; in the character of; eg when a person sues not in his own individual interest but *qua* trustee.

quadriennium utile — the period of four years following the attainment of majority, during which the reduction of any transaction may be sought on grounds of minority and lesion. *See* **enorm lesion**.

quae ab initio non valent ex post facto convalescere non possunt — that which was invalid from the beginning cannot be made better by a subsequent act. Thus a contract which is fundamentally null and void or a procedure which is fundamentally incompetent cannot be corrected by some later act.

quae perimunt causam — taking away the ground of action; used of defences or pleas which take away the ground of action; a successful defence on the merits which leads to absolvitor and constitutes *res judicata* of the issues between the parties.

quaere or quaeritur — it is questioned; the question is raised.

qualified majority voting (QMV) — a method by which the Council of the European Union adopts a measure. The Council acts either by simple majority, by unanimity, or by qualified majority vote. Where the **legal base** (qv) under which the Council is acting calls for a qualified majority vote, each member state is accorded a weighted vote based upon population but corrected in favour of less-populous member states, from, in 2003, 2 votes for Luxembourg and 10 each for Germany, France, Italy and the United Kingdom. The total of all weighted votes is 87, and 62 votes (sometimes with an additional requirement of those votes being cast by at least 10 member states) is required for the Council to act. The arithmetic is scheduled (as agreed in the Treaty of Nice) to change significantly with enlargment. **[E]**

qualified acceptance — an acceptance of an **offer** (qv) subject to a qualification so that until the qualification is itself accepted or withdrawn, the contract is not concluded.

qualified privilege. *See* **privilege**.

qualify — to establish by evidence; to authenticate.

quamprimum — as soon as possible; forthwith.

quando aliquid mandatur, mandatur et omne per quod pervenitur ad illud — when anything is ordered to be done, everything is ordered by which the performance of the order may be accomplished. Thus a decree, competently pronounced by a judge, automatically carries with it the power to enforce that decree by diligence.

quando aliquid prohibetur, prohibetur et omne quod devenitur ad illud — when anything is forbidden, everything which amounts to the forbidden thing is also forbidden. This is the counterpart of the preceding maxim. It is most often found in patent cases where the patent right is infringed under the colour or pretext that something else is being used than that which has been patented. Further, an agreement between a creditor and a bankrupt may be struck at if, in truth, it is really a device to effect an unfair preference.

quando res non valet ut ago, valeat quantum valere potes — when a thing is not valid as I do it, it may still be valid to some extent. Thus if a bill of exchange or promissory note is, for want of some particular, invalid for summary diligence, it may still be excellent evidence to support an action for payment.

quantitative restriction — a measure which imposes a total or partial restraint on imports, exports or goods in transit. **[E]**

quanti minoris — for how much the less. *See* **actio quanti minoris**.

quantum — how much; the extent of the damages payable; thus in a reparation action it is necessary first to establish liability and then to determine *quantum*.

quantum lucratus — as much as he has been enriched, as of gain or profit in an action based on the redress of unjustified enrichment rather than on contract. Cf *quantum meruit*.

quantum meruit — as much as he has earned or deserves. Thus where services have been rendered or work has been performed under a contract which does not fix the amount to be paid,, the gap in the contract may be filled by an implied term under which payment *quantum meruit*, that is a fair remuneration or market value, is deemed to be due in respect of the work or services.

quantum valeat — as much as it is worth; for what it is worth. Evidence the competency or relevancy of which is doubtful may be admitted for subsequent consideration *quantum valeat*.

quarter days — Candlemas, Lammas, Martinmas and Whitsunday, which fall on the 28th February, 28th May, 28th August and 28th November respectively.

quasi — as if; as though.

quasi-contract — an obligation to avoid or redress unjustified enrichment created by force of law and not by contract, such as recompense, restitution and *negotiorum gestio*.

quasi-delict — a confusing term, perhaps best used for cases of strict liability to make reparation irrespective of intention or negligence (eg liability under the praetorian edict *nautae, caupones, stabularii* (qv)).

Queen's and Lord Treasurer's Remembrancer — the holder of two Exchequer offices who now combines a number of miscellaneous responsibilities including the collection of fines and penalties, auditing the accounts of sheriff clerks and procurators fiscal, and more exotic activities such as administering treasure trove and caring for the Regalia of Scotland.

Queen's Counsel — a senior and experienced member of the Faculty of Advocates (or of the English Bar), appointed as such as an honour by the Sovereign. Upon appointment the Queen's Counsel 'takes silk', which refers to his entitlement to wear a silk gown. Since 2002 the distinction has also been conferred on solicitors and solicitor advocates.

Queen-in-Parliament — the sovereign legislature of the United Kingdom, comprising the **monarch** (qv), the **House of Lords** (qv) and the **House of Commons** (qv).

quem nuptiae demonstrant — whom the marriage indicates or points out. See *pater est quem nuptiae demonstrant*.

quh . . . — in early Scots, equivalent to 'wh', eg quha, who; quhare, where; quharever, wherever; quhat, what; quhatsumever, whatsoever; quhen, when; quhile or quhill, while; quhilk, which; quhilom, formerly; quhose, whose.

qui alterius jure utitur eodem jure uti debet — he who exercises the right of another ought to exercise the same right. Thus rights exercised by an agent can never be greater in extent or character or used differently from those which the principal could exercise himself.

qui approbat non reprobat — one who approbates may not reprobate. Thus a person may not take advantage of a benefit conferred upon him by one part of a deed or contract and disregard or dispute another portion which may impose some unwelcome condition on the benefit.

qui facit per alium facit per se — he who acts by another acts himself: the principle of vicarious liability. Thus an employer is liable in delict for the consequences of his employee's negligence in the course of carrying out his duties, and a principal is liable for his agent's actions done on his behalf.

qui haeret in litera haeret in cortice — who holds by the letter holds by the bark. Thus the law looks to the substance of deeds to ascertain the parties' intentions, not just the 'skin deep' words which might cloak intention.

qui in utero est, pro jam nato habetur, quoties de ejus commodo quaeritur — in any question which may arise touching its rights or interests, a child in the womb is held as already born. Thus if a right vests whilst a child is *in utero*, the child, after its birth, is entitled to the rights of a living person from the date of its conception.

qui jure suo utitur nemini facit injuriam — he who asserts his own right does wrong to no one. Thus a proprietor is entitled to build right up to the boundary of his neighbour's property.

qui non negat fatetur— he who does not deny, admits: an important rule of written pleadings. If an opportunity to answer has been given, a statement that is not denied is held to have been admitted.

qui potest et debet vetare, jubet si non vetat — he who can and ought to forbid, orders if he does not forbid. Thus if an officer unjustifiably orders his ordinary soldiers to fire upon a crowd, the soldiers, who are bound by obedience, may be excused, but if a superior officer is standing by and hears the orders being given and does nothing about it, he is just as responsible for the order as if he had given it himself. Cf *qui tacet consentire videtur*.

qui suum recipit licet a non debitore, non tenetur restituere — he who receives that which is due to him, although it be not from his debtor, is not liable in **repetition** or **restitution** (qv). When a payment is made under the mistaken belief that it is due, repetition can be required under the *condictio indebiti*. Where, however, the friend of the debtor pays off the debt for him and later he is unable to get reimbursement from the debtor, he cannot then insist on repetition on the basis that he was not the true debtor in the obligation.

qui tacet consentire videtur — he who does not object is held as consenting; silence imposes consent. Where a party to an action knows it has been conducted in his name and takes no step to disclaim it, he is held by his silence to have authorised it. Cf *qui potest et debet vetare, jubet si non vetat*.

qui totum dicit nihil excipit — he who says everything, excepts nothing. Thus a general disposition of his estate by a testator carries the whole estate; it cannot be maintained that some particular thing, of which no mention is made, is excepted.

quid juratum est — what has been sworn; that which has been deponed to. In a formal reference to the oath of a party, the truth of what the party says under oath is not a matter for decision. The only question is what the party has actually said under oath.

quid juris? — what is the law?

quid pro quo — something, usually of similar or equal value, given in return for something else; the price paid for goods.

quid valet nunc — what it is now worth.

quilibet est rei suae arbiter — everyone is the judge of his own affairs; one may do what one pleases with one's own.

quilibet juri pro se introducto renunciare potest — a person may renounce a right which exists solely for his own use or benefit.

quinquennial prescription — the five-year **prescription** (qv).

quisque scire debet cum quo contrahit — everyone ought to know with whom he contracts. Some obligations are not binding because of the position or character of the person granting them, notwithstanding the *bona fides* of the grantee. Thus an obligation entered into by a minor without the consent of his curator may be reduced even if the other party was unaware of the minority. Likewise, a good title can never be acquired in respect of stolen goods, even by an innocent purchaser.

quo animo? — with what intention?

quoad . . . — as regards . . .

quoad fiscum — as regards the rights of the Crown.

quoad omnia — as regards all matters.

quoad potest — in so far as one is able; to the extent of one's powers.

quoad sacra — as regards sacred things.

quoad ultra — as regards the rest. In pleadings in civil actions it is common practice for part of a party's averments to be admitted, and *quoad ultra denied,* by the other party.

quoad valet seipsum — as regards its real value; so far as it is worth.

quoad valorem — as regards the value; to the extent of the value.

quocunque — in whatever way; in any way.

quod ab initio non valet in tractu temporis non convalescit — that which is invalid from the beginning does not become more valid by the lapse of time.

quod constat curiae operae testium non indigit — what is clear to the court does not need the aid of witness: the principle of judicial knowledge.

quod fieri debet facile praesumitur — that which ought to be done is easily presumed. Thus where something is done as required by law, it is presumed to have been done properly. If a deed appears to have been executed in accordance with the due formalities, it is presumed that the witnesses were present and saw the granter subscribe or heard him duly acknowledge his signature.

quod non apparet non est — that which does not appear, does not exist. Thus if some thing is not produced or some fact is not proved, the court will not regard it as existing.

quod nullius est fit domini regis — that which is the property of no one becomes the property of the Sovereign. Thus, subject to statutory exceptions, heritage that falls vacant reverts to the Crown and moveable property abandoned by its owner belongs to the Crown.

quod nullius est fit occupantis — that which is the property of no one becomes the property of the person finding it or taking possession of it. Thus moveable property (such as game) which has never had an owner becomes the property of the hunter who takes it. The fact that the property had never had an owner distinguishes this maxim from the previous maxim.

quomodo constat? — how does it appear? How is it shown?

quomodo desiit possidere — in what way he lost possession. When vindicating or claiming possession of a lost or stolen moveable subject it is necessary to show previous possession and how it came to be lost.

quorum — of whom; in the context of members of a body attending a meeting, the minimum number of members who must be present to constitute a valid meeting. The word is singular, not plural.

quorum usus consistit in abusu — the use of which consists in consuming them. Thus **fungibles** (qv) perish in being used.

quota —
   (1) a share or proportion;
   (2) a restriction on the volume of trade in a particular product. within the European Community eg a fishing quota or agricultural quota. Such quotas may be traded between private parties. **[E]**

quovis tempore — at whatever time; at any time.

r

R — Regina, the Queen, or Rex, the King.

racial discrimination — the unlawful treatment of some persons less favourably than others on the ground of their race, colour, nationality (including citizenship), or ethnic or national origin. *See also* **direct racial discrimination** and **indirect racial discrimination**.

rack rent — the maximum rent obtainable for a heritable property, based on its full annual value.

raise —
   (1) to draw up eg a document;
   (2) to institute or bring an action.

ranking — the placing of the competing creditors of an insolvent person in an order of priority for the purpose of distribution of his property to them. In a sequestration of the estate of an insolvent, or a trust deed for his creditors, or in a competition between his creditors on the proceeds of diligence or in a multiplepoinding or other process of ranking, the estate or fund *in medio* must be distributed to those creditors in the order of priority in which they are entitled to be paid their debts, that is to say in accordance with their respective rights and preferences as fixed by various enactments and rules of law.

ranking agreement — a contract, or clause in a contract or security, determining the **ranking** (qv) of the parties between themselves in insolvency.

ranking and sale — an obsolete judicial form of action whereby the heritable property of an insolvent person was sold and the proceeds divided among his creditors according to their several rights and preferences.

rape — the crime of having sexual intercourse with a female against her will.

rapporteur — lit. reporter. Committees within the **Community institutions** (qv) appoint a *rapporteur* with responsibility for minutes, drafting, and various related functions. *See also* **Judge–Rapporteur. [E]**

ratification — the confirmation of a decision or agreement, for example, when the legislative body of a state confirms a government's action in signing a treaty.

ratio. See ratio decidendi.

ratio decidendi — literally the reason of the decision; the principle of law justifying and underlying the decision of a court; the ground on which a case is decided, and which may be used as a precedent in subsequent cases.

ratio scientiae — the reason of knowledge. The grounds on which a witness's knowledge of the facts of which he has given evidence is based is his *ratio scientiae*. If it is **hearsay** (qv), that evidence may be valueless.

ratione — by reason; on account of.

ratione contractus — because of the contract.

ratione delicti — because of the delict.

ratione originis — because of one's origins.

ratione rei sitae — because of the position or situation of the property.

re infecta — the thing not having been done; performance having failed.

real burden — an encumbrance on land constituted in favour of the owner of other land in his capacity as owner of that other land. The encumbered land is known as the burdened property. The other land is known as the benefited property. Title Conditions (Scotland) Act 2003, s 1. A form of subordinate **real right** (qv).

real evidence — any thing (including a human being) tendered as evidence in court, as distinct from written or spoken evidence. In court the significance of any real evidence produced must always be explained by a human being.

real raiser — *See* **multiplepoinding**.

real right (*jus in re*) — a right in a thing enforceable against all persons entitling the holder of the real right to follow and vindicate it in whose hands soever the thing comes. Real rights are the most important units – the building blocks - of property law. The real rights consist not only of the right of ownership but also of several defined categories of **subordinate real right** (qv) that is a real right in a thing owned by another person or *jus in re aliena*. In principle the types of real right recognised by Scots law form a closed list or *numerus clausus* (qv). Contrast **personal right** and *jus ad rem*.

real warrandice. *See* **warrandice**.

reasoned opinion — an administrative measure adopted by the European Commission and addressed to a member state, before enforcement proceedings are brought against that state in the European Court of Justice, setting out the reasons why and the respects in which the Commission believes the state to have failed to fulfil an obligation under Community law. **[E]**

reasoning — term sometimes used, stemming from the obligation imposed by article 253 of the EC Treaty that all measures adopted by a **Community institution** (qv) be 'reasoned' (*motivé*), for the (sometimes extensive) preambular justification found in all Community legislation; a measure which is insufficiently reasoned is legally flawed and so liable to **annulment** (qv). **[E]**

rebus integris — matters being complete or intact. Where nothing has been done following a purported agreement or contract, then, the matter being intact and neither party having altered his position, it may be permissible to resile without penalty, eg where there was a verbal agreement to sell heritage but no missives or conveyance followed. Where there has been *rei interventus* (qv), then *res non est integra* and the parties may not resile. Cf **res non est integra**.

rebus sic stantibus — matters so standing; in the existing state of things.

rebut — to counter an opponent's case with evidence or argument.

recall — to cancel: used of (1) court decrees, orders and interlocutors; and (2) some diligences notably arrestments and inhibitions.

receiver — an individual, who must be an **insolvency practitioner** (qv), appointed by the holder of a **floating charge** (qv) or the court to control and manage a limited company in the place of its directors in the interests of the holder of the floating charge and other creditors and the company itself.

reclaim — to submit an interlocutor pronounced by a Lord Ordinary in the Outer House of the Court of Session or by the vacation judge to the Inner House for review, ie to appeal.

reclaiming motion — a motion by which a party **reclaims** (qv). Formerly the procedure was by reclaiming note.

recommendation — a measure adopted by a Community institution which lacks binding force (cf **regulation, directive, decision**). **[E]**

recompense —
  (1) an obligation for redress of unjustified enrichment at another's expense arising from work or services or an uncertain amount or the act of the enriched party;
  (2) a remedy redressing unjustified enrichment.

reconsideration stage — **stage** (qv) in the legislative process of the **Scottish Parliament** (qv) for a public bill or **private bill** (qv) after being passed by the Parliament following a challenge to its legislative competence under the statutory procedures provided in the **Scotland Act 1998** (qv). This enables a Bill to be amended by the Parliament to make it legislatively competent, before it receives the **royal assent** (qv).

reconvention — the rule of jurisdiction which enables a person to counterclaim or bring a cross-claim against another who, although otherwise beyond the jurisdiction of the court, has voluntarily submitted himself to its jurisdiction by bringing principal action there.

record —
  (1) a document forming part of the **process** (qv) of a civil action and comprising the written pleadings of the parties (the record remains 'open' until, when finally adjusted, it becomes a closed record by order of the court);
  (2) to enter or 'record' a document in an official record such as the General Register of Sasines which is a register of title deeds (but not the Land Register of Scotland, which is a register of title, not title deeds);
  (3) the list of a person's criminal convictions.

Red Mass — a solemn Mass of the Holy Spirit celebrated at the outset of the judicial year and attended principally by judges, sheriffs, counsel and solicitors who are Roman Catholics.

reddendo — by handing over; the clause in a feu charter formerly indicating the obligation to pay feuduty. *See* **feu**; **feudal tenure**.

redeemable — subject to a right of redemption. Thus the holder of a heritable security has only a redeemable right in the property, whereas a proprietor has an absolute irredeemable right to it.

reduce — to set aside or annul, usually by an action of reduction, a deed, contract, decree or award. *See* **improbation**.

reduction. *See* **reduce**.

redundancy payment — compensation payable under statute by an employer to an employee who is dismissed because his job has ceased to exist through contraction, mechanisation, reorganisation etc.

re-engagement order — an order made by an employment tribunal requiring the employer of an employee who has been unfairly dismissed to re-engage him in employment comparable to that from which he was dismissed, or other suitable employment. Cf **reinstatement order**.

re-examination — the further examination, subject to certain restrictions, of a witness in court by the party who called him, following cross-examination by another party.

reference to oath. *See* **oath on reference**.

referendum — a vote on a specific question put to the entire electorate. Referenda are neither necessary nor legally binding in United Kingdom law but are used occasionally to resolve matters of great constitutional significance such as membership of the European Union or whether **devolution** (qv) should be granted.

referring court or tribunal — a court or tribunal of a member state of the European Community which makes an order for reference to the European Court of Justice for a **preliminary ruling** (qv). **[E]**

regalia — royal rights; rights of the Crown.

Regiam Majestatem — 'The Auld Lawes and Constitutions of Scotland', being an early manual of laws and practice dating from the fourteenth century, first printed in 1609 as edited by Sir John Skene. Some jurists have doubts as to the authenticity of some of the early material.

regalia majora — royal rights of the Sovereign which are personal or pertain to the Crown as guardian of the public interest and consequently inalienable without parliamentary sanction, eg rights of navigation over the sea between the foreshore and the offshore territorial limits and navigable rivers, and such prerogatives as the exercise of clemency to criminals.

regalia minora — royal proprietary rights which the Crown may exercise as it pleases and which may alienate, eg salmon fishings, mines, forests and highways.

region — one of the nine areas into which mainland Scotland was divided for local government purposes. The local authority was the regional council. Abolished in 1996 reorganisation of local government.

Register of Community Interests in Land — a register established by the Land Reform (Scotland) Act 2003.

Register of Inhibitions and Adjudications — a register kept by the Keeper of the Registers of Scotland in which are recorded inhibitions, adjudications, reductions and notices of litigiosity. Recording in the register is a prerequisite to certain proceedings and actions.

Register of Insolvencies — a public register maintained by the Accountant in Bankruptcy, containing details of sequestrated estates and protected trust deeds.

register of sasines — a public register in which all deeds affecting rights and interests in heritable property required to be recorded for effect. The former particular registers of sasines were abolished in 1868, leaving the **General Register of Sasines** (qv), which is being progressively superseded by the **Land Register of Scotland** (qv).

Registers Direct — service providing online access to certain of the registers maintained by the **Registers of Scotland** (qv).

Registers of Scotland — the government agency, based in Edinburgh, responsible for the administration of the 15 state registers, including the two land registers.

Registrar — an officer of the European Court of Justice and of the Court of First Instance responsible for acceptance, transmission and custody of documents, keeping the register and effecting service. **[E]**

Registration Appeal Court — in disputes over the registration of voters, appeal against a decision of a registration officer may be taken to the Sheriff and from there on a point of law, by way of stated case, to the Registration Appeal Court, which consists of three judges of the Court of Session, appointed by Act of Sederunt.

registration for execution — the registration of a deed in the Books of Council and Session or the Sheriff Court Books, which *ipso facto* endows it, for the purpose of enforcement by diligence, with the character of a court decree. An extract of the registered deed automatically contains a warrant for diligence.

registration for preservation — the registration of a deed in the Books of Council and Session or the Sheriff Court Books in order to preserve it and to enable copies or extracts, the equivalent of the original, to be made.

registration for publication — the registration or recording of a deed relating to heritable property in the General Register of Sasines, thus formally publishing it and *ipso facto* giving effect to it at that date. Cf **registration of title**.

registration of title — registration of a deed relating to land in the **Land Register of Scotland** (qv), which is gradually superseding the General Register of Sasines. Registration has the effect of vesting in the person registered as entitled a real right in the land ranked according to the date of registration, the right being guaranteed by the state.

regular marriage — a marriage is regular or irregular depending on its mode of constitution. A regular marriage is either religious (that is solemnised by a minister of the Church of Scotland, or a clergyman of a religious body approved by regulations, or other approved celebrant) or civil. A civil marriage is solemnised by an authorised registrar of births, deaths and marriages. Cf **irregular marriage**.

regulation — a measure adopted by a Community institution which has general application, is binding in its entirety and is directly applicable in all member states; it is anologous to legislation of general application. **[E]**

regulatory impact assessment — the evaluation of a proposed regulation and its associated policy before it is put in place that shows what the likely consequences will be, including the likely risks, benefits and costs associated with all of the possible options.

rei depositae proprietas apud deponentem manet, sed et possessio — the right of property in a thing deposited remains with the depositor, as does the right of possession. Thus the property in silver left in a bank's safe, or luggage deposited in a left luggage office, does not pass from the person leaving it. The maxim does not apply to fungibles such as cash deposited at a bank.

rei interitus — the destruction of a thing or its ceasing to exist. Performance may not be enforceable if property referred to in a contract is physically destroyed or, for the purposes of the contract, ceases to exist.

rei interventus — the intervention of a thing or act. When one party, to the knowledge of the other, acts to his own disadvantage on the faith of an obligation, contract or trust not properly constituted in a written document, both parties may be bound it. In respct of documents executed on or after 1 August 1995, the common rule law of *rei interventus* is replaced by a statutory version under the Requirements of Writing (Scotland) Act 1995, s 1.

rei vindicatio — a claim to vindicate a thing; the claim by an owner of a thing (*res*) against the current possessor for delivery of the thing. *See* **jus in re**; **jus possidendi**; **real right**; *ubi meam rem invenio, ibi vindico*. The holder of a **subordinate real right** (qv) in a thing also has right to vindicate it. *See* **jus in re.**

reinstatement order — an order made by an employment tribunal requiring an employer to treat an employee who has been unfairly dismissed in all respects as if he had not been dismissed. Cf **re-engagement order**.

reinsurance — the taking out of insurance by the insurer to protect himself from the risk embodied in the original insurance policy granted by the insurer to the insured.

rei publicae interest ut sit finis litium — it is in the public interest that there should be a known termination of litigation after which further appeal becomes impossible, or the raising of claims is barred by lapse of time.

relevancy; relevant —
(1) the pertinence of evidence to a fact in issue in a litigation;
(2) in civil litigation a plea to the relevancy affirms that even if the facts averred by the pursuer are true, he is not entitled to the remedy he seeks. Similarly a charge in criminal procedure is irrelevant if the facts libelled by the prosecution do not constitute a criminal offence. A plea to the relevancy may be the subject of debate before evidence is heard, and if the pleadings fail to support the case being made or lack appropriate specification, dismissal of that case may follow.

relevant market — a market in competing goods and services which are sufficiently homogenous to satisfy the same consumer demand, and so by reference to which the economic effects of an anti-competitive arrangement are assessed.

reliance interest — the interest which a contracting party has, in an action of damages for breach of contract, to recover expenses or other losses incurred in reliance on the contract. Contrast **expectation interest** (qv); **restitution interest** (qv).

relict — widow or widower. *See jus relictae.*

relocation. *See* **tacit relocation.**

remand —
(1) the committal of an accused person, in custody or on bail, upon the adjournment of criminal proceedings;
(2) to commit a person in those circumstances.

remissio injuriae — forgiveness of the offence; condonation as a defence in an action of divorce founded on adultery.

remission *ob contingentiam. See* **contingency.**

remit —
(1) to refer a case or some portion of it to another court or judge or to an official, either absolutely or for some particular purpose (eg remit to the Court of Session, to the sheriff, to an arbiter, to a man of skill or to the Auditor of Court);
(2) to extinguish, modify or reduce a sentence or penalty.

removing —
(1) the relinquishment of possession of heritable property by a tenant, either voluntarily (as by agreement or on breach of contract by the landlord) or compulsorily (which may be either ordinary removing (at the natural **ish** (qv)) or extraordinary removing (during the currency of the tenancy, through some default on the part of the tenant);
(2) an action by a landlord to displace a tenant in possession.

rent — the return, usually in money but sometimes in produce or other moveables, due by a tenant or hirer for the possession and use of the property which is the subject of the lease or hire.

rentaller — **kindly tenant** (qv).

renvoi — the application of the conflict rules of one state by the court or tribunal of another state, in order to solve a conflict of laws problem. 'Single renvoi' is the referral by the forum court to the conflict rules of a foreign state, but not to that state's renvoi rules. This may result in a reference back to the forum's domestic law ('remission') or a reference to the domestic law of a third state ('transmission'). 'Double renvoi' is the referral by the forum court to the conflict rules, including the renvoi rules) of a foreign state.

renvoi préjudiciel — the French term for **preliminary reference** (qv). **[E]**

reparation —
(1) compensation for a delict or civil wrong;
(2) that branch of the law concerned with delict.

repeal —
(1) the cancellation or termination of primary legislation by further legislation;
(2) (verb) to cancel (primary legislation).

repel — in Scots civil court procedure to reject or overrule.

repetition — repayment of money which has been paid without legal ground.

replication — reply. *See* **proof in replication.**

repone — to restore a defender against whom a decree has been pronounced in his absence and allow him to defend his case. The process is known as 'reponing', and the application is made by a reponing note. A similar procedure exists in the Inner House of the Court of Session to enable an appeal to proceed where it has been deemed to have been abandoned by some default.

reporter —
(1) a person appointed to hold a public hearing or inquiry and to report;
(2) a professional person or other man of skill to whom a court remits a question for

advice or investigation and report;

(3) a person delegated by the Principal Reporter under the Local Government etc (Scotland) Act 1994 to investigate matters concerning children, to arrange and present cases to **children's hearings** (qv) and for related purposes;

(4) a person who compiles and edits reports of court decisions for publication.

representation —

(1) a statement made by a person to influence another to enter into a contract with that person (inaccuracy in the statement may entitle the other person to rescind the contract);

(2) in the law of succession, the right of the children of a beneficiary predeceasing the deceased person to succeed to their parent's share.

representative — a person who represents or takes the place of another person.

reprobate — reject. *See* **approbate and reprobate.**

repudiate — to demonstrate by words or conduct that one does not intend to perform one's obligations under a contract. *See* **anticipatory breach.**

requisition —

(1) a demand by a creditor for the payment of a debt or the performance of an obligation;

(2) to require, by authority, that the use of something be surrendered.

res — matter, affair, thing, circumstance.

res accessoria sequitur rem principalem — an accessory follows the principal. *See accessorium principale sequitur.*

res aliena — property or some thing belonging to another.

res communes — common things; things incapable, by their nature, of being appropriated, eg light, air and running water.

res furtiva — stolen property, the right to which remains in the original owner, even if it has since passed to others acquiring it in good faith.

res gestae — things done; the facts and circumstances immediately surrounding or related to a matter at issue in a litigation and of which evidence, otherwise inadmissible, may be allowed.

res inter alios acta aliis non nocet — a thing done between certain people does not injure others. Thus dealings between two parties are generally irrelevant in a question involving different or other parties. Exceptions may occur where there is a *jus quaesitum tertio* (qv).

res ipsa loquitur — the thing speaks for itself. Thus the proof of the occurrence of an event may raise a rebuttable presumption of liability in delict.

res judicata — a case or matter decided. Thus a final judgment so disposes of an issue that it may not be raised again in a litigation between the same parties.

res merae facultatis — a matter of mere power; a right the exercise of which depends on the pleasure of the party entitled. Unlike a servitude, such a right cannot be lost by prescription.

res mercatoria. See **in re mercatoria.**

res non est integra — the matter is not complete or intact. Cf *rebus integris.*

res noviter veniens ad notitiam — things newly come to light, which may warrant the admission of further evidence or even a new trial.

res nullius — something which belongs to nobody. *See* **quod nullius est fit domini regis** and **quod nullius est fit occupantis.**

res perit suo domino — a thing perishes to its owner. Thus, unless the loss is caused by another's fault, loss following destruction or deterioration is borne by the owner of the property.

res publicae — a thing belonging to the public or the Crown on its behalf, eg a highway, the sea or a navigable river.

res religiosae — sacred things. Churches, communion plate etc are outwith the stream of commerce so long as they are dedicated to religious uses, but the principle is modified in modern practice by statute. See the Church of Scotland (Property and Endowments) Amendment Act 1933.

res sua — one's own property.

res sua nemini servit — an owner cannot have a servitude over his own property. A servitude, being a minor right, can merge with the paramount right of property. Thus, if the owner of the servient tenement acquires the dominant tenement, the servitude may be extinguished.

res universitatis — property belonging to a corporate body, contrasted with the property of an individual.

resale price maintenance — the control of the price at which the buyer of goods may resell them to a third person; may infringe competition law.

rescind — to terminate or cancel a contract. A right to rescind arises where the other party wrongly induced the contract, has repudiated it or has committed a material breach of it.

rescission — the termination or cancellation of a contract.

reservatio ut et protestatio non facit jus sed tuetur — reservation and protest do not make a right, but protect it. Thus the reservation of a right in a deed does not give the right to the granter; he had the right already. The reservation merely preserves or protects it for him.

reservation —
  (1) a clause in a deed in which the granter of the deed keeps or reserves something for himself;
  (2) a provision in an international treaty by which a party to the treaty states that certain specified provisions shall not apply to that party.

reserved matters — those matters which are reserved to the United Kingdom Parliament by the Scotland Act 1998. and therefore not within the **legislative competence** (qv) of the **Scottish Parliament** (qv), listed in Schedule 5, these include: the Constitution, Foreign Affairs, Defence, economic matters, immigration and nationality, social security and employment.

reserved power. *See* reserved matters.

reset —
  (1) to receive stolen goods knowing them to have been obtained by theft, fraud, robbery or embezzlement, and with the intention of keeping them from their owner;
  (2) the crime of so receiving such goods.

residence order — a court order regulating the arrangements as to the persons with whom a child under the age of sixteen years is to live, and during what periods. See Children (Scotland) Act 1995, section 11(2)(c).

residential establishment — an establishment which provides residential accommodation for children in need of **compulsory measures of supervision** (qv).

residuary beneficiary *or* **legatee** — a person entitled under a will to the residue of the testator's estate after the payment of debts and expenses and the disposition of **specific** (qv), **demonstrative** (qv) and **general legacies**.

resignation —
  (1) the giving up of an appointment or office;
  (2) in feudal conveyancing, formerly, the form by which a vassal returned his interest in land to the superior, permanently (*ad remanentiam*) or for transfer to another, such as a purchaser (*ad favorem*).

resolutive condition — a condition which terminates a right or obligation if a certain specified event occurs.

resolution — motion expressing the will of the **Scottish Parliament** (qv) but which does not have the force of law.

resoluto jure dantis, resolvitur jus accipientis — the right of the giver having ceased or become void, the right of the receiver also ceases. Thus if a liferenter assigns the benefit of a liferent, the right of the assignee ends on the liferenter's death.

respondeat superior — let the master answer, or be responsible, for the civil wrongs of his employee in the ordinary course of his employment.

respondent — the party in a civil appeal who, whether he was pursuer or defender in the court of first instance, defends the decision against which the appeal has been made.

respondentia — (nearly obsolete) bond or contract by which all or part of a ship's cargo is hypothecated as security for a loan, whose repayment is dependent upon maritime risks.

resting-owing —
(1) the state of an unpaid bill;
(2) due and unpaid.

restitutio in integrum — entire restoration; the restoration of a person to the position in which he would have been had the transaction or event in question not taken place.

restitution —
(1) the obligation under property law of the possessor of a thing to restore it to the owner or the holder of a subordinate real right having a higher right to possess it (*jus possidendi*) (sometimes called 'vindicatory restitution');
(2) the obligation under the doctrine of spuilzie of a vitious dispossessor or spoliator (even if he is the true owner) to restore the thing to the dispossessed former possessor;
(3) the obligation under the law of unjustified enrichment of a person who has acquired ownership of a thing *sine causa* (without legal cause) to restore ownership of the thing to the person entitled thereto (sometimes called 'enrichment restitution').

restitution interest — in actions for breach of contract, a contracting party who has conferred a benefit on the other contracting party has an interest to seek restoration of that benefit or its value. Compare **expectation interest** (qv) and **reliance interest** (qv).

restitutionary damages — a remedy requiring the surrender or giving up of unauthorised gains or profits acquired by a trustee or other **fiduciary** (qv) by virtue of his fiduciary position. Criticised as a misnomer because the remedy is neither 'restitutionary' (it involves 'giving up' rather than 'giving back') nor 'damages' properly so called (since the beneficiary suffers no loss, the remedy is not compensatory). Compare **disgorge**.

resumption — taking back; especially repossession by the landlord of part of the subjects of a lease where permitted by the terms of the lease.

retenta possessione — possession being retained. A pledge of moveables is ineffective without physical delivery to the pledgee.

retention —
(1) the withholding by one party to a contract of performance of his obligations under the contract until the other party performs his obligations under it;
(2) more particularly, retaining moveable property until a debt due by its owner is paid, ie a lien.

retentis. See **in retentis**.

retro — backward. Some events or acts are said to operate *retro*, ie with retrospective or retroactive effect.

retrocession — assignation back to the former owner of incorporeal moveable property or a right originally assigned by the former owner to the person making the retrocession. Often applied to the re-assignation by a lender to a borrower , upon repayment of a loan, of an insurance policy assigned by the borrower in security of the loan.

retrospectivity — law which has effect with reference to an event which occurred prior to the enactment of the law in question.

return day — the date by which the defender in a summary cause or small claim in the sheriff court must send a written reply to the court and, where appropriate, the date by which the pursuer must return the summons to court. The date is stated in the summons. Cf **calling date**.

reus — the defender, sometimes called *alterior*, contrasting with *actor*, the pursuer.

reverse discrimination — application of national rules within a member state of the European Community to the disadvantage of one of its own nationals or of goods originating, or producers situated, in its own territory; reverse discrimination is generally tolerated in Community law. **[E]**

reverser. *See* **wadset**.

reversion —
- (1) in relation to heritage, a right of redemption which maybe legal, as in **adjudication** (qv) for debt, or conventional, as usually set forth in the terms of a heritable security;
- (2) the right of the fiar to heritage at the end of a **liferent** (qv).

reversionary interest — the interest in heritage of the person entitled to exercise a **reversion** (qv).

review — the reconsideration of a judicial decision on appeal.

revoke —
- (1) to cancel subordinate legislation, eg a statutory instrument or bye-law; equivalent to **repeal** (qv) of primary legislation;
- (2) an order of court a synonym for **recall** (qv); and
- (3) to cancel the authority of an agent or a will or other written instrument.

rider —
- (1) a person with a **riding interest** (qv);
- (2) an addendum or qualification added by a jury to its verdict (thus a verdict of guilty of a charge of assault may be qualified by a rider that the accused had been provoked).

riding interest — the claimed interest of a creditor of a claimant in a **multiplepoinding** (qv) in the share of the fund *in medio* to which the claimant is or will be ranked.

right — a lawful claim or title to something; rights may be **real** (qv) or **personal** (qv) and may be claimed over **corporeal** (qv) or **incorporeal** (qv) **property** (qv). Rights may only be held by **persons** (qv).

right of establishment — in EC law, a fundamental Treaty right, the settlement, for an indefinite period of time, of a natural or juristic person in the territory of a member state other than his or its own for the purpose of carrying out business there. **[E]**

right of way — the right of a person, either as an individual (in the case of a right of way constituted by servitude) or as a member of the public (in the case of a public right of way), to pass by a specified or recognised route over the land of another. It may be subject to conditions and limitations specified in any grant of the right.

rights of defence — rules of natural justice applicable in contentious administrative proceedings, especially those in competition law. **[E]**

rioting — a crime which, with **mobbing** (qv), is constituted by the formation of a **mob** (qv) for a purpose to be accomplished by illegal means such as violence or intimidation to the alarm of the public.

riparian — of or relating to the bank of a river.

riparian owner — the owner of land on the bank of a river.

risk — the possibility of loss or damage. An important question in the contract of sale is the determination of the time at which the risk passes from the seller to the buyer. In matters of insurance it is the risk which is covered by the policy.

robbery — the crime of theft by means of the threat or use of personal violence.

roll of advisings. *See* **rolls.**

roll of defenders — a list of defenders which, where there are more than three, must be lodged with the summons in a civil action in the Court of Session.

roll of proofs, jury trials and special hearings. *See* **rolls.**

roll of undefended causes. *See* **rolls.**

rolls — lists of civil cases set down for hearing in the Court of Session or the sheriff court. The Court of Session rolls, which are published daily during session, include:
- (1) the adjustment roll — a list of Outer House cases in which defences have been lodged by the defender and copies of the open record have been lodged by the pursuer, and which are consequently ready for a Lord Ordinary to close the record;
- (2) the by order rolls — lists of causes in which the Court orders a hearing at which the parties must appear or be represented;
- (3) the calling list — a list of summonses lodged for calling in the Outer House, providing public intimation of actions which have been raised;
- (4) the commercial roll — a list of commercial actions determined by the commercial judge;

(5) the judgment roll — a list of Outer House cases taken to avizandum in which a Lord Ordinary is to give judgment;

(6) the motion roll — a list of motions entered in the motion sheet in the Outer House;

(7) the procedure roll — a list of preliminary pleas in the Outer House;

(8) the roll of advisings — a list of dates on which judgment will be given in the Inner House in particular cases;

(9) the roll of proofs, jury trials and special hearings — a list of causes in which proofs, jury trials or special hearings have been fixed;

(10) the roll of undefended causes — a list of Outer House causes (invariably divorce) in which the defenders have failed to enter an appearance or lodge a defence;

(11) the single bill roll — a list of motions etc to be heard by a division of the Inner House;

(12) the summar roll — a list of cases for hearing in the Inner House which are accorded priority in hearing dates;

(13) the summary trial roll — a list of cases proceeding by summary procedure under the Court of Session Act 1988, s 26.

Roman Law — the law of classical Rome and the Roman Empire, and in particular the law embodied in the *Corpus Juris Civilis* (qv).

Rome Convention, 1980 — The Convention on the Law Applicable to Contractual Obligations, adopted at Rome on 19 June 1980, which lays down uniform conflict of law rules for contract for all member states of the **European Community** (qv).

Rome Statute — shorthand for the Rome Statute of the International Criminal Court 1998 which will result in the Establishment of the International Criminal Court when ratified by 60 states.

ROS — **Registers of Scotland** (qv).

Rothesay, Duke of — the senior Scots title of the eldest living son of the Sovereign, which should be used in Scotland in preference to the title 'Prince of Wales'.

roup — auction,.

royal arms. *See* **Royal Coat of Arms**.

royal assent — the formal consent of the sovereign which is needed for bills in both the United Kingdom and Scottish parliaments before the Bill which has been passed by Parliament may become law. Upon receiving the royal assent the Bill becomes an Act and, subject to the provisions of the Act, will thereupon come into force.

Royal Coat of Arms — the official symbol of the Head of State and of the state itself. The royal arms are borne only by the **sovereign** (qv) and are also displayed, where appropriate, to mark the authority of the state, e.g. on passports, in this latter context they appear in all courtrooms and upon the covers of acts of parliament. The design of the royal arms shows the emblems of different parts of the United Kingdom in four quarters upon the shield: the three lions of England (in the first and fourth quarters) the lion of Scotland (in the second quarter) and the harp of Ireland (in the third quarter); in the Scottish version of the royal arms this design is varied by reversing the position of the arms of Scotland and England.

royal proclamation — a formal notice issued to the people by the **Sovereign** (qv); a declaration by the **Crown** (qv) having legal effect, used for example, to dissolve the Scottish and United Kingdom Parliaments. Royal proclamations dissolving the **Scottish Parliament** (qv) have passed under the **Scottish Seal** (qv) and are recorded by the **Keeper of the Registers of Scotland** (qv) in the **Register of the Great Seal** (qv).

royal seal. *See* the **Great Seal** or the **Signet**.

royal sign manual — the actual signature, or 'royal hand' of the monarch, as distinct from the **signet** (qv) of the monarch, upon an official document.

rubric —

(1) the long title of a statute, formerly written or printed in red (hence the term);

(2) the headnote of a reported case.

rule of law — a doctrine which protects all citizens from the exercise of arbitrary power, and treats all persons as subordinate to the law and as equal in the eye of the law; which ensures that the officials and organs of government are answerable in the courts of law in accordance with the law, and that fundamental constitutional liberties, human rights and private laws are safeguarded and may be vindicated by due process of law.

rule of reason —
(1) a principle of competition law, most developed (distinctly so) in United States anti-trust law, whereby a restrictive agreement or practice which is not *per se* anticompetitive ought to be subjected to a balancing test, and if its pro-competitive benefits outwigh its anticompetitive costs, it ought to fall outwith a general legislative prohibition; alternatively, the ancillary anticompetitive provisions of an agreement which is of itself unobjectionable, but the former being necessary for the latter to be practically operable;
(2) a principle under which the prohibition imposed by article 28 of the EC Treaty on **quantitative restrictions** (qv) and **measures having equivalent effect** (qv) is not applied to certain types of national measures which may restrict trade within the European Community but are justified by reference to **mandatory requirements** (qv); also known as the *Cassis de Dijon* rule. **[E]**

rules of court — rules prescribing the procedure to be followed in civil causes in the Court of Session (see the Rules of the Court of Session) and the sheriff court (see the Ordinary Cause Rules and the Summary Cause Rules). They are prescribed under statutory powers in the form of Acts of Sederunt made by the Lords of Council and Session with the advice of Rules Councils.

rules of origin — rules determining the origin of goods for customs purposes. **[E]**

ruling —
(1) generally, any decision of a court;
(2) a decision of the European Court of Justice under Articles 103 or 104 of the Euratom Treaty as to whether a proposed agreement is compatible with the provisions of the treaty. *See also* **opinion**. **[E]**

rundale land — agricultural land of which intermixed patches or ridges were formerly owned by different persons.

runrig (*or* **runridge**) **land** — agricultural land of which alternate or successive patches or ridges were formerly owned by different persons.

S

s — section of a statute.

SACRO — Safeguarding Communities - Reducing Offending; organisation which works with offenders.

safeguard clause — a provision allowing a member state to derogate temporarily from a rule of European Community law, subject to specified conditions, in order to protect its economy. Cf **protective measure**. **[E]**

safeguarder — a person appointed by a **children's hearing** (qv) or a sheriff to safeguard the interests of the child in the proceedings relating to the hearing. The word appears in the Children's Hearings Rules though not in primary legislation.

sale — a contract comprising the transfer by agreement of the ownership of property in consideration of a price.

sale or return — a form of contract of sale by which the goods are delivered to the buyer but the property in them does not pass to him until they are approved and retained. They may otherwise be returned to the seller within a reasonable period.

saltire — an X-shaped cross; a white saltire on a blue field, the national flag of Scotland; also known as the cross of St Andrew; one of the oldest national flags in the world.

salus populi (or reipublicae) suprema lex — the welfare of the people (or the state) is the highest law. Thus private interest must in certain circumstances give place to the public welfare. For example, a private house may lawfully be destroyed to check a fire which might otherwise spread throughout a town, and in wartime private interests must give way to the interests of the state in defending the country. The maxim however is dangerous and misleading. It is a principle of constitutional law for example that the public interest does not justify expropriation of vested private rights without the authority of a statute which will invariably provide compensation.

salva substantia — the substance being saved, ie not diminished, as when a liferenter is entitled to the fruits but not the capital or fee of the liferent property.

salvage — a reward, payable under maritime law or under contract, for saving or preserving an endangered vessel or its cargo. The principle has now been extended to aircraft.

salvo jure cujuslibet — reserving the right of all others. The last Act of the sessions of Scots Parliaments was usually so entitled, so as to secure the rights of others against the effects of private Acts. As a saving clause it also formerly appeared in charters of confirmation.

sanae mentis — of sound mind.

sanction — a reward or penalty for observation or contravention respectively of a rule of law.

sanctity of contract — principle that contracts must always be respected and complied with.

sasine — an act formerly symbolising the legal acquisition of heritable property. It originally involved a token physical transfer but latterly it comprised registration of the conveyance, or of a notice of title, in the **General Register of Sasines** (qv). *See* **registration for publication**.

SCCCJ — Scottish Consortium on Crime and Criminal Justice.

SCCRC. *See* **Scottish Criminal Cases Review Commission**.

SCE — **European Cooperative Society** (qv). **[E]**

schedule —
 (1) an annexe or appendix to the main body of an enactment or other writing;
 (2) 'schedule of variations' laying down a lender's standard conditions of loan differing from the statutory standard conditions for standard securities;
 (3) 'schedule of particulars' prepared by seller of property and describing the property in brief terms.

Schengen Agreement —
 (1) treaty signed in 1985 by five member states of the EEC for the gradual abolition of checks on persons crossing their common borders;
 (2) treaty by which other member states accede subsequently to the original Schengen Agreement. **[E]**

Schengen Convention — treaty signed in 1990 implementing the Schengen Agreement. Since then all member states except Ireland and the United Kingdom have acceded to the Schengen agreements; Iceland and Norway, two EEA member states, have also acceded. **[E]**

Schengen Protocol — protocol attached to the Treaty on European Union (by the Treaty of Amsterdam in 1999) integrating the Schengen *acquis* into the framework of the European Union. **[E]**

Schengenland — informal term describing the combined territory of those states party to the Schengen Agreement. **[E]**

school age — a child is of school age if he has attained five years of age and is not yet sixteen years of age: Education (Scotland) Act 1980, s 32(6). Parents have a duty to provide for every child of school age efficient education suitable to his or her age, ability or aptitude either by causing him or her to attend a public school regularly or by other means.

Schuman declaration — the formal announcement by French foreign minister Robert Schuman, on 9 May 1950, of the **Schuman plan** (qv). **[E]**

Schuman plan — the proposal for the pooling of control of coal and steel production, particularly in France and Germany, under a single authority, which formed the core of the **European Coal and Steel Community** (qv). **[E]**

sciens — knowingly.

sciens et prudens — in full knowledge; intentionally.

scienter — knowingly; the knowledge by the owner of an animal of its vicious nature, which formerly rendered him absolutely liable for damage caused by the animal. See now the Animals (Scotland) Act 1987.

scintilla juris — spark of law. Where there is no authority at all for a particular legal argument there is said to be no *scintilla juris* for it.

scire et scire debere aequiparantur in jure — to know a thing and to be bound to know it are the same thing in law. Ignorance of the law does not excuse any violation of it because everyone is bound and presumed to know the law of his own country.

scission — an operation, sometimes called 'division', by which the business of one legal person is transferred to more than one legal person. **[E]**

ScoLAG or SCOLAG — the Scottish Legal Action Group.

Scotland Act 1998 — the act of the United Kingdom Parliament which created the **Scottish Parliament** (qv) and the **Scottish Executive** (qv) and which lays down their powers and competencies.

Scotland Office — the department of the United Kingdom Government dealing with its Scottish matters, headed by the Secretary of State for Scotland, consisting of those parts of the former **Scottish Office** (qv) responsible for non-devolved matters, and now part of the Department of Constitutional Affairs.

Scots money. *See* **pound Scots**.

Scottish Cabinet, the — the senior members of the **Scottish Executive** (qv); a committee consisting of the **First Minister** (qv), the Deputy First Minister, other Scottish Ministers appointed under s 47 of the Scotland Act 1998 and the Lord Advocate.

Scottish Commission for Public Audit — committee of 5 MSP's which supervises **Audit Scotland** (qv).

Scottish Constitutional Convention — political body, existing between 1989 and 1995, composed of certain Scottish political parties and other public groups, which produced the detailed proposals for a devolution scheme, the **Claim of Right** (qv) which informed the United Kingdom Government's devolution policy and eventually resulted in the **Scotland Act 1998** (qv).

Scottish Court Service — an executive agency which is responsible for the provision of buildings, staff and services needed by the judicial system.

Scottish Criminal Cases Review Commission — public body responsible for considering convictions based on an alleged miscarriage of justice, with the power to refer deserving cases to the **High Court of Justiciary** (qv) for determination.

Scottish Environment Protection Agency — government body responsible for environmental protection in Scotland.

Scottish Executive — the statutory name for the government of Scotland created by the Scotland Act 1998 s 44, composed of the party or parties with the largest representation in the **Scottish Parliament** (qv) and answerable to that body. It consists of the **First Minister** (qv), the senior ministers of the Scottish government, and the two **Scottish Law Officers** (qv).

Scottish Executive Justice Department — Department of the **Scottish Executive** (qv) replacing the Scottish Office Home Department and the Scottish Court Administration and responsible for the supervision of civil and criminal justice, the police and fire services, legal aid and liaison with the legal profession in Scotland; also responsible for the Scottish Prison Service and the Scottish Court Service.

Scottish government — informal term for the **Scottish Executive** (qv).

Scottish Land Court — a court set up under the Small Landholders (Scotland) Act 1911 with wide jurisdiction under Acts relating to agricultural holdings, smallholdings and crofts. The court comprises a legally qualified chairman with the status of a judge of the Court of Session and six other members experienced in agriculture, one of whom must speak Gaelic.

Scottish Land Register. *See* **Land Register of Scotland**.

Scottish Law Commission — a body set up in 1965, comprising a chairman and not more than four other commissioners appointed by the Lord Advocate, to promote the reform of the law of Scotland by keeping the law under review and recommending codification, the elimination of anomalies, the repeal of unnecessary and obsolete enactments and generally the simplification and modernisation of the law. The Law Commission performs similar functions in respect of English law.

Scottish Law Officers — the **Lord Advocate** (qv) and the **Solicitor General for Scotland** (qv). *See also* **Advocate General**.

Scottish Office — prior to Scottish **devolution** (qv) all the departments of government which were concerned with Scottish affairs over the whole spectrum of government activities (eg education; environment; health; transport) for each of which, in England, there is a separate ministry, but which in Scotland were under the control of the **Secretary of State for Scotland** (qv).

Scottish Parliament —

(1) the present day legislature created by the Scotland Act 1998 and composed of members elected by the peoples of Scotland. As a statutory creation of the United Kingdom Parliament the Scottish Parliament only has those powers which are devolved to it by the United Kingdom Parliament.

(2) (Historical) the parliament of the Kingdom of Scotland which was merged with the parliament of the Kingdom of England by the Acts of Union of 1707.

Scottish Parliamentary Commissioner for Administration — the Scottish Parliamentary Ombudsman, an independent official who investigates complaints that come from members of the public claiming that they have suffered injustice because of maladministration by those public bodies that come within his jurisdiction, such as the **Scottish Executive** (qv); the **Scottish Parliamentary Corporate Body** (qv); and various Scottish public bodies and tribunals.

Scottish Parliamentary Corporate Body — organisation which provides the property, staff and services required by the Scottish Parliament.

Scottish public authority — is defined by the Scotland Act 1998, s 126, to mean any public body (except the Parliamentary corporation), public office, or holder of such an office whose functions (in each case) are exercisable only in or as regards Scotland.

Scottish Seal — The named used by the Scotland Act 1998 for the royal seal appointed by the Treaty of Union to be used in place of the Great Seal of Scotland, and still informally referred to by that name. A bill of the **Scottish Parliament** (qv) becomes law on the day when **letters patent** (qv) under the Scottish Seal signed by the monarch are recorded in the Register of the Great Seal (Scotland Act 1998 s 28).

Scottish Solicitors' Discipline Tribunal — a statutory tribunal established to investigate complaints of unprofessional conduct on the part of solicitors, inadequate professional services, breaches of the professional practice rules and the conviction of solicitors for serious crime, and to impose appropriate penalties or punishment.

Scottish Solicitors Guarantee Fund — form of professional insurance to which all practising solicitors must contribute; the fund is used to reimburse any clients who have suffered monetary loss as a result of the dishonesty of a solicitor or their staff.

Scottish statutory instrument— a **statutory instrument** (qv) made by a member of the Scottish Executive under an Act of the Scottish Parliament or under other powers devolved by the Scotland Act 1998.

SCRA — Scottish Children's Reporter Administration.

scrip certificate — certificate entitling the holder to apply for shares in a company.

scripto vel juramento — by writ or oath. In certain circumstances a party was limited in evidence to the production of his opponent's writings or, alternatively, referring to his oath. Abolished by the Requirements of Writing (Scotland) Act 1995. *See* **oath on reference**.

SCRO — Scottish Criminal Record Office.

SE — '*Societas Europaea*'. *See* **European Company**. **[E]**

se defendendo — in defending himself; in **self-defence** (qv).

SEA —
   (1) **Single European Act** (qv) **[E]**;
   (2) strategic environmental assessment: the process of assessing the total incremental and cumulative environmental effects of implementing a policy, plan or programme.

seal — a device impressed, either on wax or directly onto documents, to symbolise authenticity. It is used primarily by the Crown, corporate bodies and notaries public.

search for encumbrances —
   (1) an inspection of all relevant property and personal registers to trace the recording of the sequence of title deeds to heritable property and to ascertain the presence or otherwise of **encumbrances** (qv) affecting the property or restrictions on its disposition;
   (2) a document recording the results of such an inspection.

search warrant — a warrant to search for stolen goods or for other material or documents which might form evidence in criminal proceedings. It is granted by a sheriff or magistrate on the sworn evidence of the applicant.

secondary creditor — a creditor whose security ranks below those of another creditor. Cf **catholic creditor**.

secondary legislation — any legislation which is not an **act of parliament** (qv) or act of the **Scottish parliament** (qv), viz **statutory instruments** (qv), **Scottish statutory instruments** (qv) and **orders in council** (qv).

Secretary of State — highest rank of minister in the United Kingdom government.

Secretary of State for Scotland — senior minister of the United Kingdom government with res[ponsibility for Scottish matters, head of the **Scotland Office** (qv) and a member of the United Kingdom cabinet. Prior to **devolution** (qv), the Secretary of State for Scotland was the political head of the **Scottish Office** (qv), **keeper of the Great Seal of Scotland** (qv), and the principal government minister concerned with Scottish affairs with extensive powers and duties which ranged over the whole spectrum of government activities (eg education; environment; health; transport) for each of which, in England, there is a separate minister but most of which have now been devolved to the **Scottish Executive** (qv).

SECS — Scottish Executive Corporate Services.

secundum . . . — according to . . .

secundum allegata et probata — according to what has been alleged and proved. The decision in every litigation must proceed upon the allegations of the parties and the evidence brought in support of them, and not upon the private knowledge of the judge. Cf *judicis est judicare secundum allegata et probata*.

secundum materiam subjectam — according to the subject matter.

secured creditor — a creditor holding a security for a debt, eg a **standard security** (qv) over heritable property or pledge over moveables.

security —
   (1) something which tends to assure or to secure that an obligation will be performed, being either a personal security (eg a guarantee or **cautionary obligation** (qv) by a third party) or a real security where rights are granted over the debtor's property by pledge or heritable security;
   (2) an investment, eg stocks and shares.

securities —
   (1) more than one security;
   (2) the general collective term for stocks and shares.

sed quaere — but inquire; an expression indicating doubt of the soundness of a judgment or proposition and suggesting further consideration.

SEDD - Scottish Executive Development Department.

sederunt — they sat; an attendance list, usually incorporated in the minutes of a meeting.

sederunt book — a record of the proceedings in a sequestration, maintained by the permanent trustee, and on his discharge lodged with the Accountant in Bankruptcy.

SEJD — **Scottish Executive Justice Department** (qv).

selective distribution — the distribution of goods by a supplier through intermediaries upon criteria chosen by him.

self-defence — a special defence to a criminal charge of homicidal assault. A person is entitled to use reasonable force to ward off an attack made upon him if there is no other way of escaping from the threatened violence.

semble — it seems: a word used to introduce a legal principle or proposition which is not quite clear but which appears to be implied in a particular judgment.

semper in dubiis benigniora praeferenda — in matters of doubt the more liberal view is always to be preferred: a rule of construction that, where the words used in a deed are doubtful or ambiguous, the most liberal interpretation is to be given to them so as to carry out what, from the deed itself, appears to have been the granter's intention. More generally, preference is to be given, in cases of doubt, to the most liberal or charitable view which the words, acts or circumstances in question will admit. Thus an accused person is always entitled to the benefit of a reasonable doubt of his guilt.

semper praesumitur pro negante — the presumption is always in favour of the person who denies. Thus the onus is always on the person who affirms. It is not always necessary (or, indeed, possible) to prove the negative.

Senator of the College of Justice — a judge of the Court of Session.

senior — of counsel, a **Queen's Counsel** (qv), as distinct from an advocate or junior counsel.

sentence —
(1) to impose a penalty on a person convicted of a crime or offence;
(2) the penalty thus imposed.

sententia interlocutoria revocari potest, definitiva non potest — an interlocutory judgment may be recalled, but a definite judgment may not. Thus a judge may always recall or review a procedural decision issued by him in the course of a litigation, but he may not recall or review a definitive decision on any question of substance in the litigation submitted to him. In respect of such a definitive decision he is *functus officio* (qv).

SEPA — **Scottish Environment Protection Agency** (qv).

separatim — separately; quite apart from anything argued or pleaded.

separation — the judicial separation, short of divorce, of spouses *a mensa et thoro* (qv).

separation of powers — constitutional theory that state power is (or ought to be) divided into three branches the executive, the legislature and the judiciary all of which are, and ought to be, kept separate and independent of each other in their operation.

sequestration —
(1) the process of rendering an individual bankrupt by attaching, ingathering and setting aside his assets, heritable and moveable, and vesting them in a trustee for the benefit of the bankrupt's creditors;
(2) generally, the judicial seizure of assets to enforce a claim or to satisfy a court order.

sequestration for rent — the seizure under the order of the sheriff court of a tenant's moveable property within his house for sale to satisfy his landlord's claim for arrears of rent. Such sequestration is the diligence to enforce the landlord's right of **hypothec** (qv).

seriatim — one by one; one after another.

series rerum judicatarum — a succession of decisions deciding some particular proposition or principle.

service —
(1) the timeous delivery of a judicial writ or other formal document to another person in the prescribed manner as required by law;
(2) the duty owed by an employee to his employer under a contract of service (*locatio operarum*) to do work in the manner directed by the employer, in contrast to a contract for services (*locatio operis faciendi*), where the employer has only limited control over the manner in which the services are performed and relies on the skill and expertise of the person hired;
(3) an obsolete judicial process, known as service of heirs, by which an heir's title to a deceased person's estate was established, being either general service, which

determined the heir's general title without application to any particular property, or special service, which established his general title and his specific right to enter and be infeft in particular heritage; still occasionally used in cases of succession to heritage which opened before 10 September 1964;

(4) the obsolete duty of a vassal to a feudal superior to perform certain personal services for him.

service mark — a mark (akin to a trade mark) used in relation to services, indicating that a particular person is connected in the course of business with the provision of those services.

services — in EC law, a fundamental right under the EC Treaty; *see* **free movement of services. [E]**

services of general economic interest — universal services provided by public or private **undertakings** (qv) charged by law with that task, and to the extent which it is necessary in order to enable them to do so, are excluded from the prohibitions of competition law.

servient tenement — land subject to a servitude in favour of the proprietor of other land, called the 'dominant tenement'.

servitude — an obligation attached to land, either restricting the owner's use of it (a 'negative servitude', eg limiting the height of buildings), or obliging the owner to allow others to exercise certain rights over it (a 'positive servitude'). Under the Title Conditions (Scotland) Act 2003, s 70, no new negative servitudes can be created after 28 November 2004. *See also* **dominant tenement; servient tenement**.

session —

(1) roughly a working year of the United Kingdom Parliament; ended and begun by prorogation; the equivalent in the Scottish Parliament is 'a parliamentary year';

(2) in the Scottish Parliament the period from the date of the first meeting of the Scottish Parliament following a general election until the time when the Scottish Parliament is dissolved (approximately four years unless there is early dissolution). The nearest Westminster equivalent is 'a Parliament': a period up to five years;

(3) *see* **sessions**; **Court of Session**.

Session Cases — authorised reports containing selected decisions of the **Court of Session** (qv).

sessions — the periods in a year, separated by vacations, during which the Court of Session and the sheriff courts sit to conduct civil business. The precise dates are fixed annually.

set-off. *See* **compensation**.

sett —

(1) the constitution of a burgh (obsolete);

(2) an action by a part owner of a ship seeking an order that the other part owners acquire his share or sell their shares to him, or that the ship be sold by public roup and the proceeds divided among the part owners.

settlement —

(1) the termination of an action or legal dispute on agreed terms;

(2) the completion of a transaction relating to heritable property;

(3) a deed setting up a trust, *inter vivos* or *mortis causa*, to dispose of property subject to conditions and limitations;

(4) the arrangement constituted by such a deed.

Sewel convention — colloquial term used for the United Kingdom Government's stated policy on legislating on **devolved matters** (qv) in the United Kingdom Parliament, viz that that the United Kingdom Parliament would not normally legislate with regard to devolved matters except with the agreement of the Scottish Parliament. Named after Lord Sewel, who set out the terms of the government policy in the House of Lords on 21 July 1998 during the passage of the Scotland Bill.

Sewel motion — colloquial term used for a motion in the Scottish Parliament (qv) giving its consent to devolved matters being legislated for in a Bill in the United Kingdom Parliament, under the 'Sewel Convention' (qv).

SFO — Serious Fraud Office.

share — a proportion of the ownership of the capital of a company which confers on the shareholder a right to share in the company's profits.

shareholder — person who owns a share in a company. Shareholders have the right to attend a company's annual meeting, and to vote on the election of members of the Board of Directors and certain other company matters.

sheriff — judge of the sheriff court, which is the main inferior court in Scotland. Originally the shire reeve; the holder of an ancient office who was the king's man in the shire or county. The office was hereditary until 1746, and comprised extensive military, financial, administrative and judicial functions. The sheriff is now the judge of a sheriff court and has an almost unlimited civil jurisdiction and an extensive criminal jurisdiction. In criminal matters appeal lies to the High Court of Justiciary and in civil matters to the **Sheriff Principal** (qv) and/or to the **Inner House** (qv). Qualified persons may be appointed as temporary sheriffs. Honorary sheriffs, appointed by the sheriff principal, need not be legally qualified. They may relieve sheriffs of such duties as may be allocated to them.

sheriff clerk — the principal clerk of court in a sheriff court. He may be assisted by deputes and supported by ancillary staff.

sheriff court — the principal inferior court in Scotland, presided over by the **sheriff** (qv). Has both a civil and criminal jurisdiction. In civil matters appeal from sheriff court lies to the sheriff principal and the Inner House of the Court of Session.

sheriff court district — the area which comprises the territorial jurisdiction of a sheriff court. *See also* **sheriffdom**.

sheriff officer — an officer of a sheriff court who is responsible for serving process and executing diligence. He is generally also a **messenger-at-arms** (qv).

sheriff principal — a judge, formerly known as a **sheriff** (qv), appointed to secure the speedy and efficient disposal of business in the sheriff courts throughout his **sheriffdom** (qv). In his judicial capacity he hears appeals from sheriffs in civil cases, and appeal from him in turn lies to the Inner House of the Court of Session. He is also responsible for the administration of the sheriff courts under his authority.

sheriff substitute — the title, from 1746 to 1971, of the **sheriff** (qv).

sheriffdom — the area within which a sheriff principal exercises his jurisdiction. There are currently six sheriffdoms, each being divided into sheriff court districts.

shewer — one of two persons appointed by the Court of Session to accompany selected jurors in a civil case on a view of a place or other subject.

ship's master — on merchant vessel, the officer in command of ship, who is generally deemed to be the agent of the ship's owners.

short title — every statute of the United Kingdom and Scottish Parliaments contains a provision giving it a short title by which it can be cited.

shorthand writer — a person who makes a verbatim shorthand note of the evidence given at a proof or trial.

shrieval — adjectival form of sheriff.

SI — **statutory instrument** (qv). Cf **SSI**.

si institutus sine liberis decesserit — if the beneficiary dies childless. *See* **conditio si institutus sine liberis decesserit**.

si petitur tantum (*or si petatur tantum*) — if asked only; a payment which must be made only if the person entitled to it demands it, eg a nominal feuduty, such as one penny Scots or a peppercorn rent.

si sit incompos mentis, fatuus et naturaliter idiota — if of unsound mind, fatuous and naturally an idiot: the question which a jury formerly had to answer when considering the obsolete brieve of idiotry.

si (testator) sine liberis decesserit — if (the testator) has died without issue. *See* **conditio si testator sine liberis decesserit**.

sic utere tuo ut alienum non laedas — so use your property that you do not harm your neighbour.

Signet — Originally the personal seal of the sovereign, as distinct from the **Great Seal** (qv). Summonses in Court of Session actions and warrants for diligence in such summonses must be signeted (ie bear the imprint of the Queen's seal) to be valid and effectual. *See also* **Keeper of the Signet**.

signeting — the process of applying the **Signet** (qv) to a document.

silk — a **Queen's Counsel** (qv), so called because he wears a silk gown, and hence the use of the expression 'to take silk' to describe appointment as a QC.

simul et semel — at one and the same time.

sine — without.

sine animo remanendi — without the intention of remaining: used of a person who has left the country but who intends to return.

sine animo revertendi — without the intention of returning: used of a person who has left the country for good.

sine causa — without legal cause (or ground or justification). A person who has benefited at another's expense *sine causa* may be unjustifiably enriched and bound to redress the enrichment. *See condictio sine causa*.

sine die — indefinitely; without a day being fixed eg for the resumption of adjourned proceedings.

sine qua non — without which nothing can effectually be done; an essential condition or factor.

sine quo non **trustee** — a trustee whose concurrence is required for all acts in the administration of the trust.

single bill roll — *See* **rolls**.

Single European Act — a treaty signed in 1986, in force 1987, by the member states of the European Communities amending and augmenting in certain respects the **founding treaties** (qv). **[E]**

singular successor — a person who acquires the right to heritable or moveable property in some character other than by succesion *mortis causa*. Thus a purchaser, a donee or a creditor acquiring property are all singular successors of the previous proprietor. Cf **universal successor**.

singuli in solidum — each is liable for the whole. *See* **conjunct and several obligation**.

sist —
   (1) to stay or suspend court proceedings by order of the court;
   (2) a stay or suspension of court proceedings;
   (3) a court order staying or suspending legal proceedings;
   (4) to add another person in court proceedings as a litigant, eg as a third party with an interest intervening in a cause, as the executor of a deceased party or as the trustee or liquidator of an insolvent party; or a mandatory for a pursuer living abroad.

skat — a tribute under udal tenure payable by udallers in Orkney and Shetland to the earl or to the Crown in right of the bishop (from the Norse *skattr* — tax; tribute). Future imposition of skat was prohibited in 1974.

SLR — statute law revision; Statute Law Revision Act.

SLS — **Society of Legal Scholars** (qv).

sleep — the state into which a civil action fell when a year and a day had passed since the last step was taken in the procedure. In order to become operative again a minute of wakening was required.

sluicegate price — nominal price fixed in some common organisations of the **market** (qv) under the **common agricultural policy** (qv), essentially the world market price, sale of imported agricultural products below which will attract a levy. **[E]**

small claim — an action that may be raised under the small claims procedure, viz claims up to a value of £1,500 for money, delivery or recovery of moveable property or for performance of an obligation.

small claims court — a court conducted by the sheriff for resolving **small claims** (qv) and petty disputes rapidly and inexpensively under a relatively informal procedure.

small debt court — a court conducted before the sheriff or justices of the peace for the summary and inexpensive determination of petty claims. The sheriff's jurisdiction was latterly extended to £50 but was abolished in 1976 with the introduction of the **summary cause** (qv).

small tenancy — a tenancy of an agricultural holding controlled by the Crofters Acts as applied by the Small Landholders (Scotland) Acts.

smallholding — a form of agricultural tenancy of restricted size regulated by the Small Landholders (Scotland) Acts and similar to a **croft** (qv) but situated outside the **seven crofting counties** (qv).

SME's — small and medium enterprises.

Social Charter. *See* **European Social Charter. [E]**

social security — a system of contributions and benefits regulated by the Social Security Contributions and Benefits Act 1992 and administered under the Social Security Administration Act 1992.

societas — the contract of society or partnership.

Societas Europaea. See **European Company. [E]**

Society of Legal Scholars — (SLS). The Society of Legal Scholars in the United Kingdom and Ireland. A society for the advancement of legal education and scholarship, mainly composed of legal scholars and teachers of law in universities. (formerly known as Society of Public Teachers of Law or SPTL).

socii — partners; associates.

socius criminus — an associate or accomplice in crime; *particeps criminis.*

soft law — regulations which are not binding in that they cannot be enforced in a court of law.

SOGA — Sale of Goods Act 1979.

solatium — compensation; damages given for injury to feelings or reputation, pain and suffering and loss of expectation of life. Awards of *solatium* to members of the immediate family of a deceased person were replaced by a **loss of society** (qv) award under the Damages (Scotland) Act 1976.

solemn procedure — the procedure under which a person charged with serious crime on indictment is tried before a sheriff, or judge of the High Court of Justiciary, together with a jury of fifteen, whose decision to convict may be reached by at least eight votes.

solicitor — a lawyer who is employed to conduct legal proceedings, to give advice on legal matters, to draw up legal papers, to appear before the lower courts. The vast majority of members of the Scots legal profession are solicitors, as distinct from **advocates** (qv). All practising solicitors in Scotland are required to be members of the Law Society of Scotland; sometimes known as a law agent, a writer, a procurator or (in Aberdeen) an advocate.

solicitor advocate — a solicitor who has obtained the right to appear in person before either or both of the higher courts, viz the **High Court of Justiciary** (qv) and the **Court of Session** (qv).

Solicitor General for Scotland — a law officer of the Crown who assists the Lord Advocate and is a member of the **Scottish Executive** (qv).

Solicitors in the Supreme Courts of Scotland (SSC) — a society of solicitors practising in the Court of Session, formed in 1784 and incorporated by royal charter in 1797.

solo animo — by the mere act of the mind; by mere intention or design. The law takes no cognisance of intent until it leads to some overt act. Thus an intention to steal is not criminal until it becomes at least an attempt.

solum — soil or ground, especially that on which a building stands.

solus cum sola in loco suspecto — a man alone with a woman in a suspicious place or circumstances. The circumstances may point to adultery.

sorner — one who begs importunately with threats; a scrounger; the subject of early poor law legislation.

souming and rouming; sowming and rowming — an action relating to the servitude of pasturage in which the extent of the pasturage and the proportion to be enjoyed by each commoner is determined.

sovereign —
  (1) the person or institution which exercises supreme legal authority within a given state, in the United Kingdom it is the **Queen-in-Parliament** (qv) which is sovereign;
  (2) the reigning King or Queen.

sovereignty — the supreme legal authority within a given state.

SPA — **Special Protection Areas** (qv) and **Special Areas of** Conservation (qv).

SPCB — **Scottish Parliamentary Corporate Body** (qv).

Speaker — the presiding officer of the United Kingdom Parliament.

Special Area of Conservation — an officially designated conservation area.

special case —
  (1) proceedings to obtain, by consent, the opinion, or the opinion and judgment, of the Inner House of the Court of Session on a point of law when the parties agree as to the facts;
  (2) a form of statutory appeal by which the opinion of the Court of Session may be obtained on a point of law referred to it by an inferior court, eg the Scottish Land Court or the sheriff principal sitting as an election court.

special defence — a defence (eg alibi, insanity, incrimination or self-defence) notice of which must be given to the prosecutor before the beginning of a criminal trial.

special destination — a provision in a will or the title to heritable property indicating or directing some departure from the legally implied line of succession *mortis causa*.

Special Drawing Rights — an artificial currency unit created by the IMF out of a basket of national currencies.

Special Protection Areas — a designated environmental conservation area.

special service. *See* **service** (3).

special verdict — the verdict of a jury in a civil trial making findings of fact to enable the court to apply the appropriate law, as distinct from a verdict determining the specific issues raised.

specialisation agreement — an agreement between two or more undertakings by which the parties specialise in different areas of business, eg one party concentrates on the production of certain goods and the other party ceases to produce those goods (often in order to concentrate on another area of business), obtaining its requirements from the first party instead. **[E]**

species facti — the particular nature of the thing done; the precise circumstances attending any alleged crime or civil wrong.

specific duty — a customs duty expressed as a particular sum (eg 16 Euros) rather than as a percentage of the value of the goods. **[E]**

specific implement; specific performance — the performance of a contractual or common law obligation, other than by the payment of money. It is enforced by decree *ad factum praestandum* (qv), but damages may be awarded instead.

specific legacy — a legacy of a determinate subject; payable before any **demonstrative, general or residual legacy** (qv).

specificatio — acquisition of property by changing the formation of materials belonging to another into a new species, eg by making flour out of corn or wine out of grapes.

specification — in written pleadings, the full and proper description of the facts and circumstances and the legal propositions upon which a party founds. A lack of specification may be pled in an attack upon the relevancy of pleadings and may lead to the dismissal of an action or defence.

spei emptio — the purchase of a hope or chance, eg of the right of succession or the produce of the cast of a net.

spent conviction — a previous conviction treated through lapse of time as no longer of any effect by virtue of the legislation on rehabilitation of offenders.

spes obligationis — the hope or expectation of a future obligation.

spes successionis — the hope or expectation of future succession. It has a market value and may be used for security.

spoliatus ante omnia restituendus — a person despoiled is to be restored to his possession first. Thus a person violently deprived of goods of which he is in actual possession may recover them on proving that actual possession, even against the true owner, before questions of right are considered. *See* **spuilzie**.

spondet peritiam artis et imperitia culpae enumeratur — a person is responsible for exercising skill in his profession, and want of such skill will be regarded as a fault. Thus an employer is entitled to assume that a person will display the skill which he professes, up to a reasonable standard.

sponsiones ludicrae — obligations in jest; an agreement unenforceable because the parties did not seriously intend to be bound in law, eg a betting or gaming contract.

SPS — Scottish Prison Service.

spuilzie (pronounced 'spool(y)i')
    (1) the carrying off of, or intermeddling with, the moveable property of another without his consent;
    (2) a civil action for the restoration of spuilzied property and damages for consequential loss.

SR & O. *See* **statutory rules and orders**.

SRO — Scottish Records Office, offcial state archive which changed its name in 1999 to the National Archives of Scotland.

SSC — Society of Solicitors in the Supreme Court.

SSI —
    (1) **Scottish statutory instrument** (qv);
    (2) site of scientific interest.

SSP — second state pension.

STABEX — stabilisation of export earnings; a system of financial transfers designed to compensate **ACP countries** (qv) in the event of a reduction in their earnings from the export of certain basic (mainly agricultural) products. **[E]**

stabiliser — any mechanism adopted within the framework of the **common agricultural policy** (qv) which seeks to regulate agricultural production. **[E]**

stability pact — alternatively, the stability and growth pact; a 1997 agreement within the European Council designed to maintain fiscal discipline within **economic and monetary union** (qv). **[E]**

stabit praesumptio donec probetur in contrarium — the presumption will stand until the contrary is proved: a general rule providing that those who have the benefit of a presumption will retain it until it is overcome by proof to the contrary.

stables of advocates — **advocates** (qv) are divided into groups, known as stables, each run by an advocates' **clerk** (qv) after whom the stable is named, in 2002 there were 12 stables.

staff case — an action brought before the **Court of First Instance** (qv) by an official or other servant of the European Community against the employing **Community institution** (qv). **[E]**

Staff Regulations — the regulations governing the employment of officials of the **Community institutions** (qv). **[E]**

stages of public bills — the formal stages of consideration of a public bill by the Scottish Parliament. Stage 1 is a consideration of, and a decision on, a bill's general principles. Stage 2 is a consideration of the details of a bill by a parliamentary committee (or committees) or in a Committee of the Whole Parliament. Stage 3 is the final consideration of a bill and a decision whether it should be passed or rejected. **Reconsideration** (qv) is a further stage after a bill has been passed if a bill has been subject to a legal reference or a section 35 order preventing it from going for the royal assent.

Stair Society — a learned society founded in 1934 to encourage the study and knowledge of the history of the law of Scotland and to publish books on aspects of the subject.

stakeholder pension — a type of low-cost pension introduced in 2001.

stamp duty — a tax on a legal document, the payment of which, evidenced by impressing or affixing an official stamp, is generally essential to the enforceability of the obligations constituted by the document.

standard charge. *See* **stipend**.

standard of proof — there are two standards of proof in Scot law:
(1) in criminal cases a fact or a criminal charge must be proved 'beyond all reasonable doubt';
(2) in a civil case the standard of proof is 'on the balance of probability'.

standard conditions — statutory conditions which, subject to variations agreed by the parties, regulate a **standard security** (qv).

standard security — the only form in which an interest in land for the purpose of securing a debt by way of a heritable security may now be created. It is not effective until recorded in the General Register of Sasines or registered in the Land Register of Scotland.

standing orders — orders or rules regulating the proceedings of a body and how it conducts its business (including for example either House of the United Kingdom Parliament; the Scottish Parliament; the General Assemby of the Church of Scotland) and normally made by that body.

standstill provision — a provision of European Community law, usually part of a transitional regime, which prohibits the introduction of further measures in addition to those existing at the time when the standstill provision comes into effect. **[E]**

stare decisis — literally to stand upon decisions; to abide by precedents. Used to describe the doctrine that subsequent courts must strictly obey relevant precedents.

state aid — aid granted by a member state of the European Community or through state resources in any form whatever. **[E]**

state trading country — a state (few of which remain) in which trade (in particular external trade) is conducted through the agency of the state. **[E]**

stated case — an appeal procedure by which the decision of an inferior court or tribunal may be referred to the Court of Session or the High Court of Justiciary so that that court may pronounce on questions of law arising. In the procedure the lower court 'states a case for the opinion of' the appeal court.

statement of claim — the part of a summary cause summons in which pursuers set out details of their cases against defenders.

statement of compatibility — under the **Human Rights Act** (qv) a written statement must be attached to any legislative proposal stating that the provisions of a bill are compatible with the **Convention** (qv). In the United Kingdom parliament this is made by a minister before the Second Reading of a Bill, and in the Scottish Parliament this is made by a minister and also by the Presiding Officer before a bill is introduced.

statement of objections — a document delivered by the European Commission to an **undertaking** (qv) before the Commission reaches a decision on an alleged infringement of EC competition rules, in which the Commission sets out the allegations which it proposes to make against the undertaking. **[E]**

status — the legal standing or position of a person, eg as a minor, single person, widow etc, upon which may depend his or her legal capacity.

status quo — the existing or present situation or state of affairs.

status quo ante — the situation or state of affairs which existed before a particular date or event.

statute — a law created by a legislature, in particular:
(1) an Act of Parliament, public or private, made by the Sovereign by and with the advice and consent of Parliament and by its authority. In traditional constitutional theory the United Kingdom parliament has unlimited law-making powers;
(2) an Act of the Scottish Parliament, concerning a devolved matter, made by the Scottish Parliament, and with the consent of the Sovereign, within its authority as granted by the **Scotland Act** (qv) and provided it is compatible with the **Human Rights Act** 1998 (qv).

statutory instruments (SI) — the form in which orders, rules, regulations or other subordinate legislation are made. Statutory instruments are prescribed or enacted under the royal prerogative or statutory authority by the Queen in Council or a minister of the Crown. *See* **Scottisgh statutory instrument**.

statutory rules and orders (SR & O) — the form in which subordinate legislation was made until the end of 1947. Thereafter they took the form of **statutory instruments** (qv).

steelbow — a practice by which the landlord of a farm stocked the farm on an undertaking by his tenant to restore their equivalents at the end of the lease.

stellionate — any fraudulent or deceitful act (obsolete).

stent — a tax or duty.

stillicide. *See* **eavesdrop**.

stipend — the remuneration of a parish minister which was formerly met out of a standard charge upon local heritable property, and formerly based on **teinds** (qv). It must now be redeemed upon sale.

stipendiary magistrate — a salaried legally qualified magistrate appointed by a local authority to be a judge in a district court.

stirpes — see *per stirpes*. English adjective: 'stirpital'.

stocks — a fixed-interest security.

stop now order — order made under an EC Directive (Directive No 98/27 of 19 May 1998) and national measures implementing it (in the United Kingdom, SI 2001/1422) to stop infringements of consumer protection laws. **[E]**

stoppage in transit — the statutory right of an unpaid seller of goods who has parted with possession of the goods to stop them in transit if the buyer becomes insolvent, and to resume possession of them and retain them pending payment. See the Sale of Goods Act 1979, ss 44-46.

stouthrief — obsolete term of criminal law meaning 'masterful theft or depradation' and once often applied to robbery in dwellings or burglary.

Strasbourg — city in Alsace in the east of France which is the seat of the **Council of Europe** (qv) and the **European Court of Human Rights** (qv) and hence the place name is often used as a synonym for matters concerned with the Council of Europe and, more especially the **European Court of Human Rights** (qv) or the **European Convention of Human Rights** (qv).

Strasbourg case law/jurisprudence — colloquial expression for the judicial decisions of the **European Court of Human Rights** (qv). Under s 2 of the Human Rights Act 1998 any United Kingdom court or tribunal making a decision concerning **Convention rights** (qv) must take the decisions of the ECtHR into account.

Strasbourg Court. *See* **European Court of Human Rights**.

strict liability — liability in delict regardless of fault on the pursuer establishing the facts constituting the delict but subject to certain defences. Strict liability differs from absolute liability because in strict liability some defences such as *damnum fatale*(qv) elide liability. The principle of strict liability also arises under statute in the criminal law in certain circumstances where something is done or allowed to happen without any intention or negligence or, sometimes, even knowledge on the offender's part.

stricti juris — according to strict right or law.

structural funds — general term for various funds within the European Community budget for the amelioration of underdeveloped, declining or stagnant regions of the Community. **[E]**

structured settlement — a settlement giving a victim of personal injuries claiming damages a lump-sum and an index-linked annuity payable by the wrongdoer's insurers.

style —
(1) the name or title of a person;
(2) an approved form of a document, used as a model for drawing up similar documents.

sua sponte — voluntarily; of one's own free will.

sub judice — in the hands of the law. A matter or dispute which is *sub judice* has been brought before a court in a litigation for decision, but the decision has not yet been given.

sub modo — under condition or restriction. Thus property may be conveyed to a trustee under condition that it be applied for certain specified purposes.

sub nomine — under the name of.

sub silentio — in silence.

subfeuar — a person who holds heritable property by **subinfeudation** (qv).

subinfeudation — the grant of a sub-feu by a feudal proprietor out of his heritable estate. Prohibitions against subinfeudation are void. The power to feu or sub-feu will be extinguished as from 28 November 2004; *see* **feu, feudal tenure**.

subjects — property, generally heritable, although the expression can sometimes and in certain contexts comprehend moveables.

submission — a contract entered into between two or more parties who have debatable rights or claims against one another, by which they refer their differences to the final determination of an arbiter and oblige themselves to acquiesce in his decision.

submissions —
(1) the opinion of an Advocate-General of the European Court of Justice;
(2) the relief sought by a party to proceedings before the European Court of Justice or the Court of First Instance;
(3) arguments relied on in support of a claim for relief made by a party to such proceedings. **[E]**

subordinate legislation — Orders in Council, orders, rules, regulations, schemes, warrants, byelaws and other instruments made, or to be made, under the authority of an Act of the United Kingdom Parliament or of the Scottish Parliament.

subordinate real right — a real right in the property of another (*jus in re aliena*). The categories of subordinate real right recognised by Scots law include right in security; proper liferent; servitude; lease; and exclusive privilege. Possession and public rights of way are sometimes also so classified.

subornation of perjury — the crime of inducing a witness to commit **perjury** (qv).

subreption — obtaining gifts by concealing the truth. Cf **obreption**.

subrogation — substitution; the principle under which a person who has discharged another's debt is entitled to any related claims, securities or rights of relief vested in that other. The principle for example allows an insurer who has indemnified the insured for loss caused to the insured by a third party's delict to succeed to the rights of the insured.

subsequente copula — with subsequent carnal intercourse. Prior to 1940 intercourse allowed on the faith of a promise of marriage constituted a valid irregular marriage.

subsidiarity — a general principle of Community law, formally adopted into the EC Treaty in 1993 by the Treaty on European Union, seeking to ensure that decisions are taken and tasks implemented at the most appropriate practical level of authority, either Community or national; it is a principle which also obtains within the constitutional order of some states, eg Germany. **[E]**

subsidiary company — a company which is under the control of another company (called a holding company).

substitute — a person named as beneficiary in case the **institute** (qv) fails.

substitution — in testate **succession** (qv), an enumeration of a series of heirs or successors described in the appropriate technical language.

substitutional redress — a synonym for damages, so called because damages are substituted for literal enforcement by specific implement.

succession — the passing of property from one person to another, especially on the death of the owner, governed by deed or will or, on an intestacy, by statutory rules. Succession may be universal, under which the whole of the property, with its rights and liabilities, passes together (eg to the executor of a deceased person or a trustee on bankruptcy), or singular, where particular items of property pass to a specific person such as a purchaser or donee.

sue — to raise a civil action against a person.

sufficiently serious — in (the clearer) French, *suffisament charactérisé*; that quality of a breach of a legal duty owed by a Community institution or a member state acting within the sphere of Community law which will give rise to a right in reparation for persons injured by the breach. **[E]**

sui generis — unique.

sui juris — of full legal capacity, describing a person not under a legal disability such as minority, pupillarity or insanity.

summar roll. *See* **rolls**.

summary application — an application to a sheriff which may be disposed of either forthwith or in accordance with a summary and swift procedure prescribed by the sheriff subject to the Summary Application Rules; much used for administrative proceedings rather than proceedings enforcing a right; equivalent to a petition in Court of Session procedure.

summary cause — a civil action in the sheriff court seeking payment or the delivery of goods to the value of £1,500. It is commenced by summons under and follows the simplified procedure set out in the Summary Cause Rules.

summary decree — a decree granted by the Court of Session on the application of the pursuer in an action where the defences lodged disclose no defence to the action.

summary diligence — diligence proceedings to enforce the payment of a debt without the necessity of an action to constitute the debt. It is employed to enforce payment of bills of exchange, promissory notes, and extracts of documents of debt registered for preservation and execution in the Books of Council and Session or sheriff court books.

summary petition. *See* **summary trial**.

summary proceedings — criminal proceedings taken before a sheriff, magistrate or justice sitting alone, ie without a jury; is used for the trial of less serous offences.

summary removing — a procedure by which, where heritable property is let for a shorter period than a year, the sheriff may on summary application pronounce a decree for removing.

summary sequestration — an adaptation of the normal sequestration procedure formerly used where a debtor's assets did not exceed £300. It has now been replaced by a modified procedure under Schedule 2 of the Bankruptcy (Scotland) Act 1985 for small estates or for sequestrations where the creditors do not elect a permanent trustee.

summary suspension — the sisting of diligence by the sheriff on the summary application of a party.

summary taxation — the **taxation** (qv) of a solicitor's account by the Auditor of Court on a remit by the Court of Session granted on the summary application of the client or the solicitor during the dependence of the process in court or following decree.

summary trial —
(1) the trial of a dispute or question in the Outer House of the Court of Session by consent of the parties on application initiated by summary petition, held either in court or in chambers by an agreed simplified procedure;
(2) the trial of an accused person under **summary proceedings** (qv).

summary trial rolls. *See* rolls.

summary warrant — a warrant issued by the sheriff to the Inlabd Revenue, Customs and Excise or a local authority authorising diligence for the recovery of arrears of rates or taxes without the need for a court action.

summons — a document requiring a person to appear in court to answer a claim made against him. The originating writ in a Court of Session action (as distinct from a petition) and in a sheriff court summary cause action.

summum jus, summa injuria — extreme right is extreme injury. Thus to give one person everything he is entitled to may inflict great harm on another. This principle is a restraint in equity on the strict enforcement of a legal right or obligation.

suo nomine — in one's own name.

suo periculo — at one's own risk. *See periculo petentis*.

superior — in feudal tenure the person holding heritable property immediately from the Crown (the paramount superior) who grants land to a vassal in return for the payment of feuduty. The vassal then holds the *dominium utile* (qv) and the superior retains the *dominium directum* (qv). The vassal may in turn, as mediate superior, grant land to a sub-vassal, and so on, without limit. Feuduties may no longer be created, must be redeemed on sale and any unredeemed on 28 November 2004 will be extinguished on that date when feudal tenure is abolished: *see* **allodial**; **feu**; **feudal tenure**.

supersede —
(1) to postpone for a period, as of an extract for a decree;
(2) to replace.

support —
(1) the law on the adjacent or subjacent support from land to land or from land to buildings;
(2) an urban servitude entitling the proprietor of the dominant tenement to rest the weight of his building on the wall of the servient tenement;
(3) maintenance payable by a parent under the Child Support Act 1991 in respect of a child.

supra — above.

supra citatum — above cited (generally abbreviated '*sup cit*'), a phrase used to refer to a matter earlier or already cited.

surety — English legal term of art for a guarantor, used sometimes in Scots law instead of the indigenous term **cautioner** (qv).

surrogatum — a surrogate or substitute.

surrogatum capit naturam rei surrogati — a thing substituted partakes of the nature or character of that for which it was substituted.

survivorship clause — a clause in a will or conveyance by which a testator or granter provides that should one of several beneficiaries or grantees die before he takes his interest, it is to pass to the survivor or those who survive.

suspension — the means by which injury of rights, occasioned or threatened by court decrees, sentences or orders and diligence, is prevented, namely:
(1) a procedure in the Court of Session or sheriff court to stay the execution of diligence or threatened diligence (*see also* **suspension and interdict**);
(2) a procedure in the Court of Session to recall a decree granted *in absentia*;
(3) a procedure in the Court of Session to recall the decree of an inferior court;
(4) a procedure by which an illegal warrant or summary conviction in criminal proceedings in the sheriff court or the district court may be set aside by the High Court of Justiciary.

suspension and interdict —
(1) a procedure in the Court of Session to stay the execution of diligence where injury has taken place, eg where there has been an attachment (if a sale of the attached goods has been obtained, the remedy is suspension or suspension and interdict);
(2) a procedure in the Court of Session to prevent injury to a right by a deliberate act which is threatened or is being performed.

suspension and liberation — a procedure in the Court of Session for release from imprisonment for civil debt.

suspensive condition — a condition which prevents an obligation arising unless and until a specific future event, certain or uncertain, occurs. Cf **resolutive condition**.

sustain — in Scots court procedure – when a court agrees with and upholds a party's plea-in-law.

suum cuique tribuere — to give to everyone that which is his due: one of the three principles laid down by Justinian (*Institutes* I, 1, 3) as those upon which all rules of law are based. '*Suum cuique*' is the motto of the Faculty of Advocates.

symbolic delivery — handing over a small thing as a token to represent the transfer by law of ownership of a much larger thing by delivery.

SWSI — Social Work Services Inspectorate.

SWIFT — Society for Worldwide Interbank Financial Telecommunications; sytem which allows international transfers between banks.

t

tacit — arising by operation of law as in 'tacit **hypothec**' (qv).

tacit relocation — implied consent to the renewal of a lease if notice to terminate the lease is not given timeously. The renewal is for one year in the case of a lease for a year or more or, in the case of a lease for a shorter term, for that term. The principle applies also to certain contracts of service and (save that the renewal is indefinite) to partnerships.

taciturnity — silence of the creditor which raises a presumption that, in the relative situations of himself and the debtor, and in all the circumstances, the creditor would not have been so long silent if the debt had not been paid or other obligation implemented. *See also* ***mora*** and **acquiescence**.

tack —
(1) a lease or tenancy, especially of a farm or a mill (obsolescent);
(2) the land held on a tack;
(3) a payment levied by a feudal superior (obsolete).

tack duty or takkar duty — the rent paid by a tacksman.

tacksman — the lessee under a tack.

TAIEX — the technical assistance exchange office of the European Community. TAIEX deals with the public administrations in the applicant countries and the member states. It provides the legal texts of the ***acquis communautaire*** (qv) and assesses the legislation of the applicant countries conformity with Community legislation (screening). *See also* **Phare**. **[E]**

tailzie *or* **tailyie** (pronounced 'tile(y)i'). *See* **entail**.

takkar — the person who granted a tack.

tanquam quilibet — like any other person. The Sovereign or an official may have certain prerogatives, but in ordinary matters, such as buying and selling property, they act *tanquam quilibet*.

tantum et tale — so much and of such a kind. Subjects so described when sold are accepted by the buyer with all their advantages and faults, just as they are.

tantum praescriptum quantum possessum — there is only one prescription in so far as there has been possession. Thus continuous possession for the appropriate period is an essential prerequisite for the operation of prescription.

target price — the price which it is hoped that producers of certain **agricultural products** (qv) will be able to obtain for their produce on the open market in the European Community. **[E]**

TARIC — the integrated tariff, based on the **combined nomenclature** (qv), containing additional sub-divisions needed in order to identify goods subject to certain specific measures adopted by the European Community, such as **anti-dumping duties** (qv). **[E]**

tariff —
(1) a customs duty;
(2) a list of customs duties (eg the common customs tariff of the European Community). **[E]**

tariff heading — a division of the common customs tariff of the European Community under which particular goods are classified for customs purposes. **[E]**

tariff preference — a tariff advantage, usually in the form of a reduced level of customs duty. *See also* **generalised tariff preference**. **[E]**

taxation — the scrutiny of a solicitor's account for legal expenses or charges in litigation by the Auditor of Court.

taxative plan — a plan of property referred to in a disposition is taxative if in the event of an inconsistency between the plan and the verbal description of the property in the disposition, the plan is deemed to be correct. The opposite of taxative is **demonstrative** (qv).

technical barriers to trade — obstacles to European Community wide trade derived from eg national consumer safety or environmental standards to which goods must conform. **[E]**

teind (pronounced 'teend') — tithe; one-tenth of the annual produce of land, originally used towards the support of the clergy, and after the Reformation towards the minister's stipend. Since 1925 teinds have been standardised at a fixed standard charge.

Teind Clerk — the officer of the Court of Session, acting under the direction of the Principal Clerk of Session, in charge of the Teind Office, which is responsible for all processes dealt with by the Teind Court and the Lord Ordinary on Teinds. *See* **Commissioner of Teinds.**

Teind Court. *See* **Commissioner of Teinds.**

temere litigare — to litigate rashly or without reasonable ground.

tempus continuum — time running on without interruption during which a legal right may be exercised or not.

tempus mortis inspiciendum — the time of death is to be regarded. Thus in considering the effect of a will, it is the date of the testator's death which is important, not the date of the will. Accordingly a legacy bequeathed to a person who predeceased the testator lapses and becomes ineffectual.

tenancy — a right of occupation under a **lease** (qv).

tenant — a person who occupies in terms of a **lease** (qv) heritable property belonging to a **landlord** (qv) to whom the tenant pays periodic rent. The occupation in terms of the tenancy is for a fixed (usually renewable) period and the contract is normally subject to a number of additional terms and conditions.

tender —
(1) to offer money in payment of a debt or liability, especially (by a defender) to offer money, with expenses, in settlement of an action for the payment of damages (upon refusal of which a pursuer who is subsequently awarded only the amount tendered or less will be liable for the defender's expenses from the date of the tender);
(2) money so offered.
See also **legal tender.**

tenement —
(1) heritable property having the benefit of or burdened by a servitude (*see* **dominant tenement** and **servient tenement**);
(2) a building containing several dwellinghouses under the same roof, sometimes with common staircases and means of access, and thus combining separate ownership with common interest, regulated by special rules known as 'the law of the tenement'.

tenendas — the clause in a feu charter which sets forth the nature of the **tenure** (qv) by which the land is to be held.

tenor. *See* **proving the tenor.**

tenure. *See* **allodial, feu, feudal tenure.**

terce — liferent of one-third of the heritage of a deceased husband conferred on a widow who has not accepted provision under his will (obsolete since 1964).

term —
(1) a condition or stipulation in an agreement;
(2) a fixed period, especially the period during which an agreement is to subsist;
(3) a fixed date, especially the date on which a person must pay interest or rent, the legal terms for payment being **Whitsunday** (qv) and **Martinmas** (qv).

term days — 28th May and 28th November.

term of entry — the date on which a tenant or the purchaser of heritage enters into possession under a lease or under **missives** (qv).

terminus a quo — the point from which, used especially in expressing when a period of time begins.

terminus ad quem — the point to which; used especially in expressing when a period of time ends.

termly — (adj or adv) at each term.

territorial sea — the waters adjacent to a coastal state, extending from the coastline out to 12 nautical miles, within which that state exercises complete sovereignty with the exceptions that shipping is allowed the rights of innocent passage and transit passage.

territoriality principle — doctrine of criminal law to the effect that a court has criminal jurisdiction if the offence was committed within the forum state.

tertium quid — a third thing, having a character and qualities distinct from those of either of its two components. Thus where liquids are confused or solids are commixed the subject produced, being different from the other two, is a *tertium quid*.

tertius — a **third party** (qv).

TESSA — Tax Exempt Special Savings Account, now replaced by the **ISA** (qv).

testament — a will.

testament-dative — the former name for the confirmation of an **executor dative** (qv).

testament-testamentar — the former name for the confirmation of an **executor nominate** (qv).

testamentary writing — a will or codicil.

testate —
(1) (adj) having died leaving a valid will for the disposal, in whole or in part, of the estate of the deceased;
(2) a person who dies having left such a document.

testator — a person who dies leaving a valid will for the disposal of his estate.

testibus non testimoniis credendum est — credence should be given to the witness, not to his evidence. The character and credibility of a witness is more important than the probability or otherwise of what he says. Thus an improbable fact spoken to by an unimpeachable witness is more likely to be accepted than a probable fact spoken to by a doubtful or incredible witness.

testimonia ponderanda sunt, non numeranda — the evidence of witnesses is to be weighed, not counted. Thus the character and quality of the evidence given is more important than the number of witnesses who give it.

testimony — evidence given in the form of a declaration by a person, especially oral evidence given in court.

testing clause — the attestation clause at the end of a deed identifying any erasures or alterations, specifying the date and place of execution and naming and designating the witnesses.

TEU — Treaty on European Union (qv) **[E]**.

theft — the crime of dishonestly taking and keeping the property of another person without his consent.

Thellusson Act — The Accumulations Act 1800 (now replaced by the Trusts (Scotland) Act 1961, s 5), which, as amended, prohibits or restricts accumulations of income by trustees.

third country — for purposes of an international organisation, and particularly the European Union, any state which is not a member state of that organisation. **[E]**

third country nationals — citizens of third countries. **[E]**

third party —
(1) a *tertius*; a person who, not being a party to a transaction between others (and who would consequently more correctly be called a 'third person'), is nevertheless in some way connected with or affected by that transaction, and who in appropriate circumstances may have a *jus quaesitum tertio* (qv) conferred on him by a contract between those other people;
(2) a person who, not originally being a party to a civil action in the Court of Session or the sheriff court, is added as a party by leave of the court, commonly on the application of a defender who claims that he has a right of contribution, relief or indemnity against the third party or that the third party should be made a party along with the defender as being solely liable or jointly and severally liable with him.

third party notice — a notice served on a third party setting out the defender's claim against him and requiring him to lodge answers within a specified period.

thirlage — a burden akin to a servitude by which land was formerly astricted or thirled to a particular mill, to which grain produced on the land had to be taken for grinding, for the payment of **multures** (qv).

thole — to suffer, endure or be subjected to.

thole an assize — to stand or suffer trial. Once an accused person has tholed his assize on a criminal charge he may not be tried again on the same charge.

threshold price — the minimum import price for certain **agricultural products** (qv) imported into the European Community. **[E]**

tigni immittendi — an urban servitude permitting the dominant proprietor to fix a beam or joist in the wall of the servient tenement.

time charter — a type of maritime contract, essentially a specialised contract of carriage of goods, whereby the charter buys space on the ship but the ship owner remains responsible for the ship and its operation. The duration of the contract is the time agreed in the **charterparty** (qv).

time bar — the effect of lapse of time on a person's rights, preventing his taking steps to enforce those rights or extinguishing them entirely. *See also* **prescription**.

time order — an order made by the sheriff to adjust the rate and time of payment of instalments by a debtor, hirer or **surety** (qv) (guarantor) who has defaulted on a regulated agreement under the Consumer Credit Act 1974.

time to pay direction — where in an action the sheriff grants decree for payment of money, he may direct that payment should be made by instalments or by a lump sum.

time to pay order — where diligence under a decree has begun the sheriff may make a time to pay order providing for payment of the debt by instalments or defer payment by lump sum for a period.

timeous — within the period allowed by law.

tinsel — the forfeiture of a right or its termination by default in performing some condition.

tinsel of superiority — the forfeiture of rights of superiorities on declarator of the superior's failure to complete his defective title. Abolished from 28 November 2004.

tinsel of the feu — the forfeiture of a vassal's rights for failure to pay feuduties. *See* **ob non solutum canonem**. Abolished from 28 November 2004.

tithe — the tenth part of the produce, direct or indirect, of land, once exigible for the maintenance of the church and the clergy. Tithes continued to be exacted after the Reformation, and were latterly called '**teinds**' (qv).

title —

(1) the right to the ownership of property;
(2) the deed or other instrument constituting evidence of that right;
(3) a personal designation denoting some office, honour or dignity;
(4) the name or heading of an Act of Parliament, deed, writ, book or document.

title deed — a deed or other instrument constituting evidence of the ownership of heritable property.

title indemnity policy — an insurance policy indemnifying the owner of property against the risk of a defect in title. Sometimes provided by a seller of property to settle a dispute with the purchaser as to the sufficiency of the title.

title raider — a person who acquired superiorities and mixed estates and made money by such practices as enforcing long forgotten real burdens and leasehold casualties, and irritating feus. Those practices have been struck at by legislation abolishing superiorities and leasehold casualties.

title sheet — in registration of title, a document which sets out the boundaries of a plot and identifies the persons who have real rights in it.

title to sue — a legal right to raise an action.

titular —

(1) a layman to whom the Crown transferred the title to church land after the Reformation;
(2) (adj) having a title, if only in name.

titulus transferendi dominii — the cause or intention of conveying property, as opposed to *modus transferendi*, which is the form of conveying property.

tocher *or* **toucher** — a marriage portion or dowry.

tocher band — a marriage settlement.

Torrens land registration system — a system of registration of titles to land invented by Sir Robert Torrens, Prime Minister of Australia, under which the State is the keeper of the master record of all the titles to land and their owners. In the Torrens system, a land title certificate suffices to show full, valid and indefeasible title. The Land Registration (Scotland) Act 1979 introduced a similar system of registration of title in Scotland. It differs from the Register of Sasines which is a register of title deeds, not of title.

tort — English law term for **delict** (qv)

tota re perspecta — the whole matter being clearly in view; in all the circumstances.

toties quoties — as often as; for each time.

totting up — the accumulation of penalty points imposed and recorded in a driving licence after convictions for motoring offences. The accumulation of twelve penalty points involves automatic disqualification from holding a driving licence.

trade description — a direct or indirect indication of the quantity, quality, composition or fitness for their purpose of goods supplied or offered in the course of a trade or business. The application or use of a false trade description is an offence.

trade mark — a mark on goods indicating a connection in the course of trade between goods and the person entitled to use the mark. If registered, the mark is a certification trade mark.

traditio — handing over; delivery.

traditionibus (et usucapionibus), non nudis pactis, transferuntur rerum dominia — rights of property are transferred by delivery (and by prescription), and not by mere agreement. See, however, the Sale of Goods Act 1979.

trainee — in the legal profession, an aspirant for admission to the **Law Society of Scotland** (qv), who trains as an assistant to an admitted **solicitor** (qv), is known as a trainee solicitor for a period of 2 years.

Trans-European networks (TENs) — programmes encouraging infrastructure development to assist transfrontier Community interests, eg, the 'interoperability' of transport, telecommunications and energy services. **[E]**

transfer —
(1) to convey or voluntarily hand over property or rights in property from one person to another, cf **transmission**;
(2) to remove an action from one court to another, or from one roll to another within the same court;
(3) to effect a **transference** (qv);
(4) a document effecting a transfer, eg of shares in a company.

transfer of undertakings — the transfer from one employer undertaking to another of the employees of the former; *see* **TUPE.**

transfer pricing — the practice of paying a price different from the market price or the price ordinarily payable in an arm's length transaction in the normal course of business for the supply of goods or services between associated undertakings. **[E]**

transference — the process in the Court of Session whereby an action by or against a person is reconstituted upon his death, bankruptcy, insanity or otherwise so that it becomes an action by or against another, eg his executor, trustee or curator.

transmission —
(1) the transfer of legal rights from one person to another, eg on bankruptcy or death;
(2) the transfer of proceedings from one court to another;
(3) the sending of documents from one place (eg a court) to another.

transnational — involving more than one country; cross-frontier. **[E]**

transparent — open; easily detected; not concealed from public knowledge. **[E]**

transposition — the incorporation of European Community or European Union law into the domestic law of member states. **[E]**

transumpts —

(1) an extract, duplicate or copy of a writ or a portion thereof made or recovered for production in a litigation (obsolete).

(2) an action to recover a deed in the hands of a third person so that a transumpt could be made of it (obsolete).

travaux préparatoires — drafts and other documents drawn up in the course of preparing the final text of a legal instrument which reflect the substance of the discussions between and the views of the persons who adopted the instrument.

treason — a crime committed by compassing the death of the Sovereign or the Sovereign's consort or heir, by violating the Queen, the Sovereign's eldest daughter unmarried or the wife of the Sovereign's heir, by making war against the Sovereign within the realm, by adhering to the Sovereign's enemies or giving them aid or comfort, by disputing or hindering the succession to the Crown, by killing any judge of the Court of Session or the High Court of Justiciary whilst exercising his office, or by counterfeiting seals kept under the Act of Union of 1707.

treasure trove — coin, gold, silver, plate and bullion found in the ground, apparently abandoned, the owner being unknown. As a sub-category of ownerless things it may be claimed by the Crown, but as a matter of grace – and policy – the Crown may reward the finder.

Treasury, the — in effect the United Kingdom ministry of finance. The Treasury is headed in form by the **P**rime Minster, who holds the office of 'First Lord of the Treasury', but in substance by the Chancellor of the Exchequer.

treaty — an international agreement between two or more independent states, that defines or modifies their mutual duties and obligations.

Treaty base. *See* **legal base. [E]**

Treaty of Accession — a treaty between existing member states of the European Union and one or more applicant countries constituting formal agreement of accession of the latter to the Union, in accordance with terms set out in an accompanying **Act of Accession** (qv). **[E]**

Treaty of Amsterdam — 1997 treaty (in force 1999) making significant amendments to the EC Treaty and the Treaty on European Union. **[E]**

Treaty of Maastricht — *See* **Treaty on European Union. [E]**

Treaty of Nice — 2001 treaty (in force 2003) making amendments to the EC Treaty, essentially institutional reform preparatory to the enlargement of the European Union. **[E]**

Treaty of Paris. *See* **ECSC Treaty. [E]**

Treaty of Rome. *See* **EEC Treaty; Euratom Treaty. [E]**

Treaty of Union (1706–1707) — national treaty between the two independent kingdoms of Scotland and England which led to their union as the new state of Great Britain in 1707, with a single parliament based in Westminster. The treaty was ratified by Acts of the two Parliaments (the Acts of Union) and provided for certain safeguards to Scottish interests notably the position of the Church of Scotland and of Scots law.

Treaty on European Union ('the Maastricht Treaty') — 1992 treaty signed at Maastricht (in force 1993) making substantial amendments to the EEC Treaty and establishing the European Union (qv). **[E]**

trespass — a temporary intrusion upon the land of another without permission or legal justification. Damages are not recoverable for mere trespass in Scotland. The only remedy is interdict. Trespass has a much wider meaning in English law.

trial —

(1) In a criminal case; a full hearing of the issues of both fact and law before a judge and jury (**solemn procedure** (qv)) or before a judge sitting alone (**summary procedure** (qv));

(2) in a civil case; a full hearing of the issue of both fact and law before a judge and jury. Cf **proof** (1).

tribunal — a court, especially a person or body of persons appointed under statute to hear and determine particular questions. Thus entitlement to redundancy payments, compensation on the compulsory acquisition of land, social security benefits and the like are determined by tribunals. *See* eg **Lands Tribunal for Scotland**.

Tribunal, the — sometimes shorthand for the **Court of First Instance** (qv); from *Tribunal de première instance*. **[E]**

troïka — the European Union member state which currently holds the Presidency of the Council, together with the immediate predecessor and successor member states to that office; close co-operation within the troika seeks to ensure continuity of Council business. **[E]**

trust — a legal institution under which a person called a trustee owns assets segregated from his own private patrimony and is obliged by law to deal with those assets for the benefit of another (called the 'beneficiary') or for the furtherance of a trust purpose.

trust deed — a deed constituting a **trust** (qv).

trust deed for creditors — a deed by which an insolvent person conveys his estate to trustees for the benefit of his creditors. By statute the deed may be protected against the possibility of being suspended by sequestration proceedings.

trustee —
 (1) a person administering a **trust** (qv);
 (2) a person in whom the legal title to property is vested in trust for others, eg as an executor of the estate of a deceased person.
As to trustees in a sequestration, *see* **interim trustee** and **permanent trustee**.

truster — a person who creates a **trust** (qv) to control and manage property belonging to him.

tunc — then; *ex tunc* from then; cf *nunc*.

TUPE — the Transfer of Undertakings (Protection of Employment) Regulations (SI 1981/1794), the purpose of which is to protect employees when there is a change of employer. the TUPE Regulations implement within the United Kingdom an EC Directive (Directive No 77/187 of 14 February 1977) commonly known as 'the Acquired Rights Directive'.

turnover equalisation tax — a tax imposed on imported goods in order to make the final tax burden on them the same as that imposed on domestic goods. **[E]**

turnover tax — a sales tax. *See also* **cumulative multi-stage turnover tax**. **[E]**

turpis causa — an immoral or illegal purpose. Contracts for such a purpose are unenforceable.

tutius semper est errare ex parte misericordiae quam ex parte justitiae — it is safer to err on the side of mercy than of justice. Thus it is better that ten guilty men should go unpunished than that one innocent man should suffer unjustly.

tutius semper est errare in acquietando quam in puniendo — it is safer to err in acquitting than in punishing. *See* ***tutius semper est errare ex parte misericordiae quam ex parte justitiae***.

tutor *or* **tutrix** — the guardian of a **pupil** (qv) and (in the case of a tutor-dative) includes a reference to an adult suffering from mental disability.
 (1) The institution of tutory, and the office of tutor, of pupil children was abolished by the Age of Legal Capacity (Scotland) Act 1991 along with abolition of the status of pupillarity. They were replaced by a new statutory regime of representation and guardianship of minors by that Act as amended by the Children Act 1995.
 (2) The institution of tutory, and the office of tutor-dative, of an adult suffering from mental disability was abolished by the Adults with Incapacity (Scotland) Act 2000 and replaced by new provisions on guardianship and **intervention orders** (qv).
 (3) After 25 September 1991 any reference in any rule of law, enactment or document to the tutor of a pupil child is construed as a reference to a person entitled to act as the child's legal representative under Part I of the Children (Scotland) Act 1995: Age of Legal Capacity (Scotland) Act 1991, s 5(1).

tutor *ad litem* — under the old law prior to 25 September 1991, a tutor appointed to safeguard a pupil's interests in legal proceedings. Now replaced by a ***curator ad litem***. (qv). *See* **tutor or tutrix**.

tutor-at- law — under the law prior to 25 September 1991 a pupil's nearest male relative on his father's side, who became tutor in default of any appointment by the parents. Now abolished. *See* **tutor or tutrix.**

tutor-dative — a tutor appointed by the Court of Session or the sheriff. The office of tutor-dative was abolished by the Adults with Incapacity (Scotland) Act 2000. *See* **tutor or tutrix.**

tutor nominate — prior to 25 September 1991, a tutor named by the parents of a pupil. Tutors nominate were abolished by Age of Legal Capacity (Scotland) Act 1991, s 5. *See* **tutor or tutrix**. It is now however possible for a parent or guardian of a child to appoint a person to be guardian under the Children (Scotland) Act 1995, s 7 in the event of the death of the person or guardian. Such a guardian exercises parental responsibilities and rights.

tutory — the guardianship and legal representation of a pupil prior to 25 September 1991. After that date any reference in any rule of law, enactment or document to the tutory of a pupil child is to be construed as a reference to the entitlement to act as the child's legal representative enjoyed by a person under Part I of the Children (Scotland) Act 1995: Age of Legal Capacity (Scotland) Act 1991, s 5(1).

tying — the practice of making the conclusion of a contract subject to the acceptance of supplementary obligations.

type approval — the procedure by which a member state of the European Community certifies that a type of goods satisfies the technical requirements established by Community legislation with the consequence that all models of that type of goods are deemed to satisfy those requirements. **[E]**

u

uberrimae fidei — with perfect frankness; in the utmost good faith; the standard required in certain contracts, especially for insurance, although generally this is required more of the insured than of the insurer!

ubi id non agebatur — where that was not done.

ubi jus ibi remedium — where there is a right, there is a remedy, ie a right of action to protect the right.

ubi rem meam invenio, ibi vindico — where I find my property there I can vindicate it – the principle of **vindication** (qv).

ubi onus ibi emolumentum — where there is a burden, there is a profit or advantage. Thus rights and obligations go together.

UCTA — Unfair Contract Terms Act 1977.

udal tenure — a form of land tenure, formerly common in Northern Europe, and surviving in parts of Orkney and Shetland. Those islands were pledged in the 15th century in security of the unpaid dowry of Princess Margaret of Norway and Denmark, wife of James III. Landowners (udallers) paid skat (tax) to the Crown under udal law (Code of Magnus the Lawmender). In 1974 future imposition of skat was prohibited. Most land in Orkney and Shetland is now held on feudal tenure.

UDHR — Universal Declaration of Human Rights.

UKCS — the United Kingdom Continental Shelf; those areas of the sea bed and subsoil beyond the **territorial sea** (qv) over which the United Kingdom exercises sovereign rights of exploration and exploitation of natural resources. The extent of the UKCS is set out in orders made under section 1(7) of the Continental Shelf Act 1964.

ultimo loco — in the last place.

ultimus haeres — the last heir. On an intestacy the Crown takes as *ultimus haeres* if there are no other heirs, but may confer the residue on relatives or others by way of gift.

ultra fines compromissi — beyond the limits of the submission or reference; grounds for partial or complete reduction of an arbiter's decision.

ultra petita — beyond that which was sought. A judge cannot award more than is asked for or sued for in a litigation.

ultra vires — beyond the powers. Thus acts or deeds of those to whom powers are granted may be reduced if they exceed the substance of the delegated powers or if requisite procedures have not been observed. The term is used especially in the context of delegated legislation and the activities of central and local government, trustees and companies.

ultra vires compromissi — beyond the force or import of the submission. *See* **ultra fines compromissi**.

ultroneous — spontaneous; voluntary; as of a witness, without having been cited.

umpire. *See* **oversman**.

umquhile (pronounced 'umwhile') — (of a person) former; late; deceased.

UN — United Nations.

UNCRC — UN Convention on the Rights of the Child 1989.

UNHCHR — United Nations High Commissioner for Human Rights.

UNCITRAL — United Nations Commission on International Trade Law; founded in 1966 to promote harmonization of international trade law. Its greatest achievement is the Vienna Convention on the International Sale of Goods concluded in 1980.

undefended cause or action — an action in court in which the defender has failed to appear to contest it.

undertaking —
(1) generally, a promise; an accepted obligation;
(2) generally, a natural or legal person;
(3) in competition law, any entity engaged in economic activity, irrespective of its legal status or the manner in which it is financed; embraces therefore not only bodies corporate, publicly or privately owned or controlled, but also the state and its public authorities in some aspects of their activities, and even individuals insofar as they engage in economic activity.

underwriter —
(1) any party which provides insurance, the insurer;
(2) stockbrokers who help a company become a public listed company, so called because they underwrite (vouch for) the stock. When a company has been brought public, the shares have been underwritten.

undisclosed principal — the principal on whose behalf an agent enters into a contract without disclosing to the other contracting party that he is an agent acting for the principal.

undue influence — a vice of consent rendering **voidable** (qv) a contract, conveyance, or other transaction involving an abuse of the confidence which the victim of the undue influence has reposed either in the other party to the transaction, or in a third party (as where in a cautionary obligation undue influence is exerted on the cautioner by the principal debtor).

unfair contract terms — extreme contractual terms excluding or restricting liability for breach of contract. They were rendered void or voidable by the Unfair Contract Terms Act 1977.

unfair dismissal — a statutory ground for complaint by an employee to an employment tribunal which, if established, may involve the employer in paying compensation or reinstating or re-engaging the employee.

unfair preference — an ageement voluntarily entered into by a debtor who is knowingly insolvent which has the effect of creating a preference in favour of a creditor to the prejudice of the general body of creditors. Such a preference was formerly misleadingly known as a 'fraudulent preference'.

unfair prejudice — conduct on the part of those controlling a company which unfairly prejudices other company members usually minority shareholders. The court on petition may grant remedies to undo the prejudice such as compelling the majority to buy out the minority at a fair price.

unfit to plead — the state of a person accused of crime who by reason of his mental condition is not capable of understanding his trial. If the accused is unfit to plead his trial cannot take place. If the Crown proposed nevertheless to proceed with the case a preliminary plea of insanity in bar of trial would be made.

unico contextu — in one connection; by one and the same act; as part of a single continuous process. Thus multiple parties to a deed need not execute is *unico contextu*, at the same time and place, but a granter and his witness must so subscribe it.

UNIDROIT — The Rome institute for the Unification of Private Law, founded in 1926, has framed Principles for international Commercial Contracts and several other conventions, eg on agency in international sale of goods; factoring; international financial liaising; and stolen or illegally exported cultural objects.

uniform interpretation — alternatively, consistent or sympathetic interpretation; *interprétation conforme*; an interpretative principle whereby national law of a member state of the European Community ought to be interpreted so as to conform with Community legislation; applies primarily, but not exclusively, to the interpretation of a national measure in a field addressed by a **directive** (qv), but the directive having been implemented inadequately, not having been implemented timeously, or not having been implemented at all. **[E]**

unilateral — involving only one person. Thus a will or gift is a unilateral transaction, whereas a contract between two parties is bilateral.

Union, the. *See* **union of the parliaments**.

Union Minister for Foreign Affairs — a post proposed by the draft **Constitution of the European Union** (qv); a member and vice-president of the European Commission responsible for conducting the Union's **common foreign and security policy** (qv). **[E]**

Union of the Crowns — In 1603 James VI of Scotland became James I of England, thereby uniting the two kingdoms. This union was a purely dynastic one and did not constitute a formal legal union between the two countries or their Parliaments. *See also* **Union of the Parliaments**.

Union of the Parliaments — The term sometimes used to describe the situation in 1707 when the two countries of Scotland and England united to form the new United Kingdom of Great Britain, under the Treaty of Union, approved by Acts of the two Parliaments. The two Parliaments ceased to exist on the establishment of the new Parliament of Great Britain.

unincorporated association — a voluntary association comprising a body or society of persons who have come together for the purpose of business or trade, as a partnership or firm, or for some sporting, charitable, religious, scientific or leisure purpose.

uninfeft proprietor — an owner of property who has not completed title by registering it (ie has not 'obtained infeftment'). *See* **infeftment**. With the abolition of the feudal sytem, the concepts of uninfeft and infeftment have become out-of-date.

unitary authority — the unit of local government in Scotland since 1996 created by the Local Government etc (Scotland) Act 1994. *See also* **council**.

United Kingdom — the state comprising Great Britain (ie Scotland, England and Wales) and Northern Ireland.

universal successor — a person (eg an heir) who succeeds to the entire estate, rights and liabilities of a deceased person. Cf **singular successor**.

universitas — the whole; the entire property of an individual; an undivided collection.

unjustified enrichment — the principle that a person who has been enriched at another's expense without legal justification is bound to redress the enrichment. The cornerstone of obligations to redress unjustified enrichment (one of the main categories of the law of obligations coeval with obligations arising out of contract, unilateral promise, delict and *negotiorum gestio*). These include the obligations of **repetition** (qv), **restitution** (qv) and **recompense** (qv) (now judicially described as remedies), and at a lower level various gounds of action including the *condictiones* (qv) that is to say *prima facie* reasons for redressing the enrichment. The principle against unjustified enrichment identifies three elements (1) the enrichment of the defender; (2) at the pursuer's expense; and (3) no legal justification for the enrichment; together with (4) a defence that it would be inequitable for the court to compel redress. *See also* **condictio**; **nemo debet locupletari ex aliena jactura, recompense, repetition** and **restitution**.

unlimited jurisdiction — the jurisdiction of the European Court of Justice to substitute its own subjective appreciation for that of the **Community institution** (qv) which adopted a measure challenged in proceedings before the Court, in addition to reviewing the legality of that measure. **[E]**

unliquidated damages — damages whose amount is fixed by the court. Cf **liquidate damages**.

unum quid — one thing. The phrase is applicable where several things are for some purpose or reason taken and considered and treated together as one.

unumquodque eodem modo dissolvitur quo colligatur — an obligation is discharged in the same manner as that in which it was constituted. Thus verbal agreements may be discharged verbally, but those constituted in writing may in general only be discharged in writing.

uplift — to collect or take possession of something, especially money.

upset price — the minimum price set for property put up for auction, below which bids will not be accepted (in England, the reserve price). The upset price is usually advertised before the auction.

urban — relating to a dwellinghouse or other building in a town or city, eg an urban lease, or an urban servitude as opposed to a rural servitude.

urban development area — an area of land in a town or city designated by the Secretary of State as one in need of regeneration by an urban development corporation, which may be empowered to exercise certain local authority functions eg over planning, building control, housing and public health.

usucapio or **usucapion** — the acquisition of property under the civil law by lengthened possession similar to **positive prescription** (qv).

usufruct (Latin) *ususfructus* — equivalent in Roman law of **liferent** (qv).

usus — use; usage; custom.

usus fit ex iteratis actibus — uses that arise from repeated acts. A right acquired by use cannot be acquired by a single act: the act must be repeated before a series of acts can be held to amount to a use.

Usus modernus Pandectarum – the modern use of the Roman law of the **Pandects** (qv).

ut intus — as within: a reference in one part of a book or document to a statement in another part of it.

ut res valeat potius quam pereat — in order that the thing may avail rather than perish: a rule to give a benign interpretation to documents so as to avoid defeating their purpose.

ut supra — as above.

ut voluntas testatoris sortiatur effectum — that effect may be given to the will of a testator. If the trustee dies or declines to act, the court will appoint a **judicial factor** (qv) to give effect to the will.

uterine — descended from the same mother but not from the same father, eg half brother. Cf **consanguinean**.

uttering — the crime of tendering a forged document or banknote or a counterfeit coin with the necessary criminal intention, whether or not the result intended is achieved.

uxor sequitur domicilium viri — a wife follows her husband's domicile. The proposition is not necessarily true today since by statute a wife can now have her own domicile independent of that of her husband.

V

vacant possession — the state of heritable property which is available for sale with legal possession and which has nothing and no person (such as a tenant) in occupation to prevent a purchaser enjoying actual possession.

vacation — a period between **sessions** (qv) of the court; a recess during which the court is not generally sitting.

vacation court — a court sitting during vacation.

vacation judge — a judge sitting during vacation. In the Court of Session the judges (other than the Lord President and the Lord Justice-Clerk) sit in rotation as vacation judge to hear urgent business.

valens agere — able to act; describes a person of full age and full legal capacity. The negative is *non valens agere*. Prescription did not run against a person so described.

valentia agendi — the power or capacity to act.

Valuation Appeal Court. *See* **Lands Valuation Appeal Court**.

variable geometry — describing the situation whereby European Community law applies differently, at different times, in different member states; 'multi-speed Europe'. **[E]**

vassal — in feudal tenure the owner of the *dominium utile* (qv) of land, his right of ownership being conditional on his fulfilling certain obligations imposed by his **superior** (qv). As from 28 November 2004, the owner of the *dominium utile* will become an allodial owner. *See* **allodial**; **feu**; **feudal tenure**.

VAT — value added tax; the sales tax within the European Community, applies to both goods and services. The tax is imposed on the amount of value added to goods or services since the preceding taxable event. **[E]**

vellum — a writing material made from animal skin; a particularly strong and long lasting writing material. Historically, much used for important legal documents and still used for the record copies of United Kingdom **acts of parliament** (qv) and certain other documents granted by the sovereign under **seal** (qv).

verba accipienda sunt secundum subjectam materiam — words are to be accepted according to the subject matter of which they deal; words are to be understood in context.

verba debent intelligi cum effectu ut res magis valeat quam pereat — words ought to be read or understood as of some effect, so that the matter (ie the deed, contract etc in which the words are used) may be of some avail rather than perish. Thus, if two interpretations are possible, the one to be preferred is that which makes sense.

verba jactantia — empty, vain words; words spoken in jest.

verba sollennia — solemn or formal words; words essential to validity. At one time the word 'dispone' in a disposition was of that character.

verbal injury — the actionable wrongs of injurious words. Though intent to insult (*animus injuriandi*) was regarded as essential irrespective of patrimonial loss, some decisions have used the expression to apply to causing loss by a false but not slanderous statement.

verbatim et literatim — word for word and letter for letter; an exact copy. The phrase is usually abbreviated '*verbatim*'.

verdict — the decision of a judge or **jury** (qv) on a matter of fact.

vergens ad inopiam — approaching to want; tending to insolvency. Formerly a creditor could resort to certain measures to protect his interests if the debtor was *vergens ad inopiam*.

veritas convicii — the truth of the accusation, a defence to an action of defamation.

vertical integration — a merger or other concentration between **undertakings** (qv) operating at different economic levels.

verity — truth. In a sequestration an oath of verity that his claim was true was formerly required from a creditor.

versans in illicito — engaged in some unlawful occupation; performing an illegal act.

vertical arrangement — an arrangement between **undertakings** (qv) operating at different economic levels (eg between a manufacturer and a distributor, distributor and retailer).

vertical direct effect. *See* **direct effect**. [E]

vest — to become the property of a person, and thus transmissible to heirs and assignees. In succession, vesting may depend on survival to an ascertainable date, eg three months after the testator's death. Cf mere *spes successionis*.

vexatious litigant — a person who brings proceedings primarily for the purpose of annoying or embarrassing the defender. The Court of Session may prohibit the institution of proceedings by a vexatious litigant unless the court's approval has first been obtained.

vi aut clam aut precario — by force, by clandestine stealth or by importunate entreaty. Possession of property obtained by any of these means is regarded as precarious possession.

vi et metu — by force and fear. Contracts and conveyances so induced are probably void or voidable according to circumstances; marriages so induced are null.

vicarious liability — the liability of a person for the delictual act or omission of an employee, servant or agent. The vicarious liability is additional to the liability of the actual wrongdoer. *See* *qui facit per alium facit per se*.

vice versa — conversely.

vicennial prescription — **prescription** (qv) for twenty years.

vide — see.

vide infra — see below.

vide supra — see above.

videlicet — namely, usually abbreviated as 'viz'.

view — an inspection outwith the court by a judge or a jury of premises which are the subject matter of a litigation.

vigilantibus non dormientibus jura subveniunt — the law assists those who are watchful of their rights, not those who are careless of them. Thus prescription cancels rights which are not enforced over prescribed periods.

vindicatio (or *rei vindicatio*), **vindication** — an action (sometimes called a real action, because it is used to vindicate and recover a *res* or thing) or right of action whereby a party who has ownership (*dominium*) of property (including a trustee vested in trust property) or the holder of a subordinate real right in another's property (*jus in re aliena*) may follow the property into whose hands so ever it comes and there vindicate it. The possessor comes under an obligation to deliver the property to the owner or holder of the real right which is the counterpart of the owner's real right.

violent profits — penal damages exigible as a deterrent against a tenant unwarrantably ('violently') taking or retaining possession of heritable property. In urban property they are estimated at double the rent; elsewhere they are the greatest rent the landlord could have obtained, together with compensation for any damage.

vis et metus — force and fear. *See* *vi et metu*.

vis major — greater or superior power; *force majeure*.

visitation —
(1) a visit to a parish by the presbytery to exercise supervision, for judicial or administrative purposes or to express sympathy;
(2) the examination of records by a superior court.

visiting force — the naval, military or air force of one of certain designated countries whose members are by statute subject to the service courts of the sending country and not to the courts of the host country.

vitious intromitter — a person who, by taking possession, without authority, of the property of a deceased person, incurs unlimited liability for all the debts of the deceased.

vitium reale — a real defect. *See* *labes realis quae rei inhaeret*.

viva voce — orally.

viz. *See* *videlicet*.

voces signatae — formal words; words with a special technical meaning.

void — null; having no legal effect whatsoever, eg a purported marriage by a person under age.

voidable — apparently valid, but vitiated in some way, so that a contract, deed or obligation may be annulled or set aside by the person entitled to avoid it. Until so avoided the subject remains valid.

volens — willing.

volenti non fit injuria — no wrong is done to him who consents: the principle that a person who voluntarily (either expressly or impliedly) accepts the risk of an injury which he in fact sustains cannot then claim damages. This is a defence in an action of damages for personal injury or death.

voluntary organisation — generally a body (other than a public or local authority) whose activities are not carried on for profit.

voluntas est ambulatoria usque ad mortem — a will is ambulatory until death takes place. It may thus be altered or revoked at any time during the lifetime of the testator.

voluntas testatoris — the intention of the testator.

vouch — to confirm or answer for something.

voucher —
(1) a document or receipt confirming the payment of money;
(2) the document to be exchanged for goods or services, implying that payment has already been made.

vox emissa volat; litera scripta manet — the spoken word is transitory; writing remains. The spoken word may be forgotten, misunderstood and misrepresented, but a document speaks for itself and remains the same.

voyage charter party — specialised contract of carriage of goods by sea, whereby the charterer buys space on the ship but the shipowner remains responsible for the ship. The duration of the contract is the length of the voyage.

W

W S — Writer to the Signet. *See* **Writer**.

wadset — the obsolete conveyance of land to a creditor (the 'wadsetter') in security for or in satisfaction of a debt or other obligation with a reserved power to the debtor (the 'reverser') to recover the land on payment or performance.

waiver — an express or implied voluntary renunciation or forsaking of the assertion of a right. A superior may expressly renounce or modify conditions in a feu charter by a minute of waiver.

wakening. *See* **sleep**.

ward — a person of limited legal capacity, such as a minor or person of unsound mind, on whose behalf legal steps are taken by a guardian curator.

ward holding — the obsolete feudal tenure of land in exchange for military service.

warn — to notify the other party of intention to terminate a lease or contract of service.

warrandice — an express or implied personal obligation (personal warrandice) of a granter (eg a seller or lessor), especially of heritable property, to indemnify the granter in case of eviction on some grounds existing before the grant or sale. Problems arise in determining what constitutes 'eviction'. Personal warrandice may be:
(1) simple warrandice, where the granter undertakes not to grant any future deed which will conflict with the right transferred;
(2) warrandice from fact and deed, where the granter undertakes that he has not granted and will not grant any such deed or do anything to conflict with that right;
(3) absolute warrandice (the usual form), where it protects the buyer from anything which conflicts with that right.

Real warrandice, now abolished, was warrandice either on the sale of land by which other land ('warrandice land') was liable to be disponed in security of the principal land or, on excambion, where one party or his heirs or assigns suffered eviction and he might have back the land which was exchanged.

warrandice clause — a clause in a deed binding the granter to a warrandice.

warrandice land — land formerly held in security for other land over which a real warrandice existed: *see* **warrandice**.

warrant — a written judicial authority, eg for service of a writ, sale, search or eviction.

warrant sale — a stage in the now abolished diligence of poinding and warrant sale by which a creditor obtained a warrant from the sheriff authorising the public sale of articles which had been **poinded** (qv).

warranty — an express or implied material guarantee in a contract, breach of which justifies the other party in rescinding the contract and claiming damages.

way. *See* **right of way**.

way-going crop — a crop planted on arable land in the last year of a tenancy which an outgoing tenant may take, even if the harvest postdates removing.

wayleave — a right of passage for pipes, cables and the like over heritable property, analogous to that conferred by a servitude. Unlike a servitude in the strict sense, there is no relationship of dominant and servient tenement. The right is invariably constituted by a specific contract.

web. *See* **word wide web**.

welfare power of attorney — a power of attorney granted by an individual relating to his personal welafre.

West Lothian question — a problem arising out of the fact that there is devolution for Scotland but not England, first raised by Tam Dalyell MP (whose constituency was then West Lothian). Dalyell questioned whether a Scottish MP at Westminster after devolution should be entitled to vote upon matters (such as education) affecting England but could not vote on such matters affecting his own constituency because they would have been devolved to a Scottish Parliament. More commonly however the question is understood to refer to the fact that Scottish MPs can vote upon English matters but English MPs cannot vote on devolved matters.

Western European Union (WEU) — an intergovernmental organisation established in 1948 for the purposes of co-operation on security and defence; originally recognised by the Treaty on European Union to be 'an integral part of the development of the Union', but now effectively absorbed into the **common foreign and security policy** (qv). **[E]**

Westminster Confession — a declaration of the faith and doctrine of the Church of Scotland, drawn up in 1647, entrenched in the Union Agreement of 1707 and recognised as the 'principal subordinate standard' of the Church in the Declaratory Articles scheduled to the Church of Scotland Act 1921.

whereas — formal legalistic way of saying 'because' or 'therefore'; commonly found in contracts and in the **reasoning** (qv) of all European Community legislation.

WHISP — What's Happening in the Scottish Parliament (information bulletin of the Scottish Parliament).

white list — terms set out in a **block exemption** (qv) of expressly permitted anticompetitive practices which would otherwise be prohibited.

whitebonnet — a person who, in collusion with a party selling by auction, attends the sale to raise the price by making offers to deceive and encourage other bidders on the understanding that he will be relieved by the seller of liability should his offer not be outbid.

Whitsunday — a quarter day in Scotland (28 May: Term and Quarter Days (Scotland) Act 1990, s 1); a term day for payment of rent.

Whole court —
(1) a bench of the **Inner House** (qv) composed of the judges of more than one **Division** (qv);
(2) the European Court of Justice sitting in **plenary session**. (qv) **[E]**

whole life insurance — a life insurance policy providing payment on death, whenever this occurs. Premiums may be payable throughout life, or for a shorter period.

wilful — intentional or deliberate.

will — a deed comprising the legal expression of a person's intention as to the disposal of his property and the administration of his affairs after his death.

winding up — the process of liquidation or bringing to a close the affairs of a company by the Court.

without prejudice —
(1) in statutes or documents, the phrase introduces a saving clause creating an exception to the provision in which the phrase is used;
(2) in negotiations for the settlement of a dispute, the phrase, often used alone, indicates in correspondence that if the negotiations fail they are not to be founded on in later litigation.

witness —
(1) a person who gives evidence on oath in court;
(2) a person (an 'instrumentary witness') who signs a document indicating that he saw it signed by a party to the document or heard him acknowledge his signature;
(3) to sign a document as a witness;
(4) to see or hear something happen; to observe and remember.

worker — a natural person in, or seeking to be in, a contract of employment, in a member state of the European Community other than his own, and as such enjoying significant rights under the EC Treaty; also referred to as a migrant worker. **[E]**

worker(s') participation — provision laid down in various European Community measures requiring consultation (in some degree) with the workforce before an employer firm takes certain decisions. **[E]**

working language of the Court — the language in which most of the work, such as internal dissemination of documents and deliberation, of the European Court of Justice and the Court of First Instance is actually conducted - it being French. **[E]**

workmen's compensation — a statutory system of compensation for employees in respect of injuries arising out of their employment, whether or not the employer was at fault. It was abolished in 1948.

writ — a legally significant writing; loosely, a court summons or petition. *See also* **initial writ**.

writ or oath — obsolete restricted form of proof in which the pursuer could only prove his case by the production of his opponent's writings or by requiring that the case be put to his opponent on oath, abolished by s 11 of the Requirements of Writing (Scotland) Act 1995. *See* **oath on reference**.

Writer — a Writer to the Signet; a solicitor (obsolescent). *See* **Keeper of the Signet**.

writing — a document, whether written, typed or printed.

wrongful dismissal — a breach by an employer of the contract of employment. It is now, for practical purposes, largely superseded by statutory compensation for **unfair dismissal** (qv).

wrongous — wrongful.

WTO — World Trade Organisation.

y

yair, yare, zair *or* **zare** — a trap or cruive for fish erected across a river or bay.

year to year — the indefinite term of a contract or tenancy which will continue year after year unless and until terminated by due notice.

yield — the amount of income an investment delivers after deduction of charges (but before tax) expressed as a percentage of the amount invested. Usually expressed as an annual figure.

young person — a person aged over sixteen and under twenty-one. If found guilty of a crime or offence he may not be sent to prison but may be subject to other punishment.

Z

z . . . in early Scots equivalent to 'y', eg zeir, year.

zair *or* zare. *See* yair.